Windows Applications

WINDOWS APPLICATIONS

Ritu Choudhary

CENTRUM PRESS
NEW DELHI-110002 (INDIA)

CENTRUM PRESS
H.O.: 4360/4, Ansari Road, Daryaganj,
New Delhi-110002 (India)
Tel: 23278000, 23261597, 23255577, 23286875
B.O.: No. 1015, Ist Main Road, BSK IIIrd Stage,
IIIrd Phase, IIIrd Block, Bangalore-560085 (INDIA)
Tel: 080-41723429
Email: centrumpress@gmail.com
Visit us at: www.centrumpress.com

Windows Applications

First Edition, 2011

PRINTED IN INDIA

Printed at Tarun Offset Printers, Delhi-110053

Contents

Preface

Programs like Microsoft Word, Excel, and Power Point are Windows applications. They typically have more complex user interface requirements and therefore are usually more expensive than Internet applications. They may be designed to run totally alone, or may share information over a local area network. Typically, they do their own data processing, thus requiring less network bandwidth and server resources. Windows applications increased administration cost by requiring more time and/or more complex networks to set up new users and distribute updates. One advantage of the .Net environment is the ability to automatically update Windows applications. This has reduced administration costs and improved productivity.

Author

1

System Level Web Programming

CHARACTERISTICS

ARCHITECTURE

The primary distinguishing characteristic of systems programming when compared to application programming is that application programming aims to produce software which provides services to the user (*e.g.* word processor), whereas systems programming aims to produce software which provides services to the computer hardware. It also requires a greater degree of hardware awareness.

The architects of the earliest computer systems gave little thought to software. (The very word was still a decade in the future.) Building the machine itself was the serious intellectual challenge; converting mathematical formulas into program statements looked like a routine clerical task. The very first programs were written in pure binary notation: Both data and instructions had to be encoded in long, featureless strings of 1s and 0s.

Moreover, it was up to the programmer to keep track of where everything was stored in the machine's memory. Before you could call a subroutine, you had to calculate its address. The technology that lifted these burdens from the programmer was assembly language, in which raw binary codes were replaced by symbols such as load, store, add, sub. The symbols were translated into binary by a program called an assembler, which also calculated addresses. This was the first of many instances in which the computer was recruited to help with its own programming. Assembly language was a crucial early advance, but still the programmer had to keep in mind all the minutiae in the instruction set of a specific computer. Evaluating a short mathematical expression such as $x^2 + y^2$ might require dozens of assembly-language instructions. Higher-level languages freed the programmer to think in terms of variables and equations rather than registers and addresses. In Fortran, for example, $x^2 + y^2$ would be written simply as $X^2 + Y^2$.

Expressions of this kind are translated into binary form by a program called a compiler. With Fortran and the languages that followed, programmers finally had the tools they needed to get into really serious trouble. Three such constructs were recommended: sequencing (do A, then B, then C), alternation (either do A or do B) and iteration (repeat A until some condition is satisfied). Corrado Böhm and Giuseppe Jacopini proved that these three idioms are sufficient to express essentially all programs. Structured programming came packaged with a number of related principles and imperatives.

Top-down design and stepwise refinement urged the programmer to set forth the broad outlines of a procedure first and only later fill in the details. Modularity called for self-contained units with simple interfaces between them. Encapsulation, or data hiding,required that the internal workings of a module be kept private, so that later changes to the module would not affect other areas of the program. All of these ideas have proved their worth and remain a part of software practice today. But they did not rescue programmers from the tar pit.

PROGRAMMING LANGUAGE

The term "higher level" means that many details are handled automatically so that programmers can write less code to get the same job done. System programming languages are well suited to building components where the complexity is in the data structures and algorithms.

System programming support following features:

- Register allocation is handled by the compiler so that

programmers need not write code to move information between registers and memory.
- Programmers can use simple keywords such as while and if for control structures; the compiler generates all the detailed instructions to implement the control structures.
- *Procedure calling sequences are generated automatically*: programmers need not worry about moving arguments to and from the call stack.

EMBEDDED PROGRAMMING

Technological advancement brought the price of embedded system (ICs) lower making it possible to use them for commercial purpose. Today embedded systems are widely used in various devices performing specific functions with drastic improvement in processing power. Embedded system programming has been derived from the word embedded system. An embedded system is nothing but a special purpose system in which the computer is fully encapsulated by the device it controls. Embedded software designs have advanced enough to produce widely used devices performing specific function devices such as ATM, PDA, mobile phones etc.

Systems that hosts this embedded systems are various industrial machines, automobiles, medical equipment, cameras, household appliances, and airplanes, vending machines, toys, cellular phone and PDA. Seeing its importance and worth embedded systems programming has gained lot popularity and people are looking for companies providing this service. If you are looking for a company providing embedded systems programming then your search is over as Softage is there for you.

Softage is Russia's leading IT service provider providing best and advanced embedded systems programming. Embedded systems programming is specially dedicated to unequivocal tasks so that design engineers can optimize it by reducing the magnitude and cost of the product. In fact nowadays, embedded systems are frequently mass-produced. This has resulted in the cost savings that may be multiplied by millions of items. Apart from the other devices embedded systems also range from portable devices such as MP3 players, to large stationary installations like traffic lights or factory controllers. According to the experts embedded systems are easily programmable and are provided with a programming interface. Embedded system programming is a tough and professional work which is efficiently handled by Softage.

Backed by years of experience Softage hosts some of the best and professional programmers those are experts in embedded system software programming. Embedded systems programming is basically done in various languages such as J2e, C/C++, x86 assembler, ADSP assembler, and SQL accessing appropriate language for specific devices. All these languages are supported and provided by Softage and that too easily affordable. Thus, what you are waiting for if you are looking for embedded systems programming then Softage is there for you.

WINDOWS PROGRAMMING

When the program calls a function or interacts with the Operating System (OS) by calling one of the OS's service functions, the function's instructions executed in similar way and the execution continue sequentially until the end of the last instruction of the main program. In this traditional way of programming the program only need one main function to start the execution. Nowadays, in event driven programming environment such as Windows, the interaction between the program and the OS is a message-based interaction. In this interaction the program start in a wait mode until the user create an event like for example, press a key or click a mouse button.

The OS generates appropriate message and inserts it in application's message queue. The program, when it ready, should dispatch the messages (read a message from the queue and send it back to the OS) one message after another for time scheduling purpose. After that, the OS then send the message again to the program and the program respond by taking appropriate actions. In this kind of interaction, a simple program need at least two functions, the main function that start the message loop (WinMain ()) and the other called by the OS (Windows Function())and respond to the passed message.

UNIX PROGRAMMING

The Unix systems programming API has been standardised by a large number of POSIX standards documents from the IEEE. For the majority of programmers the most important of these is POSIX 1003.1 which covers process primitives and environments, directories and files, I/O primitives and device specific functions. One of the unusual characteristics of POSIX 1003.1 is its use of the C language throughout. Whereas IEEE standards would normally be expected to be language independent, the history of Unix is so bound up with C that this was the only feasible route. The document claims that it will be the basis for definitions that are independent of particular programming languages. In fact, new language dependent versions have arisen, such as Ada (POSIX 1003.5) and Fortran.

Irrespective of the formal standards mechanisms, designers of libraries for other languages have used POSIX 1003.1 as the specification for their own libraries. For example, tcl [Ousterhout] and Perl have well-developed Unix bindings that copy the syntax, and rely on the semantics, of POSIX 1003.1. Java is the latest flavour in programming languages for all sorts of excellent reasons, despite some serious shortcomings. It is a full O/O language (although not as pure as SmallTalk or Eiffel); it is based on C/C++, but avoids the worst of both languages (not completely, though); by use of a virtual machine it is cross-platform (although some vendors have variant versions); it has a rich set set of libraries that deal with, for example, graphics and networking.

These are combining to produce the "Web programming" environment where applications or applets are written once to run on any platform. Java extends the open authoring environment of HTML to an open programming environment. Java currently lacks the depth of hooks into the POSIX API that tcl and Perl have. The standard must continue to have this lack or it will lose its universal applicability. However, *extensions* by *non-standard* libraries can supply this depth, as long as they are done in an appropriate manner.

This paper reports on a project to make the POSIX API available to Java applications or applets using a non-standard library. It encapulates POSIX calls within Java methods for a new set of classes in the posix package. This project must be contrasted in aims and methods to the Microsoft policy with J++: their attempt is to make J++ the best environment for doing Windows programming in Java J++, and this implicitly rejects the notion of a cross-platform environment. It may even turn out to be difficult for the programmer using J++ to be certain of how general their code is. The statements from Microsoft do not seem to dispel any uncertainty.

WEB SHELL

LINKERS

On Unix variants the term loader is often used as a synonym for linker. Because this usage blurs the distinction between the compile-time process and the run-time process, this article will use "linking" for the former and "loading" for the latter. However, in some operating systems the same program handles both the jobs of linking and loading a program; see "dynamic linking".Computer programs are typically comprised of several parts or modules; these parts, if not all contained within a single object file, refer to each other by means of symbols.

Typically, an object file can contain three kinds of symbols:

- Defined symbols, which allow it to be called by other modules.
- Undefined symbols, which call the other modules where these symbols are defined.
- Local symbols, used internally within the object file to facilitate relocation.

When a program comprises multiple object files, the linker combines these files into a unified executable program, resolving the symbols as it goes along. Linkers can take objects from a collection called a "library". Some linkers do not include the whole library in the output; they only include its symbols that are referenced from other object files or libraries. Libraries exist for diverse purposes, and one or more system libraries are usually linked in by default.

The linker also takes care of arranging the objects in a program's address space. This may involve "relocating" code that assumes a specific base address to another base. Since a compiler seldom knows where an object will reside, it often assumes a fixed base location (for example, zero). Relocating machine code may involve re-targeting of absolute jumps, loads and stores. The executable output by the linker may need another relocation pass when it is finally loaded into memory (just before execution). This pass is usually omitted on hardware offering virtual memory — every program is put into its own address space, so there is no conflict even if all programs load at the same base address.

COMMUNIATION

The basic job of any linker is simple: it binds more abstract names to more concrete names, which permits programmers to write code using the more abstract names. That is, it takes a name written by a programmer such as get line and binds it to "the location 612 bytes from the beginning of the executable code in module iosys."

Or it may take a more abstract numeric address such as "the location 450 bytes beyond the beginning of the static data for this module" and bind it to a numeric address. A linkers is used in the development of computer programming in systems. The earliest computers were programmed entirely in machine language. Programmers would write out the symbolic programs on sheets of paper, hand assemble them into machine code and then toggle the machine code into the computer, or perhaps punch it on paper tape or cards. If the programmer used symbolic addresses at all, the symbols were bound to addresses as the programmer did his or her hand translation. If it turned out that an instruction had to be added or deleted, the entire program had to be hand-inspected and any addresses affected by the added or deleted instruction adjusted. The problem was that the names were bound to addresses too early. Assemblers solved that problem by letting programmers write programs in terms of symbolic names, with the assembler binding the names to machine addresses. If the program changed, the programmer had to reassemble it, but the work of assigning the addresses is pushed off from the programmer to the computer. Libraries of code compound the address assignment problem. Since the basic operations that computers can perform are so simple, useful programs are composed of subprograms that perform higher level and more complex operations.

Computer installations keep a library of pre-written and debugged subprograms that programmers can draw upon to use in new programs they write, rather than requiring programmers to write all their own subprograms. The programmer then loads the subprograms in with the main program to form a complete working program. Programmers were using libraries of subprograms even before they used assemblers. By 1947, John Mauchly, who led the ENIAC project, wrote about loading programs along with subprograms selected from a catalog of programs stored on tapes, and of the need to relocate the subprograms' code to reflect the addresses at which they were loaded. Perhaps surprisingly, these two basic linker functions, relocation and library search, appear to predate even assemblers, as Mauchly expected both the program and subprograms to be written in machine language.

The relocating loader allowed the authors and users of the subprograms to write each subprogram as though it would start at location zero, and to defer the actual address binding until the subprograms were linked with a particular main program. With the advent of operating systems, relocating loaders separate from linkers and libraries became necessary. Before operating systems, each program had the machine's entire memory at its disposal, so the program could be assembled and linked for fixed memory addresses, knowing that all addresses in the computer would be available. But with operating systems, the program had to share the computer's memory with the operating system and perhaps even with other programs, This means that the actual addresses at which the program would be running weren't known until the operating system loaded the program into memory, deferring final address binding past link time to load time.

Linkers and loaders now divided up the work, with linkers doing part of the address binding, assigning relative addresses within each program, and the loader doing a final relocation step to assign actual addresses. As systems became more complex, they called upon linkers to do more and more complex name management and address binding. Fortran programs used multiple subprograms and common blocks, areas of data shared by multiple subprograms, and it was up to the linker to lay out storage and assign the addresses both for the subprograms and the common blocks. Linkers increasingly had to deal with object code libraries. Including both application libraries written in Fortran and other languages, and compiler support libraries called implicitly from compiled code to handle I/O and other high-level operations.

Programs quickly became larger than available memory, so linkers provided overlays, a technique that let programmers arrange for different parts of a program to share the same memory, with each overlay loaded on demand when another part of the program called into it. Overlays were widely used on mainframes from the advent of disks around 1960 until the spread of virtual memory in the mid-1970s, then reappeared on microcomputers in the early 1980s in exactly the same form, and faded as virtual memory appeared on PCs in the 1990s. They're still used in memory limited embedded environments, and may yet reappear in other places where precise programmer or compiler control of memory usage improves performance. With the advent of hardware relocation and virtual memory, linkers and loaders actually got less complex, since each program could again have an entire address space.

Programs could be linked to be loaded at fixed addresses, with hardware rather than software relocation taking care of any load-time relocation. But computers with hardware relocation invariably run more than one program, frequently multiple copies of the same program. When a computer runs multiple instances of one program, some parts of the program are the same among all running instance (the executable code, in particular), while other parts are unique to each instance. If the parts that don't change can be separated out from the parts that do change, the operating system can use a single copy of the unchanging part, saving considerable storage.

Compilers and assemblers were modified to create object code in multiple sections, with one section for read only code and another section for writable data, the linker had to be able to combine all of sections of each type so that the linked program would have all the code in one place and all of the data in another.

WORKING

Program Loading

In some cases loading just involves copying the data from disk to memory, in others it involves allocating storage, setting protection bits, or arranging for virtual memory to map virtual addresses to disk pages.

Relocation

Compilers and assemblers generally create each file of object code with the program addresses starting at zero, but few computers let you load your program at location zero. I. a program is created from multiple subprograms, all the subprograms have to be loaded at non-overlapping addresses. Relocation is the process of assigning load addresses to the various parts of the program, adjusting the code and data in the program to reflect the assigned addresses.

In many systems, relocation happens more than once. It's quite common for a linker to create a program from multiple subprograms, and create one linked output program that starts at zero, with the various subprograms relocated to locations within the big program. Then when the program is loaded, the system picks the actual load address and the linked program is relocated as a whole to the load address.

Symbol Resolution

When a program is built from multiple subprograms, the references from one subprogram to another are made using symbols; a main program might use a square root routine called sqrt, and the math library defines sqrt. A linker resolves the symbol by noting the location assigned to sqrt in the library, and patching the caller's object code to so the call instruction refers to that location. Although there's considerable overlap between linking and loading, it's reasonable to define a program that does program loading as a loader, and one that does symbol resolution as a linker. Either can do relocation, and there have been all-in-one linking loaders that do all three functions. The line between relocation and symbol resolution can be fuzzy. Since linkers already can resolve references to symbols, one way to handle code relocation is to assign a symbol to the base address of each part of the program, and treat relocatable addresses as references to the base address symbols.

TWO-PASS LINKING PROCESS

Now we turn to the general structure of linkers. Linking, like compiling or assembling, is fundamentally a two pass process. A linker takes as its input a set of input object files, libraries, and perhaps command files, and produces as its result an output object file, and perhaps ancillary information such as a load map or a file containing debugger symbols. Each input file contains a set of *segments,* contiguous chunks of code or data to be placed in the output file. Each input file also contains at least one *symbol table.*

Some symbols are exported, defined within the file for use in other files, generally the names of routines within the file that can be called from elsewhere. Other symbols are imported, used in the file but not defined, generally the names of routines called from but not present in the file. When a linker runs, it first has to scan the input files to find the sizes of the segments and to collect the definitions and references of all of the symbols It creates a segment table listing all of the segments defined in the input files, and a symbol table with all of the symbols imported or exported. Using the data from the first pass, the linker assigns numeric locations to symbols, determines the sizes and location of the segments in the output address space, and figures out where everything goes in the output file. The second pass uses the information collected in the first pass to control the actual linking process. It reads and relocates the object code, substituting numeric addresses for symbol references, and adjusting memory addresses in code and data to reflect relocated segment addresses, and writes the relocated code to the output file.

It then writes the output file, generally with header information, the relocated segments, and symbol table information. If the program uses dynamic linking, the symbol table contains the info the runtime linker will need to resolve dynamic symbols. In many cases, the linker itself will generate small amounts of code or data in the output file, such as "glue code" used to call routines in overlays or dynamically linked libraries, or an array of pointers to initialization routines that need to be called at program startup time. Whether or not the program uses dynamic linking, the file may also contain a symbol table for relinking or debugging that isn't used by the program itself, but may be used by other programs that deal with the output file. Some object formats are relinkable, that is, the output file from one linker run can be used as the input to a subsequent linker run. This requires that the output file contain a symbol table like one in an input file, as well as all of the other auxiliary information present in an input file. Nearly all object formats have provision for debugging symbols, so that when the program is run under the control of a debugger, the debugger can use those symbols to let the programmer control the program in terms of the line numbers and names used in the source program.

Depending on the details of the object format, the debugging symbols may be intermixed in a single symbol table with symbols needed by the linker, or there may be one table for the linker and a separate, somewhat redundant table for the debugger. A few linkers appear to work in one pass. They do that by buffering some or all of the contents of the input file in memory or disk during the linking process, then reading the buffered material later.

RELOCATION

When a compiler or assembler generates and object file, it generates the code using the unrelocated addresses of code and data defined within the file, and usually zeros for code and data defined elsewhere. As part of the linking process, the linker modifies the object code to reflect the actual addresses assigned. For example, consider this snippet of x86 code that moves the contents of variable a to variable b using the eax register.

```
mov a,%eax
mov%eax,b
```

If a is defined in the same file at location 1234 hex and b is imported from somewhere else, the generated object code will be: A1 34 12 00 00 mov a,%eax A3 00 00 00 00 mov%eax,b Each instruction contains a one-byte operation code followed by a fourbyte address. The first instruction has a reference to 1234 (byte reversed, since the x86 uses a right to left byte order) and the second a reference to zero since the location of b is unknown. Now assume that the linker links this code so that the section in which a is located is relocated by hex 10000 bytes, and b turns out to be at hex 9A12.

The linker modifies the code to be:

```
A1 34 12 01 00 mov a,%eax
A3 12 9A 00 00 mov%eax,b
```

That is, it adds 10000 to the address in the first instruction so now it refers to a's relocated address which is 11234, and it patches in the address for b. These adjustments affect instructions, but any pointers in the data part of an object file have to be adjusted as well. On older computers with small address spaces and direct addressing, the modification process is fairly simple, since there are only only one or two address formats that a linker has to handle. Modern computers, including all RISCs, require considerably more complex code modification. No single instruction contains enough bits to hold a direct address, so the compiler and linker have to use complicated addressing tricks to handle data at arbitrary addresses. In some cases, it's possible to concoct an address using two or three instructions, each of which contains part of the address, and use bit manipulation to combine the parts into a full address. In this case, the linker has to be prepared to modify each of the instructions appropriately, inserting some of the bits of the address into each instruction.

In other cases, all of the addresses used by a routine or group of routines are placed in an array used as an "address pool", initialization code sets one of the machine registers to point to that array, and code loads pointers out of the address pool as needed using that register as a base register. The linker may have to create the array from all of the addresses used in a program, then modify instructions that so that they refer to the appropriate address pool entry.

COMMAND LANGUAGES

Every linker has some sort of command language to control the linking process. At the very least the linker needs the list of object files and libraries to link. Generally there is a long list of possible options: whether to keep debugging symbols, whether to use shared or unshared libraries, which of several possible output formats to use. Most linkers permit some way to specify the address at which the linked code is to be bound, which comes in handy when using a linker to link a system kernel or other program that doesn't run under control of an operating system. In linkers that support multiple code and data segments, a linker command language can specify the order in which segments are to be linked, special treatment for certain kinds of segments, and other application-specific options.

There are four common techniques to pass commands to a linker:

- *Command line:* Most systems have a command line or the equivalent, via which one can pass a mixture of file names and switches. This is the usual approach for Unix and Windows linkers. On systems with limited length command lines, there's usually a way to direct the linker to read commands from a file and treat them as though they were on the command line.

Embedded in Object Files

Some object formats, notably Microsoft's, permit linker commands to be embedded inside object files. This permits a compiler to pass any options needed to link an object file in the file itself. For example, the C compiler passes commands to search the standard C library.

Separate Configuration Language

A few linkers have a full fledged configuration language to control linking. The GNU linker, which can handle an enormous range of object file formats, machine architectures, and address space conventions, has a complex control language that lets a programmer specify the order in vhich segments should be linked, rules for combining similar segments, segment addresses, and a wide range of other options. Other linkers have less complex languages to handle specific features such as programmer-defined overlays.

LOADER [MH}

It is the Loader's function to fix absolute addresses for the relocated values in a relocatable module, thereby converting a relocatable module into an "executable" output file. The Loader is usually called automatically by the Linker but it may also be called separately by the user.

As indicated below, several different Loaders are (optionally) available for use with Introl-C and, if the user has elected to obtain such optional Loaders, a variety of executable output file formats can be generated, depending on the Loader being used. Each resident Introl-C compiler package, and each Introl-C cross-compiler package, nominally includes a single, specific type of Introl Loader which is considered as being the "standard" Loader for that compiler's particular host system configuration. For resident Introl-C Compiler packages, the 'standard' Loader that is furnished is an "operating system dependent" type of Loader which generates an output file that is executable on that particular Compiler's host system. For cross-compiler versions of Introl-C, the "standard" Loader furnished is typically a "hex" type Loader that generates a file of output load records, which can be either Motorola S-Records, intel Hex, Tektronix Hex, or Tektronix Extended Hex at user option. Besides the "standard" Loader that accompanies any given Compiler type, it is also possible for the user to optionally obtain and use other compatible "cross-Loaders" which generate output formats unrelated to the Compiler's host operating system. For example, "hex-type" Loaders are optionally available for use with resident versions of Introl-C; "operating system dependent" type Loaders are optionally available for use with cross-compiler versions; etc. There are, therefore, several different species of Loaders, (as well as several different types of related Standard Libraries) that may potentially be used under Introl-C. The "standard" Loader supplied with your Introl-C package, as well as any other Loaders that may have been optionally ordered, are described in detail in the Loader Appendix of this Linker Reference Manual. This Loader section describes the general features that are common to all Loader types.

Normally the input to the Loader is expected to be a relocatable file which has no unresolved external references; if unresolved references do exist in its input, loading will normally not be successful. A Loader option is provided, however, to force a file to be loaded even if it contains unresolved references. Usually a relocatable file has to be linked before it can be used as input to the Loader. It is also possible, of course, to assemble a file which makes no external references and then use the relocatable output file produced by the Assembler directly as input to the Loader (ie without having actually linked it)

FUNCTIONS

- Allocate space in memory for the program (allocation).
- Resolve symbolic references between object programs (linking).
- Adjust all address dependent locations, such as address constraints, to correspond to the allocated space (relocation).

- Physically place the machine instruction and data into memory(loading) for execution.
- *Loader*: System program that performs the loading function.
- *Linker (or linkage editor)*: System program that performs the linking operations (*i.e.* linking and relocation).

TYPES

Absolute loader

Performs Loading Only:

- *Object program contains*:
  H card (or record)
  T cards (or record)
  E card (or record)
- Check the starting address and memory size required (*i.e.* specified in H record), load Text records into memory sequentially, and then jump to the starting address specified by End record.

COMMAND LINE

The "standard" Loader supplied with your Introl-C package is normally automatically called by the Linker when the Linker pass finishes. However, linker command line options exist that mav be used to alternatively force the Linker to automatically call other optional Loaders. Situations also arise when it is desirable to explicitly call the Loader alone, without first executing the Linker. When such situations arise, the Loader may be independently called by the user with a loader command line of the general form:

```
<c>ld <file> {<option>}
```

where <c>ld represents the Introl filename of the specific Loader being called, <file> is the name of the (linked) relocatable module which is to be loaded, and (<option>) represents zero or more Loader option specifiers.

Each of the potentially usable Introl Loaders is uniquely identified by a 3-letter Loader filename, the last two letters of which are always "ld". The <c> designator indicated in the "<c>ld" loader call on the command line therefore represents the first letter in the three-letter Loader name. For example, to call the Introl hex type of Loader, which has the filename "hld", the "<c>ld" entry on the command line would actually become "hld". For further specifics on the names of the loaders which can be legally accessed. The relocatable file that is input to the Loader is expected to have a filenarne extension; if none is specified, the default filename extension ".RL" is assumed. Normally the name of the executable output file will be identical to the name of the input file, but with a filename extension typically added by the Loader. The filename extensions each Loader appends are discussed in the Loader Appendices to this manual.

LOADER OPTIONS

Each type of Loader available for use with the Introl-C has its own, generally unique set of options. When the Loader is being called separately, Loader options are specified directly on the loader command line when the Loader is being automatically called by the Linker, Loader options are specified on the link command line, together with the Linker options. If Loader options are specified on the link command line, any such options (ie those that do not apply to the Linker) will be automatically sent on to the Loader. For the most part Linker and Loader option specifiers tend to be distinct, so that there is little ambiguity when Loader options are specified on the link command line.

LIBRARY FILES

A library file is a file which contains one or more linkable object modules of the type produced by the Introl Assembler. When a file is compiled and assembled, the result is exactly one linkable module which is placed into a file. This file is actually a library which happens to contain only a single module. When the user links a program, one or more of these "libraries" are specified on the link command line. Usually the "libraries" are those produced as a result of a compilation and contain only a single module, however, they may also contain several modules. The Library Manager, "libman", is a program which allows the user to place several modules into a single library file. When the user has a large set of modules which are commonly used in programs, it is usually convenient to place them all in one library and then simply specify the library once on the link command line. The Linker will extract only those modules it requires in order to satisfy the external references of the program. The Linker is designed to automatically search the "Standard Library", libc.R, if it still has external references to satisfy after it has exhausted all the alternatives provided by the modules specified an the link command line. For many C programs, the Standard Library is usually where most of the external references are satisfied. Many users find it useful to add to, or modify routines in, the Standard Library. The Library Manager is the utility program which allows the user to create new libraries and also to maintain existing ones.

MODES

The Library Manager has three modes of operation: Direct Mode, Interactive Mode, and Command File Mode. The most convenient to use for simple additions and deletions to the library is the Direct Mode. For more extensive modifications the user may instead wish to use Interactive mode. The third mode is the Command File mode which causes the Library Manager to read its commands from a file rather than getting them from the user terminal.

- *Direct Mode*: In Direct Mode the user is permitted to specify a single command on the library manager command line. When the Library Manager is called, it executes this single command function and then immediately exits from the Library Manager. When modifying libraries, however, a single command function is often all that is necessary to accomplish the change desired by the user. When Direct Mode is being used, the desired command is specified right on the command line, following the <lib> library specification. Any Library Manager command may be used in the Direct Mode.
- *Interactive Mode*: if no command is specified on the

Library Manager call line, the Library Manager will enter its Interactive Mode of operation. In Interactive Mode the Library Manager will print a colon (".") as a promet and will accept a succession of commands directly from the user terminal. Interactive Mode is useful when the user must make extensive changes to a library, or when the user wishes to step through the library checking and/or changing modules in an "interactive" manner. Once selected, the Interactive Mode will remain in effect until the user enters a "quit" or "omit" command.

- *Command File Mode*: One of the commands which the user can specify as an Interactive code or a Direct Mode command entry is the "Comfile" command. This command instructs the Library Manager to read subsequent instructions from a command file. When a "Comfile command is entered, the Library Manager will read from the file specified until it reads a "quit" or "omit" command or, alternatively, until it reaches the end of the file. when exiting the Command File Mode, the Library Manager will return to whatever mode it was in before the Command File Mode was entered. If the Command File Mode was entered as the result of a Direct Mode command, then the Library Manager will terminate when Command File Mode is exited. If entered from the Interactive Mode, it will return to the Interactive Mode.

ASSEMBLER

DEFINITION

An assembler is a program that converts simple commands into machine code. The simple commands, written in an assembly language, are used in groups to perform more complicated tasks.

FUNCTION

The function of the assembler is to translate programs written in the assembler language into object modules. The code will then be in a suitable form for processing by the Linkage

Editor. The assembler language is a symbolic representation of machine language. The correspondence between the two can be best understood by examining the listings produced by an assembler. The assembler, like the linkage editor, is supplied as part of VSE, CMS, and MVS, and executes under control of the appropriate control program. It accepts, as input, a source program written in the Assembler Language.

This consists of three types of instructions:

- C Machine instructions.
- C Assembler instructions.
- C Macro instructions.

As expected with an IBM language, code can also be copied in from a source statement library (VSE) or a pds (MVS) or MACLIB (CMS).

INTERPRETER

DEFINITION

- An interpreter runs program code by converting it to machine code on the fly. You save some time in the front by avoiding the compiling and linking steps, but interpreters generally run slower because they have to convert the same code (in a loop, say) again and again. An example of a common interpreter is the one that executes.bat files.
- An *interpreter* is also a program that translates a high-level language into a low-level one, but it does it at the moment the program is run. You write the program using a text editor or something similar, and then instruct the interpreter to run the program. It takes the program, one line at a time, and translates each line before running it: It translates the first line and runs it, then translates the second line and runs it etc. The interpreter has no "memory" for the translated lines, so if it comes across lines of the program within a loop, it must translate them afresh every time that particular line runs.

Consider this simple Basic program:

- 10 FOR COUNT = 1 TO 1000

- 20 PRINT COUNT * COUNT
- 30 NEXT COUNT
- Line 20 of the program displays the square of the value stored in COUNT and this line has to be carried out 1000 times. The interpreter must also translate that line 1000 times, which is clearly an inefficient process. However, interpreted languages do have their uses, as we will see in a later section.
- Examples of interpreted languages are Basic, JavaScript and LISP
- The Interpreter pattern discusses: defining a domain language (*i.e.* problem characterization) as a simple language grammar, representing domain rules as language sentences, and interpreting these sentences to solve the problem. The pattern uses a class to represent each grammar rule. And since grammars are usually hierarchical in structure, an inheritance hierarchy of rule classes maps nicely.
- An abstract base class specifies the method interpret(). Each concrete subclass implements interpret() by accepting (as an argument) the current state of the language stream, and adding its contribution to the problem solving process.

STRUCTURE

- Interpreter suggests modeling the domain with a recursive grammar. Each rule in the grammar is either a "composite" (a rule that references other rules) or a terminal (a leaf node in a tree structure). Interpreter relies on the recursive traversal of the Composite pattern to interpret the "sentences" it is asked to process.

COMPILER

DEFINITION

A compiler completely converts program code to machine code once. The computer user runs the machine code in the form of an executable command, ending in.exe say. Because the translation is complete before execution, compiled code is much faster. The translation process should also report the presence of errors in the source program.

Source Program → Compiler → Target Program

↓

Error Messages

There are two parts of compilation. The analysis part breaks up the source program into constant piece and creates an intermediate representation of the source program. The synthesis part constructs the desired target program from the intermediate representation. *Compilers* were the first sort of translator program to be written.

The idea is simple: You write the program, then hand it to the compiler which translates it. Then run the result. The compiler takes the file that you have written and produces another file from it. In the case of Pascal programs, for instance, you might write a program called my Prog.pas and the Pascal compiler would translate it into the file myProg.exe which you could then run. If you tried to examine the contents of myProg.exe using, say, a text editor, then it would just appear as gobbledy-gook. The compiler has another task apart from translating your program. It also checks it to make sure that it is grammatically correct. Only when it is sure that there are no grammatical errors does it do the translation. Any errors that the compiler detects are called compile-time errors or syntax errors. If it finds so much as one syntax error, it stops compiling and reports the error to you.

COMPILER PHASES

The compiler has a number of phases plus symbol table manager and an error handler:

Input Source Program

↓

Lexical Analyser

↓

Syntax Analyser

↓

Symbol Table Manager | Semantic Analyser | Error Handler

↓

Intermediate Code Generator

↓

Code Optimizer

↓

Code Generator

↓

Out Target Program

The cousins of the compiler are:

- Preprocessor.
- Assembler.
- Loader and Link-editor.

Front End vs Back End of a Compilers. The phases of a compiler are collected into front end and back end. The front end includes all analysis phases end the intermediate code generator.

The back end includes the code optimization phase and final code generation phase. The front end analyses the source program and produces intermediate code while the back end synthesizes the target program from the intermediate code.

A naive approach (front force) to that front end might run the phases serially:

- Lexical analyser takes the source program as an input and produces a long string of tokens.
- Syntax Analyser takes an out of lexical analyser and produces a large tree.
- Semantic analyser takes the output of syntax analyser and produces another tree.
- Similarly, intermediate code generator takes a tree as an input produced by semantic analyser and produces intermediate code.

Minus Points

- Requires enormous amount of space to store tokens and trees.

- Very slow since each phase would have to input and output to and from temporary disk

ADVANTAGES

Choosing the right C compiler for your embedded-system projects may be a bigger challenge than you expect. The embedded-system-industry trend is moving from using assembly to using the higher level languages. Assembly language gives you more control over your code size and execution speeds. However, embedded C is easy to understand and portable from platform to platform. Another benefit is that developing code in C generally improves your product time to market. These features are advantageous if you expect your firmware to have longevity or if your staff changes periodically. A variety of embedded-C compilers is available in the market today. Embedded-C compilers are available as shareware from controller-or processor-IC vendors; or from high-end, reputable software companies whose selling prices often reflect the sophistication of the software. Some compiler-software companies have great advertisements and competitive prices but inferior products. So, how do you choose your compiler software for now and for the future?

There are many issues to consider when choosing your compiler. The most important are ANSI compliance, size and speed optimizations, portability, and supporting tools. Adherence to the ANSI standard for the C language is critical for about 80 to 85% of code. This feature facilitates portability from part to part, as well as from software platform to software platform. ANSI-compliant software also integrates easy-to-understand code into your library. This type of code—if it is well-written—will have a shelf life like a good red wine. Even if portability is not an issue, it is important to understand how the compiler differs from ANSI and whether those differences will impact your development.

If the compiler of interest is ANSI-compliant, you should then examine the software's machine-code-generation capability. You might ask whether the compiler output code is optimized for small code (because memory is precious in controllers or processors) or whether the application executes in a timely or time-accurate manner. These features are somewhat mutually exclusive, but the compiler software should be able to optimize one or the other. Portability between platforms is critical in larger companies that have a diverse range of products.

However, it can also be convenient in smaller companies that may want the flexibility to quickly change controllers during development. Portability allows you to change quickly from one controller to another during application development. It also makes your code libraries more valuable over time.

If you want to easily complete your programming projects, the compiler cannot stand on its own. Every compiler needs an integrated suite of other tools. This tool suite should have, at a minimum, an integrated development environment that comes complete with a simulator and a hardware-debugging interface. Sometimes, you can mix and match these tools from other vendors, but use the vendor for your compiler as a first source.

It can be difficult and frustrating to mix and then match tools from various vendors. Some other characteristics that make up a good compiler are the availability of code libraries and library support. This concept does not fit into organizations with the NIH (not-invented-here) philosophy. An NIH organization deserves everything it gets (or doesn't get). Libraries with code that implements useful functions help expedite your projects to completion.

Many times, these libraries have gone through evaluations and debugging to ensure their value. Some of the final details in your compiler evaluation have to do with customer service. You need to ask whether your compiler company supports your questions and helps with its software bugs. You will find this information in the company's application-notes library, discussion forums, and software-release history. Although frequent releases can be a sign of responsiveness, they can also be an indication of serious stability concerns. The ideal compiler vendor has more support than you'll ever need.

In the past, most firmware designers would write embedded-firmware programs in assembly language. The embedded-C compiler transforms your source code into machine code. The C compiler you use determines the size as well as the execution time of your code. Many ways exist for determining these factors, so running your own test programs is also important. Don't depend on the results from a compiler-software company that runs its own tests. Many times, these companies can consciously or unconsciously skew the results.

2

Windows Operating System

PROCESS

We see an operating system as the programs that make the hardware useable. In brief, an operating system is the set of programs that controls a computer. Controlling the computer involves software at several levels. We will differentiate kernel services, library services, and application-level services, all of which are part of the operating system. Processes run Applications, which are linked together with libraries that perform standard services.

The kernel supports the processes by providing a path to the peripheral devices. The kernel responds to service calls from the processes and interrupts from the devices. The core of the operating system is the kernel, a control program that functions in privileged state (an execution context that allows all hardware instructions to be executed), reacting to interrupts from external devices and to service requests and traps from processes. Generally, the kernel is a permanent resident of the computer.

It creates and terminates processes and responds to their request for service. Operating Systems are resource managers. The main resource is computer hardware in the form of processors, storage, input/output devices, communication devices, and data. Some of the operating system functions are: implementing the user interface, sharing hardware among users, allowing users to share data among themselves, preventing users from interfering with one another, scheduling resources among users, facilitating input/output, recovering from errors, accounting for resource usage, facilitating parallel operations, organizing data for secure and rapid access, and handling network communications.

OBJECTIVES

Modern Operating systems generally have following three major goals. Operating systems generally accomplish these goals by running processes in low privilege and providing service calls that invoke the operating system kernel in high-privilege state.

HARDWARE

An abstraction is software that hides lower level details and provides a set of higher-level functions. An operating system transforms the physical world of devices, instructions, memory, and time into virtual world that is the result of abstractions built by the operating system.

There are several reasons for abstraction.

- *First,* the code needed to control peripheral devices is not standardized. Operating systems provide subroutines called device drivers that perform operations on behalf of programs for example, input/output operations.
- *Second,* the operating system introduces new functions as it abstracts the hardware. For instance, operating system introduces the file abstraction so that programs do not have to deal with disks.
- *Third,* the operating system transforms the computer hardware into multiple virtual computers, each belonging to a different program. Each program that is running is called a process. Each process views the hardware through the lens of abstraction.
- *Fourth,* the operating system can enforce security through abstraction.

MANAGE RESOURCES

An operating system controls how processes (the active agents) may access resources (passive entities).

PLEASANT AND EFFECTIVE USER INTERFACE

The user interacts with the operating systems through the user interface and usually interested in the "look and feel" of the operating system. The most important components of the user interface are the command interpreter, the file system, on-line help, and application integration. The recent trend has been towards increasingly integrated graphical user interfaces that encompass the activities of multiple processes on networks of computers.

One can view Operating Systems from two points of views: Resource manager and Extended machines. Form Resource manager point of view Operating Systems manage the different parts of the system efficiently and from extended machines point of view Operating Systems provide a virtual machine to users that is more convenient to use. The structurally Operating Systems can be design as a monolithic system, a hierarchy of layers, a virtual machine system, an exokernel, or using the client-server model. The basic concepts of Operating Systems are processes, memory management, I/O management, the file systems, and security.

CONCEPTS

The CPU (Central Processing Unit) is the heart of any computer, but the operating system is the brain. Unfortunately, understanding exactly how these things really work can be difficult, because it's fairly hard to "play" with the operating system that you are actually using. You can do quite a bit with sophisticated debuggers, but eventually you run into confusion and difficulty. And, as you try more complex tasks, you run the risk of interfering with the real machine's operating system. Finally, modern CPU's are very complex, and that complexity can make it more difficult to understand basic concepts.

Therefore thought it would be interesting to emulate CPU's and other hardware in software. By doing that, we can present simple ideas and build on that understanding. We'll start very simply, and build from there, eventually demonstrating more advanced concepts like virtual memory, disk filesystems, and even multitasking.

FUNDAMENTAL CONCEPT:

Fundamental concept of computer operating systemstarts with the structure of the OS. Conceptually, an operating system can be broken down into the kernel, shell and system utilities. The kernel is the core of the operating system, and in some cases, the distinction between the kernel and the shell is clear; in others, the distinction is only conceptual. A process is a program in execution.

New processes are spawned when needed and terminated to free memory and other resources. Files are a method of organizing the information on disk. Files are usually organized in an inverted tree-like structure. A system call is a program that requests something from the operating system. The roles of an operating system vary with the hardware and user programs it was designed to work with. The earliest operating systems were designed to help applications interact with hardware.

This has grown to the point that the operating system now defines the machine. The operating system provides an interface to the underlying hardware, the application programs, and the user.

The *operating system* manages:

- Hardware
- CPU
- Memory
- Device Drivers
- I/O
- Applications

There are four basic types of operating systems:

- Real time operating system
- Single user, single task operating system
- Single user, multi task operating system
- Multi user operating system

HISTORY

History of operating system was started with the first generation computers. They operated on a purely mechanical basis. There was no concept of an operating system. The user fed data and the program into the computer using punched cards. The programs were debugged using front panel switches and lights. The second-generation computers were batch systems where the jobs and instructions were put together so that they could be processed without interruptions.

The third generation computers used the concepts of multiprogramming and time-sharing. Spooling batch systems were the first and simplest of multiprogramming systems. The major advantage was that the output from the jobs was available as soon as the job was completed. The fourth generation saw the advent of modern operating systems for PCs, workstations and servers and also includes networking and distributed operating systems.

The early *operating systems* were diverse, with each vendor producing their own operating systems specific to their hardware. This continued until the 1960s when IBM developed the S/360 series of machines, where all machines ran the same operating system, OS/360. CP/M (Control Program for Microcomputers) was the first generic operating system for microcomputers. Before CP/M, every brand of computer had its own unique operating system.

Because of this, programs could not be shared between computers and software had to be rewritten for every type of computer. The nearest to the operating system was the "job control language" (JCL) required to submit a program for execution on the mainframe. CP/M was a complete software development environment that enabled to write software that was machine-independent, and move CP/M itself to other computers. OS/2 was the first operating system to provide intrinsic multitasking based on hardware support. It was text-mode only and allowed only one program to be on the screen at a time, even though other programs could be running in the background.

CONCEPTS OF REAL-TIME OPERATING SYSTEMS

FUNDAMENTALS

To most people, embedded systems are not recognizable as computers. Instead, they are hidden inside everyday objects that surround us and help us in our lives. Embedded systems typically do not interface with the outside world through familiar personal computer interface devices such as a mouse, keyboard and graphic user interface. Instead, they interface with the outside world through unusual interfaces such as sensors, actuators and specialized communication links.

Real-time and embedded systems operate in constrained environments in which computer memory and processing power are limited. They often need to provide their services within strict time deadlines to their users and to the surrounding world. It is these memory, speed and timing constraints that dictate the use of real-time operating systems in embedded software.

BASI ERNEL SERVICES

The "k nel" of a real-time operating system ("RTOS") provides an "abstraction layer" that hides from application software the hardware details of the processor (or set of processors) upon which the application software will run..

In providing this "abstraction layer" the RTOS kernel supplies five main categories of basic services to application software. The most basic category of kernel services, at the very center of Figure, is Task Management. This set of services allows application software developers to design their software as a number of separate "chunks" of software—each handling a distinct topic, a distinct goal, and perhaps its own real-time deadline. Each separate "chunk" of software is called a "task." Services in this category include the ability to launch tasks and assign priorities to them. The main RTOS service in this category is the scheduling of tasks as the embedded system is in operation. The Task Scheduler controls the execution of application software tasks, and can make them run in a very timely and responsive fashion.

The second category of kernel services, shown at the top of Figure, is Intertask Communication and Synchronization. These services make it possible for tasks to pass information from one to another, without danger of that information ever being damaged. They also make it possible for tasks to coordinate, so that they can productively cooperate with one another. Without the help of these RTOS services, tasks might well communicate corrupted information or otherwise interfere with each other. Since many embedded systems have stringent timing requirements, most RTOS kernels also provide some basic Timer services, such as task delays and time-outs. These are shown on the right side of Figure. Many (but not all) RTOS kernels provide Dynamic Memory Allocation services. This category of services allows tasks to "borrow" chunks of RAM memory for temporary use in application software. Often these chunks of memory are then passed from task to task, as a means of quickly communicating large amounts of data between tasks. Some very small RTOS kernels that are intended for tightly memory-limited environments, do not offer Dynamic Memory Allocation services.

Many (but not all) RTOS kernels also provide a "Device I/O Supervisor" category of services. These services, if available, provide a uniform framework for organizing and accessing the many hardware device drivers that are typical of an embedded system. In addition to kernel services, many RTOSs offer a number of optional add-on operating system components for such high-level services as file system organization, network communication, network management, database management, user-interface graphics, etc. Although many of these add-on components are much larger and much more complex than the RTOS kernel, they rely on the presence of the RTOS kernel and take advantage of its basic services. Each of these add-on components is included in an embedded system only if its services are needed for implementing the embedded application, in order to keep program memory consumption to a minimum.

GENERAL OPERATING SYSTEMS

Many non-real-time operating systems also provide similar kernel services. The key difference between general-computing operating systems and real-time operating systems is the need for " deterministic " timing behaviour in the real-time operating systems. Formally, "deterministic" timing means that operating system services consume only known and expected amounts of time. In theory, these service times could be expressed as mathematical formulas. These formulas must be strictly algebraic and not include any random timing components. Random elements in service times could cause random delays in application software and could then make the application randomly miss real-time deadlines – a scenario clearly unacceptable for a real-time embedded system.

General-computing non-real-time operating systems are often quite non-deterministic. Their services can inject random delays into application software and thus cause slow responsiveness of an application at unexpected times. If you ask the developer of a non-real-time operating system for the algebraic formula describing the timing behaviour of one of its services (such as sending a message from task to task), you will invariably not get an algebraic formula. Instead the developer of the non-real-time operating system (such as Windows, Unix or Linux) will just give you a puzzled look. Deterministic timing behaviour was simply not a design goal for these general-computing operating systems. On the other hand, real-time operating systems often go a step beyond basic determinism. For most kernel services, these operating systems offer constant load-independent timing: In other words, the algebraic formula is as simple as:*T(message_send) = constant*, irrespective of the length of the message to be sent, or other factors such as the numbers of tasks and queues and messages being managed by the RTOS.

TASK SCHEDULING

Most RTOSs do their scheduling of tasks using a scheme called "priority-based preemptive scheduling." Each task in a software application must be assigned a priority, with higher priority values representing the need for quicker responsiveness. Very quick responsiveness is made possible by the "preemptive" nature of the task scheduling. "Preemptive" means that the scheduler is allowed to stop any task at any point in its execution, if it determines that another task needs to run immediately.

The basic rule that governs priority-based preemptive scheduling is that at every moment in time, "The Highest Priority Task that is Ready to Run, will be the Task that Must be Running." In other words, if both a low-priority task and a higher-priority task are ready to run, the scheduler will allow the higher-priority task to run first. The low-priority task will only get to run after the higher-priority task has finished with its current work. What if a low-priority task has already begun to run, and then a higher-priority task becomes ready? This might occur because of an external world trigger such as a switch closing. A priority-based preemptive scheduler will behave as follows: It will allow the low-priority task to complete the current assembly-language instruction that it is executing. But it won't allow it to complete an entire line of high-level language code; nor will it allow it to continue running until the next clock tick.

It will then immediately stop the execution of the low-priority task, and allow the higher-priority task to run. After the higher-priority task has finished its current work, the low-priority task will be allowed to continue running. This is shown in Figure, where the higher-priority task is called "Mid-Priority Task." Of course, while the mid-priority task is running, an even higher-priority task might become ready. This is represented in Figure by "Trigger_2" causing the "High-Priority Task" to become ready. In that case, the running task ("Mid-Priority Task") would be preempted to allow the high-priority task to run.

When the high-priority task has finished its current work, the mid-priority task would be allowed to continue. And after both the high-priority task and the mid-priority task complete their work, the low-priority task would be allowed to continue running. Each time the priority-based preemptive scheduler is alerted by an external world trigger (such as a switch closing) or a software trigger (such as a message arrival), it must go through the following 5 steps:

- Determine whether the currently running task should continue to run. If not ...
- Determine which task should run next.

- Save the environment of the task that was stopped (so it can continue later).
- Set up the running environment of the task that will run next.
- Allow this task to run.

FIXED-TIME TASK SWITCHING

The time it takes to do task switching is of interest when evaluating an operating system. A simple general-computing (non-preemptive) operating system might do task switching only at timer tick times, which might for example be ten milliseconds apart. Then if the need for a task switch arises anywhere within a 10-millisecond timeframe, the actual task switch would occur only at the end of the current 10-millisecond period. Such a delay would be unacceptable in most real-time embedded systems.

In more sophisticated preemptive task schedulers, the scheduler may need to search through arrays of tasks to determine which task should be made to run next. If there are more tasks to search through, the search will take longer. Such searches are often done by general-computing operating systems, thus making them non-deterministic. Real-time operating systems, on the other hand, avoid such searches by using incrementally updated tables that allow the task scheduler to identify the task that should run next in a rapid fixed-time fashion. On the other hand, the horizontal solid green line shows the task switching time characteristic of a real-time operating system. It is constant, independent of any load factor such as the number of tasks in a software system.

For, in fact, the term "real-time" does not mean "as fast as possible" but rather "real-time" demands consistent, repeatable, known timing performance. Although a non-real-time operating system might do some faster task switching for small numbers of tasks, it might equally well introduce a long time delay the next time it does the same task switch. The strength of a real-time operating system is in its known, repeatable timing performance, which is also typically faster than that of a non-deterministic task scheduler in situations of large numbers of tasks in a software system. Most often, the real-time operating system will exhibit task-switching times much faster than its non-real-time competitor when the number of tasks grows above 5 or 10.

COMMUNICATION

Most operating systems, including RTOSs, offer a variety of mechanisms for communication and synchronization between tasks. These mechanisms are necessary in a preemptive environment of many tasks, because without them the tasks might well communicate corrupted information or otherwise interfere with each other. For instance, a task might be preempted when it is in the middle of updating a table of data. If a second task that preempts it reads from that table, it will read a combination of some areas of newly-updated data plus some areas of data that have not yet been updated.

New Yorkers would call this a "mish-mash." These updated and old data areas together may be incorrect in combination, or may not even make sense. An example is a data table containing temperature measurements that begins with the contents "10 C." A task begins updating this table with the new value "99 F", writing into the table character-by-character.

If that task is preempted in the middle of the update, a second task that preempts it could possibly read a value like "90 C" or "99 C." or "99 F", depending on precisely when the preemption took place. The partially updated values are clearly incorrect, and are caused by delicate timing coincidences that are very hard to debug or reproduce consistently. An RTOS's mechanisms for communication and synchronization between tasks are provided to avoid these kinds of errors. Most RTOSs provide several mechanisms, with each mechanism optimized for reliably passing a different kind of information from task to task.

Probably the most popular kind of communication between tasks in embedded systems is the passing of data from one task to another. Another kind of communication between tasks in embedded systems is the passing of what might be called "synchronization information" from one task to another. "Synchronization information" is like a command, where some commands could be positive, and some negative. Most RTOSs offer a semaphore or mutex mechanism for handling negative synchronization (sometimes called "mutual exclusion").

These mechanisms allow tasks to lock certain embedded system resources for their use only, and subsequently to unlock the resource when they're done. For positive synchronization, different RTOSs offer different mechanisms. Some RTOSs offer event-flags, while others offer signals. And yet others rely on message passing for positive synchronization as well as data passing duties.

DETERMINING HIGH-SPEED MESSAGE

Intertask message communication is another area where different operating systems show different timing characteristics. Most operating systems actually copy messages twice as they transfer them from task to task via a message queue.

The first copying is from the message-sender task to an operating system-owned "secret" area of RAM memory (implementing the "message queue"); and the second copying is from the operating system's "secret" RAM area to the message-receiver task. Clearly this is non-deterministic in its timing, as these copying activities take longer as message length increases. An approach that avoids this non-determinism and also accelerates performance, is to have the operating system copy a pointer to the message and deliver that pointer to the message-receiver task without moving the message contents at all. In order to avoid access collisions, the operating system then needs to go back to the message-sender task and obliterate its copy of the pointer to the message. For large messages, this eliminates the need for lengthy copying and eliminates non-determinism.

DYNAMIC MEMORY ALLOCATION

Determinism of service times is also an issue in the area of dynamic allocation of RAM memory. Many general-computing non-real-time operating systems offer memory allocation services from what is termed a "Heap." The famous "malloc" and "free" services known to C-language programmers work from a heap. Tasks can temporarily borrow some memory from the operating system's heap by calling "malloc", and specifying the size of memory buffer needed. When this task (or another task) is finished with this memory buffer it can return the buffer to the operating system by calling "free." The operating system will then return the buffer to the heap, where its memory might be used again, perhaps as part of a larger buffer. Or perhaps it may in the future be broken into several smaller buffers.

Heaps suffer from a phenomenon called "External Memory Fragmentation" that may cause the heap services to degrade. This fragmentation is caused by the fact that when a buffer is returned to the heap, it may in the future be broken into smaller buffers when "malloc" requests for smaller buffer sizes occur. After a heap undergoes many cycles of "malloc"s and "free"s, small slivers of memory may appear between memory buffers that are being used by tasks. These slivers are so small that they are useless to tasks. But they are trapped between buffers that are being used by tasks, so they can't be coagulated ("glued") together into bigger, useful buffer sizes. Over time, a heap will have more and more of these slivers.

This will eventually result in situations where tasks will ask for memory buffers ("malloc") of a certain size, and they will be refused by the operating system—even though the operating system has enough available memory in its heap. The problem: That memory is scattered in small slivers distributed in various separate parts of the heap. In operating system terminology, the slivers are called "fragments", and this problem is called "external memory fragmentation." This fragmentation problem can be solved by so-called "garbage collection" (defragmentation) software. Unfortunately, "garbage collection" algorithms are often wildly non-deterministic – injecting randomly-appearing random-duration delays into heap services. These are often seen in the memory allocation services of general-computing non-real-time operating systems. This puts the embedded system developer who wants to use a general-computing non-real-time operating system into a quandry: Should the embedded system be allowed to suffer occasional randomly-appearing random-duration delays if/when "garbage collection" kicks in?... Or, alternatively, should the embedded system be allowed to fragment its memory until application software "malloc" requests to the heap are refused even though a sufficient total amount of free memory is still available? Neither alternative is acceptable for embedded systems that need to provide service continually for long periods of time.

Real-time operating systems, on the other hand, solve this quandry by altogether avoiding both memory fragmentation and "garbage collection", and their consequences. RTOSs offer non-fragmenting memory allocation techniques instead of heaps. They do this by limiting the variety of memory chunk sizes they make available to application software. While this approach is less flexible than the approach taken by memory heaps, they do avoid external memory fragmentation and avoid the need for defragmentation. For example, the "Pools" memory allocation mechanism allows application software to allocate chunks of memory of perhaps 4 or 8 different buffer sizes per pool. Pools totally avoid external memory fragmentation, by not permitting a buffer that is returned to the pool to be broken into smaller buffers in the future.

USESY

Real-time and embedded systems are used in many applications such as airborne computers, medical instruments and communication systems. Embedded systems are characterized by limited processor memory, limited processing power, and unusual interfaces to the outside world. Real-time requirements impose stringent time deadlines for delivering the results of embedded processing. RTOS kernels hide from application software the low-level details of system hardware, and at the same time provide several categories of services to application software. These include: task management with priority-based preemptive scheduling, reliable intertask communication and synchronization, non-fragmenting dynamic memory allocation, and basic timer services. The issue of timing determinism is important in differentiating general-computing operating systems from real-time operating systems.

This issue crops up in many parts of operating system kernels, such as task schedulers, dynamic memory allocation and intertask message communication. While general-computing operating systems often offer non-deterministic services in these areas, fully deterministic solutions are needed for real-time and embedded systems. A number of real-time operating systems implement these solutions in their compact high-performance kernels.

GOALS AND FUNCTIONS

GOALS

Developing a single application for multiple platforms is a difficult task. The most significant issue is the need for a clean solution for developing Graphical User Interfaces [GUI's]. FOX aims to address this by providing a single GUI library that can run on different computer hardware and operating system environments. The benefits to application vendors and developers are clear:

Reducing Effort

After development, your FOX based application is only a compile away from running on other operating systems. When multiple hardware and software combinations are required by customers operating in a heterogeneous environment, using a single GUI system such as FOX is clearly the most cost-effective method to achieve the goal.

Availability of Software on other Platforms

Without the necessity of additional development work, the cost of which would have to be amortized over the number of sales, additional revenues can be engendered by having your software be available on multiple hardware and software environments. Software development is a costly undertaking; because of this, software vendors typically limit the number of platforms to a small subset of the platforms being used by *all* customers, effectively leaving certain customers in the dark. FOX allows applications to be developed on one platform, then simply recompile the application on a number of other hardware/software systems. Because the cost of doing so is negligible, this approach will be able to generate positive cashflow even with low sales volumes.

Captive Audience

If the application you're developing is available on all platforms, you may be able to create a captive customer base on hardware/software systems where your competitor is absent; you may in fact even be able to charge premium prices. Using the additional revenues derived from these customers, your product will be able to derive a steady addional revenue stream which will allow you to compete more aggressively against your single-platform competitor.

Higher Quality

For programmers, the benefits of multi-platform development v.s. single platform development are the additional confidence and code quality that compiling under different environments will give. For example, I have compiled FOX on a number of different systems, and different compilers will discover different types of code bugs. By compiling on all these different systems, FOX has gotten quite a bit better in the course of time.

Control your Destiny

Programmers understand it as a matter of course that they need to continually work to track the changes in a system's API's. But what if the system vendor is also your competitor? In such a case, you *will* loose, sooner or later. The FOX GUI Library provides a platform-independent escape hatch that relies only on core system facilities which can be expected to be present on any modern operating system.

Approach

FOX attains the goal of platform independence by eliminating all system dependencies from its public interfaces. In fact, a typical FOX application may not even need to include any system-specific header files at all! By not including *e.g.* X-Windows header files, applications can not even accidentally slip up and introduce platform dependencies. This strategy is also carried out inside FOX itself.

Thus, large parts of FOX are in fact defined entirely in FOX itself. The only dependencies are concentrated in a few select base classes where this couldn't be avoided. The following salient points highlight some fundamental benefits of FOX *vis-a-vis* other purported platform independent toolkits:

Eliminate all Platform Specific Header Files

Applications should only include header files from FOX, and a few header files for such basic system services as opening files etc.

Internal Layering

FOX itself relies largely on FOX base classes, and therefore a large fraction of FOX itself is platform independent as well.

Rely only on low-level system facilities

FOX relies only on core system facilities, and does NOT wrap native GUI libraries or toolkits.

This has the following benefits:

- *Identical behaviour*: The behaviour will be close to identical on all systems, as the behaviour is completely controlled by the FOX implementation, rather than some underlying library.
- *Identical looks*: FOX applications will look the same no matter what system you're running it on.
- Ability to *subclass:* Because FOX is written from the ground up in C++, and is NOT a C++ wrapper around some other legacy toolkit or library, FOX Controls may be subclassed and extended by application programmers. Moreover, if these additions can be

done by calling upon FOX built-in facilities, those additions will be platform independent also.

- *Higher Quality*: It is a given in software development that those facilities which are most frequently used are the ones which are most stable. Thus, by using core system facilities instead of higher-level transient API's, the impact of the underlying system's instability is minimized. A chain is as strong as the weakest link, and while I can not control the quality of the links, I can minimize the number of them.
- *Higher Speed*: Eliminating layers between FOX and the underlying system not only increases the application's quality, it will also make it faster, and reduce memory overhead.
- *Go to the Bedrock*: FOX's core facilities needed from the target system are things like mouse/keyboard event handling, and basic graphics facilities such as drawing of lines and rectangles [and some other system facilities]. In most operating systems, these are fairly mature API's and not subject to much change. If you want to build a big building, you need to go down to the solid bedrock. This is what FOX does.

Fox is Extensible

The FOX library is designed to be open-ended and extensible. What this means is that unlike other libraries which take the approach of wrapping legacy GUI toolkits, FOX may be extended with *Custom Controls* and Widgets which will set your application apart from the others. Building Custom Controls is extremely easy in FOX, as it is essentially just a matter of C++ subclassing.

Fox is Available Under Library GNU Public License

Since FOX is distributed in source form under LGPL, you have the ability to make changes or extensions to FOX to suit your needs.

Having FOX inspected by 1000's of programmers all over the world will iron out any bugs it may have very quickly.

This process is already under way. I care a great deal about software quality; I imagine, so do you.

In the course of my programming life, I have ran into many situations where the bugs I needed to fix were not in my own code, but in someone else's, and of course I didn't have the source.

Thus, the quality of my own software was limited by the quality of someone else's. Problem is, the developers of the libraries and software I depend on are frequently not motivated to make their software correct.

This has made me a firm believer in the *GPL* or *Open Source* model of software development. FOX was started in part because I didn't want to explain to our customers that the reason X or Y didn't work was because of the broken software or libraries on their machine. The only way one can create high-quality applications is to bring as much of the underlying system under one's control as possible. Hence the *Go to the Bedrock* philosophy.

Purpose

The purpose of this HOWTO is to describe a methodology for managing multiple operating systems on a single computer system. It is intended for Linux users who have a basic familiarity with both Linux and LILO installations. Nothing here is terribly complex however, considering the amount of time it takes to install some operating systems it can be relatively time consuming.

It is different from other methods in that it doesn't require multiple operating systems on the boot disk. Instead it uses a fixed internal disk containing a single primary operating system and a selection of removable disks with one or more operating systems installed on each of them. If you absolutely have to have two, three, or four different operating systems on a single disk and are trying to get them to behave with each other, this HOWTO is not for you.

Its specific goals are:

- A primary/operational disk that once configured and installed is rarely changed. This includes not having to repartition or otherwise modify the disk it resides on.

- Easy selection of multiple alternative operating systems at boot time without having to go through more than one or two menu selections.
- No need to modify the BIOS, LILO, or any other configuration to access an O/S once it is installed.
- Easy addition/removal of operating systems depending on requirements at the moment.
- Inexpensive and scalable to allow for an increasing number of operating systems and versions as time goes on.

OPERATING SYSTEM FUNCTIONS

Usually Operating system is there to manage all pieces of a complex system Imagine what will happen if three programs running on a computer all try to print their output simultaneously on the same printer. The first few lines might be from program one and the next few lines might be from program two and so on with the result resulting in chaos. The operating system can bring order to potential chaos by buffering all the output destined for the printer on the disk.

The primary task of operating system is to keep track of who is using which resource, to grant resource request, to account for usage, and to meditate conflicting request from different programs and users. When a computer has multiple users, the need for managing and protecting the memory, input/output devices and other resources are even more apparent. This need arises because it is usually necessary to share expensive resource such as tapes drives and phototypesetters. Operating systems perform basic tasks, such as recognizing input from the keyboard, sending output to the display screen, keeping track of files anddirectories on the disk, and controlling peripheral devices such as disk drives and printers. For large systems, the operating system has even greater responsibilities and powers. It is like a traffic cop—it makes sure that different program and usersrunning at the same time do not interfere with each other. The operating system is also responsible for security, ensuring that unauthorized users do not accessthe system. The set of software products that jointly controls the system resource using these resources on a computer system is known as operating system. Examples are Unix, Windows.

Idea

The operating system is the core software component of your computer. It performs many functions and is, in very basic terms, an interface between your computer and the outside world. In the section about hardware, a computer is described as consisting of several component parts including your monitor, keyboard, mouse, and other parts. The operating system provides an interface to these parts using what is referred to as "drivers". This is why sometimes when you install a new printer or other piece of hardware, your system will ask you to install more software called a driver.

Role of driver

A driver is a specially written program which understands the operation of the device it interfaces to, such as a printer, video card, sound card or CD ROM drive. It translates commands from the operating system or user into commands understood by the the component computer part it interfaces with. It also translates responses from the component computer part back to responses that can be understood by the operating system, application program, or user.

The operating system provides for several other functions including:

- System tools (programs) used to monitor computer performance, debug problems, or maintain parts of the system.
- A set of libraries or functions which programs may use to perform specific tasks especially relating to interfacing with computer system components.

The operating system makes these interfacing functions along with its other functions operate smoothly and these functions are mostly transparent to the user.

Operating System Concerns

As mentioned previously, an operating system is a computer program. Operating systems are written by human programmers who make mistakes. Therefore there can be errors in the code even though there may be some testing before the product is released. Some companies have better software quality control and testing than others so you may notice varying levels of quality from operating system to operating system. Errors in operating systems cause three main types of problems: System crashes and instabilities-These can happen due to a software bug typically in the operating system, although computer programs being run on the operating system can make the system more unstable or may even crash the system by themselves. This varies depending on the type of operating system. A system crash is the act of a system freezing and becoming unresponsive which would cause the user to need to reboot. Security flaws-Some software errors leave a door open for the system to be broken into by unauthorized intruders. As these flaws are discovered, unauthorized intruders may try to use these to gain illegal access to your system. Patching these flaws often will help keep your computer system secure. Sometimes errors in the operating system will cause the computer not to work correctly with some peripheral devices such as printers.

NECESSITY

The big problems are when users try to install older software apps on the newest operating systems or when the latest software version does not have the same functionalities as the older ones. There are many situations where incompatibilities get in the way of proper functionality and where they cannot be repaired. The release of a new version of a certain software platform does not necessarily ask for an upgrade, because usually the latest versions of an application may require the presence of the newest operating system and the computer hardware might not support it. On the other hand, it is possible that the latest version of an application does not have the features of the previous version or shows a higher number of bugs than the older editions. Web developers and generally programmers don't need the complexity of the graphical interface of a new operating system. Instead, what they are interested in is having their development tools functioning at full capacity on a compatible operating system. Usually, software companies do not provide access to the older releases and if you reinstall the operating system, the software version you are used to work with might not be available anymore. As a consequence, the existence of older software databases is completely justified. These websites allow you to download both current versions of certain software apps, as well as various older versions.

If you need to download older software editions, you could find them on existing databases, like Old Version. com or OldApps.com for example. Even if the trend is to update your applications constantly, chances are that you use a software app that, on a new release, would also require a higher processor speed or came bundled with unnecessary plugins. It is recommended to carefully select the development tools you are working with in order to avoid frequent software updates or changes of the operating system.

NECESSITY WITH WINDOWS XP AND VISTA

Why do we now have to deal with registry problems on the new operating systems, Windows XP and Vista when we didn't have to worry about our registries so much with Windows 98 and 95? Doesn't it seem like a new, improved operating system would give us less problems. In this article, we're going to discuss these things and see if we can make some sense of the irony that newer operating systems need more attention than older ones!

Hierarchal Structure

A Windows Operating System's registry is organized in a hierarchal structure exactly the same way your documents are arranged in your Word program. There is one major directory in your registry which would be the equivalent of your MyDocuments folder. Under that directory, there are many, many, many directories and each one of these directories may or may not have files contained in them. Certainly, way down at the bottom in the very lowest directory there are lots of files. Now, multiply this MyDocuments structure by 5 and you have something that looks very much like a Windows Registry.

A Long Trip

Many times, the command you give at your keyboard or mouse spans across many registry directories and needs to travel back and forth through the registry to carry out one command. So, you can see that one little keystroke needs to wend its way through a lot of files before it is executed. When these files become disorganized the trip can become much longer.

Tangible Programs

When we add a program or anything tangible to the computer, we add entries to the registry. When that tangible program is removed, many of the entries are left behind. These entries that are no longer needed are known as registry corruption. There are other forms of registry corruption, but this is a common one. It is important to note viruses, spyware, adware and malware are all tangible programs and most of us use spyware cleaners daily to remove these things from our computer. Since these parasites are a lot more prevalent now than they were in Windows 98's hay-day, and they are usually, a lot bigger and more complicated than they used to be, removing them leaves much more corruption nowadays than it used to. As time goes on, this registry corruption causes the computer to act up. The computer will probably slow down at first and after the corruption gets more plentiful, the computer is likely to suffer crashes.

Function

What all this means is in today's world, we have many more tangible programs in the form of viruses/spyware and such that are being added and removed regularly from our operating system; probably thousands times more than 10 years ago. Add to this fact newer Windows operating systems and their tangible programs are way larger than the early Windows operating systems and their tangible programs and you can see how registry corruption has become a much bigger issue than it used to be! It is easy enough to take care of registry corruption. Just install a good registry cleaner on your computer and run it periodically and your computer will be fine! The best time to run a registry cleaner is after spyware and/or viruses have been removed. By the way, you do have a good spyware cleaner installed on your computer.

TYPES OF OPERATING SYSTEM

There are many types of operating systems. The most common is the Microsoft suite of operating systems. They include from most recent to the oldest:

WINDOWS XP PROFESSIONAL EDITION

A version used by many businesses on workstations. It has the ability to become a member of a corporate domain.

WINDOWS XP HOME EDITION

A lower cost version of Windows XP which is for home use only and should not be used at a business.

WINDOWS 2000

A better version of the Windows NT operating system which works well both at home and as a workstation at a business. It includes technologies which allow hardware to be automatically detected and other enhancements over Windows NT.

WINDOWS ME

A upgraded version from windows 98 but it has been historically plagued with programming errors which may be frustrating for home users.

WINDOWS 98

This was produced in two main versions. The first Windows 98 version was plagued with programming errors but the Windows 98 Second Edition which came out later was much better with many errors resolved.

WINDOWS NT

A version of Windows made specifically for businesses offering better control over workstation capabilities to help network administrators.

WINDOWS 95

The first version of Windows after the older Windows 3.x versions offering a better interface and better library functions for programs. There are other worthwhile types of operating systems not made by Microsoft. The greatest problem with these operating systems lies in the fact that not as many application programs are written for them. However if you can get the type of application programs you are looking for, one of the systems listed below may be a good choice.

UNIX

A system that has been around for many years and it is very stable. It is primary used to be a server rather than a workstation and should not be used by anyone who does not understand the system. It can be difficult to learn. Unix must normally run an a computer made by the same company that produces the software. UNIX is a multi-user and multi-tasking operating system. It is very popular operating system used in microcomputers to Supercomputer. It provides the command line interface. It was developed at AT&T Bell Laboratories of USA. It was specially developed at AT&T for their own minicomputers. Microsoft Company of USA also developed a version of UNIX, which is named as XENIX. It is mainly used in network environment because it has powerful security features

LINUX

Linux is similar to Unix in operation but it is free. It also should not be used by anyone who does not understand the system and can be difficult to learn.

APPLE MACINTOSH

Most recent versions are based on Unix but it has a good graphical interface so it is both stable (does not crash often or have as many software problems as other systems may have) and easy to learn. One drawback to this system is that it can only be run on Apple produced Hardware.

SINGLE USER

Single-user allows one single user to login at a time. There is no user account database which makes the level of security low and so users cannot protect their files from being viewed, copied or deleted. Examples of this type are DOS and Windows 98.

List of single user operating system:

- MS-DOS
- Amiga OS
- Classic Mac OS (System 1 through Mac OS 9).
- Windows 1.0
- Windows 2.0
- Windows 3.0
- Windows 3.1x
- Windows 95
- Windows 98
- Windows ME

MULTI-USER

The Multi-user has a user database account which states the right that users have on certain resources. They are more secure than the single user since access is limited. Example of this is UNIX. In computing, an operating system that enables several users to access centrally stored data and programs simultaneously over a network. Each user has a terminal, which may be local (connected directly to the computer) or remote (connected to the computer via a modem and a telephone line). The growth of the internet has given rise to new forms of application level multi-user systems. Multi-user online games and meeting software are examples of a growing range of collaboration and interaction systems.

Multi-access is usually achieved by time-sharing: the computer switches very rapidly between terminals and programs so that each user has sole use of the computer for only a fraction of a second but can work as if she or he had continuous access. Multi-user systems are becoming increasingly common in the workplace, and have many advantages – such as enabling employees to refer to and update a shared corporate database. The travel industry uses a multi-user system to manage bookings of airline tickets; travel agents around the world using the system can access information on available seats as readily as an airline's own office.

Networked/Work alone

Stand alone are usually not connected to a network and thus cannot access networked resources. They are usually more secured than and remote users cannot log into the computer. A network operating System uses a standard communication protocol for UNIX networks and over the internet(we have the TCP/IP). For Novell Netware internetwork Packet Exchange /Sequenced Packet Exchange (IPX/SPX). They are less secure than Standalone and should be protected (most times by creating user accounts. More examples are Windows NT 5.0, Windows 98,

MULTI-TASKING/SINGLE TASKING

Multitasking allows one or more programs to run, at time. Each process is given a prioritised amount of time on the processor. Single-user allows are programs to run at a time. It is usually faster than multi-tasking Systems +as some time is taken to in switching in multi-user. But multi-user is more efficient as they allow other tasks to run when a task is not performing any operation. Single-users are more robust, as multi-programs are require to communicate with each other which can cause synchronization problems (deadlock)

Multi Processor/Single Processor: Some Operating System allows for more than one processor to use on the system. This allows more than one task to be run, at a time, on different processors. Windows NT/2000 supports multi processors (up to). Single Processor, Multitasking involves running each of the processor for a given time slice or a single processor where with multi processor, they can all run at the same.

TIME SHARING OF OPERATING SYSTEM

The last dozen years of computer usage have seen great strides. In the early 1950's, the problems solved were largely in the construction and maintenance of hardware; in the mid-1950's, the usage languages were greatly improved with the advent of compilers; now in the early 1960's, we are in the midst of a third major modification to computer usage: the improvement of man-machine interaction by a process called time-sharing. Much of the time-sharing philosophy, expressed in this paper, has been developed in conjunction with the work of an MIT preliminary study committee, chaired by H. Teager, which examined the long range computational needs of the Institute, and a subsequent MIT computer working committee, chaired by J. McCarthy. However, the views and conclusions expressed in this paper should be taken as solely those of the present authors.

Before proceeding further, it is best to give a more precise interpretation to time-sharing. One can mean using different parts of the hardware at the same time for different tasks, or one can mean several persons making use of the computer at the same time.

The first meaning, often called multiprogramming, is oriented towards hardware efficiency in the sense of attempting to attain complete utilization of all components. The second meaning of time-sharing, which is meant here, is primarily concerned with the efficiency of persons trying to use a computer. Computer efficiency should still be considered but only in the perspective of the total system utility. The motivation for time-shared computer usage arises out of the slow man-computer interaction rate presently possible with the bigger, more advanced computers. This rate has changed little (and has become worse in some cases) in the last decade of widespread computer use.

In part, this effect has been due to the fact that as elementary problems become mastered on the computer, more complex problems immediately become of interest. As a result, larger and more complicated programs are written to take advantage of larger and faster computers. This process inevitably leads to more programming errors and a longer period of time required for debugging.

Using current batch monitor techniques, as is done on most large computers, each program bug usually requires several hours to eliminate, if not a complete day. The only alternative presently available is for the programmer to attempt to debug directly at the computer, a process which is grossly wasteful of computer time and hampered seriously by the poor console communication usually available. Even if a typewriter is the console, there are usually lacking the sophisticated query and response programs which are vitally necessary to allow effective interaction. Thus, what is desired is to drastically increase the rate of interaction between the programmer and the computer without large economic loss and also to make each interaction more meaningful by extensive and complex system programming to assist in the man-computer communication.

To solve these interaction problems we would like to have a computer made simultaneously available to many users in a manner somewhat like a telephone exchange. Each user would be able to use a console at his own pace and with-out concern for the activity of others using the system. This console could as a minimum be merely a typewriter but more ideally would contain an incrementally modifiable self-sustaining display. In any case, data transmission requirements should be such that it would be no major obstacle to have remote installation from the computer proper. The basic technique for a time-sharing system is to have many persons simultaneously using the computer through typewriter consoles with a time-sharing supervisor program sequentially running each user program in a short burst or quantum of computation. This sequence, which in the most straightforward case is a simple round-robin, should occur often enough so that each user program which is kept in the high-speed memory is run for a quantum at least once during each approximate human reaction time (~.2 seconds).

In this way, each user sees a computer fully responsive to even single key strokes each of which may require only trivial computation; in the non-trivial cases, the user sees a gradual reduction of the response time which is proportional to the complexity of the response calculation, the slowness of the computer, and the total number of active users. It should be clear, however, that if there are n users actively requesting service at one time, each user will only see on the average 1/n of the effective computer speed. During the period of high interaction rates while debugging programs, this should not be a hindrance since ordinarily the required amount of computation needed for each debugging computer response is small compared to the ultimate production need.

Not only would such a time-sharing system improve the ability to program in the conventional manner by one or two orders of magnitude, but there would be opened up several new forms of computer usage. There would be a gradual reformulation of many scientific and engineering applications so that programs containing decision trees which currently must be specified in advance would be eliminated and instead the particular decision branches would be specified only as needed. Another important area is that of teaching machines which, although frequently trivial computationally, could naturally exploit the consoles of a time-sharing system with the additional bonus that more elaborate and adaptive teaching programs could be used. Finally, as attested by the many small business computers, there are numerous applications in business and in industry where it would be advantageous to have powerful computing facilities available at isolated locations with only the incremental capital investment of each console.

But it is important to realise that even without the above and other new applications, the major advance in programming intimacy available from time-sharing would be of immediate value to computer installations in universities, research laboratories, and engineering firms where program debugging is a major problem.

Implementation problems

As indicated, a straightforward plan for time-sharing is to execute user programs for small quantums of computation without priority in a simple round-robin; the strategy of time-sharing can be more complex as will be shown later, but the above simple scheme is an adequate solution. There are still many problems, however, some best solved by hardware, others affecting the programming conventions and practices. A few of the more obvious problems are summarized:

Hardware Problems:

- Different user programs if simultaneously in core memory may interfere with each other or the supervisor program so some form of memory protection mode should be available when operating user programs.
- The time-sharing supervisor may need at different times to run a particular program from several locations. (Loading relocation bits are no help since the supervisor does not know how to relocate the accumulator, etc.) Dynamic relocation of all memory accesses that pick up instructions or data words is one effective solution.
- Input-output equipment may be initiated by a user and read words in on another user program. A way to avoid this is to trap all input-output instructions issued by a user's program when operated in the memory protection mode.
- A large random-access back-up storage is desirable for general program storage files for all users. Present large capacity disc units appear to be adequate.
- The time-sharing supervisor must be able to interrupt a user's program after a quantum of computation. A program-initiated one-shot multivibrator which generates an interrupt a fixed time later is adequate.

- Large core memories (*e.g.* a million words) would ease the system programming complications immensely since the different active user programs as well as the frequently used system programs such as compilers, query programs, etc. could remain in core memory at all times.

Programming Problems:

- The supervisor program must do automatic user usage charge accounting. In general, the user should be charged on the basis of a system usage formula or algorithm which should include such factors as computation time, amount of high-speed memory required, rent of secondary memory storage, etc.
- The supervisor program should coordinate all user input-output since it is not desirable to require a user program to remain constantly in memory during input-output limited operations. In addition, the supervisor must coordinate all usage of the central, shared high-speed input-output units serving all users as well as the clocks, disc units, etc.
- The system programs available must be potent enough so that the user can think about his problem and not be hampered by coding details or typographical mistakes. Thus, compilers, query programs, post-mortem programs, loaders, and good editing programs are essential.
- As much as possible, the users should be allowed the maximum programming flexibility both in choices of language and in the absence of restrictions.

Experimental Time-Sharing System

Having briefly stated a desirable time-sharing performance, it is pertinent to ask what level of performance can be achieved with existent equipment. To begin to answer this question and to explore all the programming and operational aspects, an experimental time-sharing system has been developed. This system was originally written for the IBM

709 but has since been converted for use with the 7090 computer. The 7090 of the MIT Computation Center has, in addition to three channels with 19 tape units, a fourth channel with the standard Direct Data Connection. Attached to the Direct Data Connection is a real-time equipment buffer and control rack designed and built under the direction of H. Teager and his group. [This group is presently using another approach (ref.9) in developing a time-sharing system for the MIT 7090.]

This rack has a variety of devices attached but the only ones required by the present systems are three flexowriter typewriters. Also installed on the 7090 are two special modifications (*i.e.* RPQ's): a standard 60 cycle accounting and interrupt clock, and a special mode which allows memory protection, dynamic relocation and trapping of all user attempts to initiate input-output instructions. In the present system the time-sharing occurs between four users, three of whom are on-line each at a typewriter in a foreground system and a fourth passive user of the back-ground Fap-Mad-Madtran-BSS Monitor system similar to the Fortran-Fap-BSS Monitor System (FMS) used by most of the Center programmers and by many other 7090 installations.

Significant design features of the foreground system are:

- It allows the user to develop programs in languages compatible with the background system,
- Develop a private file of programs,
- Start debugging sessions at the state of the previous session, and
- Set his own pace with little waste of computer time.

Core storage is allocated such that all users operate in the upper 27,000 words with the time-sharing supervisor (TSS) permanently in the lower 5,000 words. To avoid memory allocation clashes, protect users from one another, and simplify the initial 709 system organization, only one user was kept in core memory at a time. However, with the special memory protection and relocation feature of the 7090, more sophisticated storage allocation procedures are being implemented. In any case, user swaps are minimized by using

2-channel overlapped magnetic tape reading and writing of the pertinent locations in the two user programs. The foreground system is organized around commands that each user can give on his typewriter and the user's private program files which presently (for want of a disc unit) are kept on a separate magnetic tape for each user.

For convenience the format of the private tape files is such that they are card images, have title cards with name and class designators and can be written or punched using the off-line equipment. (The latter feature also offers a crude form of large-scale input-output.) The magnetic tape requirements of the system are the seven tapes required for the normal functions of the background system, a system tape for the time-sharing supervisor that contains most of the command programs, and a private file tape and dump tape for each of the three foreground users. The commands are typed by the user to the time-sharing supervisor (not to his own program) and thus can be initiated at any time regardless of the particular user program in memory. For similar coordination reasons, the supervisor handles all input-output of the foreground system typewriters. Commands are composed of segments separated by vertical strokes; the first segment is the command name and the remaining segments are parameters pertinent to the command.

Each segment consists of the last 6 characters typed (starting with an implicit 6 blanks) so that spacing is an easy way to correct a typing mistake. A carriage return is the signal which initiates action on the command. Whenever a command is received by the supervisor, "WAIT", is typed back followed by "READY." when the command is completed. While typing, an incomplete command line may be ignored by the "quit" sequence of a code delete signal followed by a carriage return. Similarly after a command is initiated, it may be abandoned if a "quit" sequence is given. In addition, during unwanted command typeouts, the command and output may be terminated by pushing a special "stop output" button.

The use of the foreground system is initiated whenever a typewriter user completes a command line and is placed in a waiting command queue. Upon completion of each quantum, the time-sharing supervisor gives top priority to initiating any waiting commands. The system programs corresponding to most of the commands are kept on the special supervisor command system tape so that to avoid waste of computer time, the supervisor continues to operate the last user program until the desired command program on tape is positioned for reading.

At this point, the last user is read out on his dump tape, the command program read in, placed in a working status and initiated as a new user program. However, before starting the new user for a quantum of computation, the supervisor again checks for any waiting command of another user and if necessary begins the look-ahead positioning of the command system tape while operating the new user. Whenever the waiting command queue is empty, the supervisor proceeds to execute a simple round-robin of those foreground user programs in the working status queue. Finally, if both these queues are empty, the background user program is brought in and run a quantum at a time until further foreground system actively develops.

Foreground user programs leave the working status queue by two means. If the program proceeds to completion, it can reenter the supervisor in a way which eliminates itself and places the user in dead status; alternatively, by a different entry the program can be placed in a dormant status (or be manually placed by the user executing a quit sequence). The dormant status differs from the dead status in that the user may still restart or examine his program. User input-output is through each typewriter, and even though the supervisor has a few lines of buffer space available, it is possible to become input-output limited. Consequently, there is an additional input-output wait status, similar to the dormant, which the user is automatically placed in by the supervisor program whenever input-output delays develop. When buffers become near empty on output or near full on input, the user program is automatically returned to the working status; thus waste of computer time is avoided.

MANAGEMENT

RULES

When programming in a GUI operating system, you allocate operating system resources for widgets, images, fonts, and other graphical objects. Since there is a platform limit on the amount of resources you can allocate, you must be careful to free any objects that you allocate in your application. If you allocate a resource and do not free it when you are done with it, your application is "leaking" resources. An application that repeatedly leaks resources will eventually consume all of the available resources, forcing the user to reboot the operating system. Fortunately, SWT makes resource allocation and disposal a straightforward process. There are only two rules that you need to remember when allocating and freeing SWT resource-based objects:

Rule 1

This is a simple rule. SWT makes it easy for you to remember when operating s,stem resources are allocated: *all* SWT resource-based objects (like *Colour, Cursor, Display, Font, GC, Image, Printer, Region, Widget and subclasses*) allocate any needed operating system resources in their constructor. There are no exceptions to this rule. There are no methods in SWT (other than constructors) that allocate operating system resources that the programmer must manage. If you didn't call the constructor, then you don't need to free the resources, so don't call dispose on the object. For example, in the following line of code, an operating system font is allocated:

Font font = new Font
(display, "Courier", 10, SWT.NORMAL);

Since you called the *Font* constructor to create the resource, you must dispose the font when you are finished with it, as follows:

```
font.dispose();
```

In the following line of code, however, a constructor is not called:

```
Font font = control.getFont ();
```

Therefore, you must not call dispose. The font variable does contain an operating system font resource, but you did not allocate it. If you were to dispose of this font, you would be leaving the control without a font! The results are undefined.

So, if you are using *any* getter that returns an SWT resource-based object that you did not allocate, do not dispose the object. This rule occasionally leads to API that seems artificial.

For example, GC.getClipping (Region) forces the programmer to create a *Region* in order to get the clipping region from a *GC*. Although it might have been a bit "prettier" to provide GC.getClipping () that returned a *Region*, this would break the rule because it would have to allocate an operating system resource outside of a constructor. While it could be documented that the programmer needs to free the *Region* returned by GC.getClipping (), programmers don't always read the documentation.

Making the programmer call the constructor for the *Region* makes it clear that it is the*programmer's* responsibility to free the resource.

Rule 2

When you dispose a *Shell*, its children are disposed. In fact, disposing any *Composite* will dispose all of the *Composite*'s children. Disposing a *Menu* disposes all menu items. Disposing a *Tree* or *TreeItem* disposes all child items. Why does this make sense? Apart from the obvious burden of having to dispose each child if this were not the case, the fact that a widget cannot exist in the operating system without a parent implies that when the parent is disposed, the child *must* also be disposed.

What about the fonts and colours that you created and set into a *Widget*? Since they are not children of the widget, they are not disposed when the parent is disposed. A widget will never dispose a resource that you allocated. To do so would mean that the widget was breaking rule 1. Because fonts and colours can be shared by different widgets, disposing a resource in one widget would dispose it in another, leading to unpredictable results.

Extensions to Rule 2

There are two extensions to rule 2. These are places where a relationship exists that is not strictly a parent-child relationship, but where it still makes sense for rule 2 to apply.

- *MenuItem.setMenu*: Disposing a cascade *MenuItem* that has a submenu set with setMenu (Menu) disposes the submenu. This is a natural extension of rule 2. It would be a burden to the programmer to dispose each individual submenu. It's also common behaviour in most operating systems to do this automatically. Both Windows® and X dispose submenus when a cascade menu item is disposed.
- *Control.setMenu*: Disposing a *Control* that has a pop-up menu set with setMenu (Menu) disposes the pop-up menu. Many application programmers expected this behaviour, even though many operating systems don't do this automatically. Leaving the application programmer responsible for disposing a pop-up menu when disposing the *Control* led to temporary leaks. (The leak was only temporary because the pop-up menu is eventually disposed when the shell is disposed).

FREE

The operating system frees all of a program's resources when the program exits. Why not just rely on this? Operating system resources are not infinite. If your program doesn't free up resources as they are no longer needed, it can run out of resources. It can also cause other programs to run out of resources. So waiting until the program exits to free up resources is generally a bad idea. Leak tools exist to help detect resource leaks. You can use the *Sleak* tool to look for leaks in your SWT application.

JAVA LANGUAGE A GARBAGE COLLECTION

The Java language successfully uses a garbage collector

to manage the memory used by Java objects. Why doesn't SWT use the Java garbage collector to manage operating system resources too? Many Java programmers ask this question. We will answer it with the following discussion on finalization.

FINALIZATION

Most attempts to use the Java garbage collector to manage operating system resources involve finalization. When an object is about to become garbage, the garbage collector sends it the finalize message. This seems like a logical place to free the resource, right?

One of the main reasons that this statement is true is that there is no guarantee how soon after an object becomes garbage that the finalize method for the object will run. Even if you could predict this time interval for a particular VM, you certainly couldn't guarantee it for new versions of the VM.

"The Java programming language does not specify how soon a finalizer will be invoked, except to say that it will happen before the storage for the object is reused.... If an uncaught exception is thrown during the finalization, the exception is ignored and finalization of that object terminates." Releasing operating system resources is critical to correct program execution. Freeing resources at some unknown time in the future (or not at all) typically leads to program failure. Here are some examples of typical problems encountered when using finalization:

- If a non-garbage object references another object, that object is not garbage and won't be collected. If the object has operating system resources that it frees in its finalize method, those resources will never be freed because finalize will never be called. This is a classic programming error because it's easy to hang on to objects accidentally in an inner class or a static variable.
- It is possible to starve other operating system processes by creating lots of "garbage resources" that have not yet been finalized. When another program attempts to acquire a resource, it fails because it

cannot run the Java finalizer. SWT could run the finalizer if it couldn't get a resource, but other programs (*i.e.* non-Java programs or even Java programs running in a different VM)-and operating system calls that allocate and free resources internally-can't run the Java finalizer.

- Some resources are very limited. For example, only a small number of cached HDCs are available on Windows 98. It is essential to free these up right away, instead of waiting for finalization.
- Different types of resource are shared on the same operating system heap, so a failure to acquire one resource may be caused by failure to free another. For example, on Windows 98, HBRUSH and HFONT are both allocated from the GDI heap, so failure to create an HBRUSH can happen if too many HFONTs are awaiting finalization. This can cause applications to have some strange dependencies on the timing of finalizer runs.

The non-deterministic nature of finalization is sufficient reason to avoid using it to free resources, but even if we decided to go against conventional wisdom and implement a resource management scheme using finalization, we would still face many other problems. The implementation would require the addition of some very complex, platform-specific code that would be difficult to get right, and tough to debug. Here are a few examples of some of the tricky issues that would need to be carefully coded around in each object's finalize method:

- Operating system objects can have subtle limitations on when particular objects can be disposed. For example in the X Window System, a GC can contain a Font. If you dispose the Font before the GC, you leave the operating system in an indeterminate state. The following quote from *The Java Language Specification* hints at the complexity of the code that would be required to handle such limitations for each object finalizer:

The Java programming language imposes no ordering on finalize method calls. Finalizers may be called in any order, or even concurrently." Add to this that for some operating systems, subtle platform behaviour in this area may be undocumented and can change in future versions of the operating system.

- On some platforms, operating system resources need to be disposed in the UI thread. According to *The Java Language Specification*:

"... the language does not specify which thread will invoke the finalizer for any given object."

This means that SWT finalize methods would need to synchronize with the UI thread, which would mean that there would be a significant cost overhead for each dispose. In addition, given the previous point that disposal order is important for some resources, we think it is possible to get into a deadlock situation if we are trying to reorder multiple concurrent threads that are trying to synchronize with the UI thread.

- The Java objects that model operating system objects need to capture all of the subtle relationships between the operating system objects. For example, on Windows, an HBRUSH can be referenced in the operating system by an HDC, but not referenced in Java code. When the Java object representing the HBRUSH becomes garbage, freeing it will cause unexpected results. In fact, it's necessary to break the reference from the HDC first before attempting to free the HBRUSH. If these relationships are not captured and managed, it is possible for a resource to be finalized when there are still references to it in the operating system.
- Freeing some resources automatically frees others. For example, on Windows, destroying a parent HWND automatically destroys the children HWNDs. On some operating systems, freeing a top level window also frees the icon associated with the window. Different rules for freeing resources need to be custom coded on a per platform basis.

- Freeing resources can be time consuming, so a critical memory allocation may need to wait until finalization is complete.
- Long waits in finalizers can also make it difficult to get good benchmarks when you are trying to performance tune your code.

Our final point against finalization is this: SWT keeps as much state in the operating system as possible to simplify the implementation (less code, smaller objects). If we were to use finalization, we could not store resources only in the operating system. We would have to hold on to them in Java code so that they would not get garbage collected. For example, when you set a *Font* into a *Button,* SWT sets the font resource in the OS button. The *Button* doesn't keep a reference to the font resource, because it doesn't need to. The state is in the operating system. In order to determine the *Button*'s font, we query the OS. There is no point caching the font resource in Java code, because it just takes up space and complicates the *Button* code, which now has to make sure there are no stale cache problems.

Given that there are many problems when trying to use finalization to free resources, we think it's dangerous to offer it as a solution in SWT, which is designed to expose operating system functionality. We believe it is reasonable to expect programs to explicitly free operating system resources. We see this as simply a fact of life because the current generation of operating systems do not support garbage collection.

OS PROCESS

For our optimization system, there are mainly three categories of "human" customers:

- Application developers create and build system components such as modeling language environments and solvers as part of a larger optimization system. The components together take care of such generic functions as managing data, solving optimization problems, and presenting solutions nicely.
- Modelers work in a modeling language environment

or GUI to build optimization models and get acceptable solutions.

- Users run application packages that perform optimization at some stage through the optimization system. Users are usually the ultimate customers of any optimization system.

Modelers and application developers may see optimization in different ways. For modelers, a mathematical program is an abstract representation to be analysed and understood; for application developers, a mathematical program is a concrete instance to be represented, communicated and solved.

Modelers benefit most immediately from innovations that help people to choose and experiment with optimization software. Some application developers are also modelers, while others deal mainly with the inputs and outputs of optimization models set up by modelers. Users may not even realise that they are running optimization system components such as solvers, although they are often aware of optimization goals, such as minimizing costs or maximizing profits.

DEVICE

Any device connected internally or externally to a computer and used in the transfer of data. A personal computer or workstation processes information and, strictly speaking, that is all the computer does. Data (unprocessed information) must get into the computer, and the processed information must get out. Entering and displaying information is carried out on a wide variety of accessory devices called peripherals, also known as input/output (I/O) devices. Some peripherals, such as keyboards, are only input devices; other peripherals, such as printers, are only output devices; and some are both.

The monitor is the device on which images produced by the computer operator or generated by the program are displayed on a cathode-ray tube (CRT). Electron guns—one in a monochromemonitor, three in a colour monitor—irradiate phosphors on the inside of the vacuum tube, causing them to glow. The flat-panel displays on most portable computers, known as liquid-crystal displays (LCDs), use two polarizing filters with liquid crystals between them to produce the image. The computer keyboard, based on the typewriter keyboard, contains keys for entering letters, numbers, and punctuation marks, as well as keys to change the meaning of other keys. The function keys perform tasks that vary from program to program. The mouse is a device that is rolled on the desktop to move the cursor on the screen. A ball on the bottom of the mouse translates the device's movements to sensors within the mouse and then through the connecting port to the computer. There are also mice that substitute optical devices for mechanical balls, and mice that use infrared rather than physical connections.

The trackball is essentially an upside-down mouse, with the ball that is used to move the cursor located on the top rather than on the bottom. The joystick is a pointing device used principally for games. The light pen performs the same functions as a mouse or trackball, but it is held up to the screen, where its sensors detect the presence of pixels and send a signal through a cable to the computer.The graphics, or digitizing, tablet is a pad with electronics beneath the surface which is drawn upon with a pointed device, called a stylus. The shapes drawn appear on the monitor's screen. The most common input, or storage, device in personal computers or workstations is a hard disk drive, a stack of magnetized platters on which information is stored by heads generating an electrical current to represent either 1 or 0 in the binary number system. The device is called hard because the platters are inflexible, and is called a drive because it spins at 3600 revolutions or more a minute, within a sealed case. Diskettes, made of flexible film like that used in recording tape, are usually stored within a hard shell and are spun by their drives at about 360 revolutions per minute.

Data can also be stored and retrieved with light, the light of a laser beam reading a pattern of pits on an optical disk. The most familiar type of optical disk is the CD-ROM (compact disk-read only memory). Another kind of optical disk is the WORM (write once read many times).

As a consequence of their greater efficiency and speed, disk drives have quickly replaced tape drives as the primary means of data and program storage. Tape drives are still in use for backup storage, copying the contents of a hard disk as insurance against mechanical failure or human error. The scanner converts an image of something outside the computer, such as text, a drawing, or a photograph, into a digital image that it sends into the computer for display or further processing. The image is viewed as a graphics image, not a text image, so it can be altered with a graphics program but cannot be edited with a word-processing program, unless the scanner is part of a character-recognition system. To digitize photographs, a scanner may dither the image (put the dots a varying amount of space apart), or use the tagged image file format (TIFF), storing the image in 16 gray values. Some scanners can use standard video cameras to capture images for the computer.

The printer puts text or other images produced with a computer onto paper or other surfaces. Printers are either impact or nonimpact devices. Daisy-wheel or thimble printers are so called from the shape of the elements bearing raised images of the characters. Their speed, perhaps 30 characters per second, is now considered unacceptably slow. Dot-matrix printers produce their images by striking a series of wire pins, typically, 9, 18, or 24, through the ribbon in the pattern necessary to form the letter, number, line, or other character.

Ink-jet printers carry their ink in a well, where it is turned into a mist by heat or vibration andsprayed through tiny holes to form the pattern of the character on paper. Laser printers are similar to photocopying machines. The quality of laser-printer output is the highest generally available. The modem connects one computer to another, ordinarily through the telephone lines, to exchange information.

COMPUTER STORAGE DEVICES

Computer storage devices can be classified into either primary storage, secondary storage, or tertiary storage. Each of these storage devices are used to store certain files and data and are accessed in different ways by the computer's CPU.

Primary Computer Storage Devices

Primary storage refers to the computer's memory, which connects directly to the computer's CPU. The computer's memory evolved into what is now known as random access memory (RAM) which is a volatile form of storage. Volatile storage means that you totally lose data when you switch the system off. Aside from the RAM, two other primary storage areas can be found; these are on the CPU itself; the Processor registers and the Processor cache. The Processor register is some form of small storage which resides on the CPU and can contain data which can be accessed quickly. The processor registers are measured by the amount of data the can hold, that is either, 8 bit, 32 bit or 64 bit. Processor cache on the other hand is used by the CPU for reducing the time it takes to access the main memory. It stores data coming from the most frequently used applications of the CPU. During normal operations, the CPU checks the processor cache before checking the main memory, making the processing time faster.

Secondary Computer Storage Devices

These storage devices are external in nature and non-volatile as compared to primary storage devices. Secondary storage devices do not lose data even when they are turned off. Hence, they are the ideal back-upand data storage devices. Examples of secondary storage devices include; CD and DVD; flash memory; floppy disks; paper and magnetic tape; RAM disks, also called SSDs; ZIP drives; and punch cards. Since secondary storage devices are not attached to the computer's CPU, it takes a longer time for the CPU to access them. Secondary storage devices need to be formated before they can store data. Secondary storage devices are formated based on a filesystem format data are organized into files and directories. It also includes other pertinent information about the data, which is described in what is called the metadata.

Tertiary Computer Storage Devices

This type of computer storage device is not as popular as the other two storage device types. Its main use is for storing data at a very large-scale. This includes optical jukeboxes and tape libraries. Tertiary storage devices require a database to organize the data that are stored in them, and the computer needs to go through the database to access those data.

Offline Storage

Aside from these three types of computer storage devices, there is also another type-offline or disconnected storage. It is not directly connected to the computer and is used as a transfer medium only. Offline storage devices are remotely located and accessed as per need only. This storage device also needs human intervention to be read properly by the main computer system. Offline storage aside, from its use as a data transmission medium, can also serve as a good back-up device since it is remotely located, hence it will not be affected by any disaster that might hit the direct source of data. Offline storage also provides good security for data since you ca

COMPUTER STORAGE DEVICES

Awhile back, we covered the different types of hardware used with computers. You know, basic hardware and the extra hardware you can buy separately, etc. (You can read here for that article). Knowing what kinds of storage devices are available can keep you from using up too much space on your computer's hard drive. They can also help keep your computer's hard drive from crashing, along with keeping it running at top speed.

Floppy Disk

They are plastic square disks, usually with a silver or black sliding piece going across the top. These disks come in a variety of colours and they hold about 144 million bytes. (Bytes are characters, symbols and letters).

Zip Disk

They look like a floppy disk, but they are a little thicker. This disk also comes in a variety of colours and holds about 200 MB of data.

CD + RW Disc (Compact Disc Rewriteable)

This disc looks like a regular CD. The only difference is that you can write on this disc and erase it as many times as you want. It works just like a floppy disk or a zip disk. A CD + RW disc holds about 650 MB.

CD + R Disc (Compact Disc Recordable)

This one is a CD that you can record on. It's mostly used to record audio and once it's been written on, you cannot rewrite or erase anything off of it. This compact disc comes in different sizes, but they are usually silver in colour. (Some CDs are black in colour and they actually don't get as many scratches on them as the silver ones do. They are also a lot less fragile).

Removable Hard Drive

This is a disk drive in which a plastic or metal case surrounds the hard drive. It can be inserted and removed just like a floppy disk. It holds about 2 GB of data.

Internet Hard Drive

This one is a service on the Internet that provides storage space to computer users. This service offers about 25 MB of space, but it could be more, depending on the service type.

Flash Drive

This a storage device that comes in many colours and has a stick shape to it. They are very small in size, but they can hold anywhere between 256 MB and 3 GB of material on them.

PC Card

This is a thin credit card size device that fits into a PC card slot, usually on a notebook computer. This card simply adds storage to most notebooks.

Smart Cards

These are the size of an ATM card. When inserted into a smart card reader, they can read and update data for you.

Storage Tape

This one is a magnetically coated ribbon of plastic, capable of storing large amounts of data at a very low cost. Usually, storage tapes are a little bigger than audio tapes. Older computers used tape and tape drives, but even today, some people still back their systems up with storage tape. These tapes hold between 20 GB to about 110 GB of data. An external tape drive can be purchased separately as well, but those are even harder to find.

Miniature Mobile Storage Media

This is used mostly with handheld computers and digital cameras.

Memory Stick

This is a rectangular shaped disk that is used mostly with digital cameras and notebook computers. They hold approximately 128 MB as well.

Micro Drive: This is a square disk that has 1 GB of space and is used with digital cameras and handheld computers.

Smart Media Disc

This is a square disk that has 2 MB to about 128 MB of space on it. It's used with digital cameras, handheld computers and photo printers. There you go! These are just some of the storage devices that are available today. So, the next time you want to save something that takes up a large amount of space on your hard drive, think twice about it and consider using one of these storage devices instead. One of these devices could save you a lot of space on your hard drive and keep your system running at its best!

MEMORY AND FILE MANAGEMENT

MEMORY

Memory is the electronic holding place for instructions and data that the computer's microprocessor can reach quickly. When the computer is in normal operation, its memory usually contains the main parts of the operating system and some or all of the application programs and related data that are being used. Memory is often used as a shorter synonym for random access memory (RAM).

This kind of memory is located on one or more microchips that are physically close to the microprocessor in the computer. Most desktop and notebook computers sold today include at least 16 megabytes of RAM, and are upgradeable to include more. The more RAM you have, the less frequently the computer has to access instructions and data from the more slowly accessed hard disk form of storage. Memory is sometimes distinguished from storage, or the physical medium that holds the much larger amounts of data that won't fit into RAM and may not be immediately needed there.

Storage devices include hard disks, floppy disks, CD-ROM, and tape backup systems. The terms auxiliary storage, auxiliary memory, and secondary memory have also been used for this kind of data repository. Additional kinds of integrated and quickly accessible memory are read-only memory (ROM), programmable ROM (PROMO), erasable programmable ROM (EPROM). These are used to keep special programs and data, such as the basic input/output system, that need to be in the computer all the time.

The memory is a resource that needs to be managed carefully. Most computers have a memory hierarchy, with a small amount of very fast, expensive, volatile cache memory, some number of megabytes of medium-speed, medium-price, volatile main memory (RAM), and hundreds of thousands of megabytes of slow, cheap, non-volatile disk storage. It is the job of the operating system to coordinate how these memories are used.

The part of the operating system that manages the memory hierarchy is the memory manager. It keeps track of parts of memory that are in use and those that are not in use, to allocate memory to processes when they need it and de-allocate it when they are done, and to manage swapping between main memory and disk when main memory is too small to hold all the processes.

Systems for managing memory can be divided into two categories: the system of moving processes back and forth between main memory and disk during execution (known as swapping and paging) and the process that does not do so (that is, no swapping and ping).

Mono Programming without Swapping or Paging

The most simple memory management scheme is to run one program at a time, sharing the memory between that program and the operating system. As shown in the diagram bellow, there are three variations of this type. The operating system may be at the bottom of the memory in TAM (random access memory), as shown in the diagram 1, or it may be in ROM (read-only memory) at the top of the memory, as shown in diagram 2, or the device drivers may be at the top of the memory in a ROM and the rest of the system in RAM down bellow. With the system organised in this way, only one process at a time can be running. As soon as the user types a command, the operating system copies the request program from a disk to memory and executes it. When the process finishes, the operating system displays a prompt character and waits for a new command. When it receives the command, it loads a new program into memory overwriting the first one.

Mono Programming with Fixed Partitions

It is often desirable to allow multiple processes to run at the same time, even on simple operating systems in which multiprogramming is sometimes used. On time-sharing systems, having multiple processes in memory at once means that when one process is blocked waiting for the I/O to finish, another one can use the CPU. This way, multiprogramming increases the CPU utilisation. It is however preferable to be able to run two or more programs at once even on personal computers.

Swapping

The process of organising memory into fixed partitions on batch system is simple compared to time sharing systems or graphically oriented personal computers. On batch systems, each job is loaded into a partition when it gets to the head of the queue. It stays in memory until it has finished. As long as enough jobs can be kept in memory to keep the CPU busy all the time, there is no reason to use anything more complicated. On time-sharing machines, sometimes there is not enough main memory to hold all the currently active processes, therefore excess processes must be kept on disk and brought in to run dynamically. Swapping as an approach to memory management consists of bringing each process in its entirety, running it for a while, then putting it back on the disk.

The Scenario

The problem we are trying to overcome is simply this: You want to develop some kind of file or text editor, and you want your program to be able to load, edit and save files of any size. In fact, you want your program to load and edit the largest sized file possible. Under 32bit Windows this is a 4Gb file.

MEMORY MANAGEMENT

Let's forget about actually editing a large file for the moment, and concentrate just on loading a file into your application. So, your have a 4Gb file saved on your hard disk, and you want to load this file so you can preview any portion of it. Let's assume that our first application will be a simple hex file viewer, with no editing capabilities. The first decision to take is what memory facilities we will use to gain access to the file's contents.

To make this decision, we need to know what memory facilities are available to our program, and base our decision on that. Because our file viewer will be a 32bit Windows program capable of running under Windows 9x and NT/2000, we have the following facilities at our disposal.

VIRTUAL MEMORY

Another strategy for managing memory is the virtual memory, which allows programs to run even when they are only partially in main memory. The basic idea behind this strategy is that the combine size of the program, data, and stack may exceed the amount of physical memory available for it. The operating system keeps those parts of the program currently in use in main memory, and the rest on the disk.

Virtual memory can also work in a multiprogramming system, with bits and pieces pf many programs in memory at once. While a program is waiting for a part of itself to be brought in, it is waiting for I/O and cannot run, so the CPU can be given to another process, the same way as for any other multiprogramming system. Most virtual memory systems use a technique called paging.

Every 32bit process in Windows has a 4Gb virtual address space, regardless of the amount of physical RAM you have installed. Of this total virtual space, only 2Gb is available for an application's private use. Actually, the available space slightly less than this-128Kb less in WinNT and 4Mb less in Win9x).

There are a variety of methods to allocate memory from this 2Gb region of space. All depend on how much memory needs to be allocated, and what its intended use is.

Malloc and New

The simplest is to use the standard C or C++ memory allocation routines (malloc and new[], respectively). Both of these methods use the memory allocation facilities provided by the operating system. In Visual C++ 6.0, malloc and new[] use VirtualAlloc internally. Anyway, malloc and new[] are only really meant for allocating lots of small objects, not one gigantic memory region.

HeapAlloc

The second method to allocate memory in Windows is to use the Heap function – HeapAlloc (or the older LocalAlloc and GlocalAlloc). These functions are also meant for allocating many small objects though-just like malloc and new[]-and are also implemented by calls to VirtualAlloc.

VirtualAlloc

The third way to allocate memory in Windows is to use

VirtualAlloc directly. This method is much more flexible because it allows you to specify where you want the memory to be in your address space, and allows you to reserve a region of memory without actually allocating any space from it.

Memory-Mapped-Files

The forth way to allocate memory is by using Memory Mapped Files. Rather than allocating memory, a memory-mapped file is a reserved region of the 2Gb address space, which has mapped into it a region a file stored on disk. The great thing about memory-mapped-files is that they free the programmer from having to do any direct file reading or writing. Simply reading and writing to the memory-mapped view causes the file's contents to be accessed. The operating system provides clever page caching to make memory-mapped files a very quick way to read/write to a file.

DOS

DEFINITION

DOS (Disk Operating System) was the first widely-installedo perating system for personal computers. (Earlier, the same name had been used for an IBM operating system for a line of business computers.) The first personal computer version of DOS, called PC-DOS, was developed for IBM by Bill Gates and his new Microsoft Corporation. He retained the rights to market a Microsoft version, called MS-DOS. PC-DOS and MS-DOS are almost identical and most users have referred to either of them as just "DOS." DOS was (and still is) a non-graphical line-oriented command-or menu-driven operating system, with a relatively simple interface but not overly "friendly" user interface. Its prompt to enter a command looks like this: C:>

The first Microsoft Windows operating system was really an application that ran on top of the MS-DOS operating system. Today, Windows operating systems continue to support DOS (or a DOS-like user interface) for special purposes by emulating the operating system.

In the 1970s before the personal computer was invented, IBM had a different and unrelated DOS (Disk Operating System) that ran on smaller business computers. It was replaced by IBM's VSE operating system. DOS stands for Disk Operating System. DOS controls the computer's hardware and provides an environment for programs to run. Everything you can do with a GUI can be done at the DOS prompt. There are many flavours of *DOS operating system*like MS-DOS, PC DOS, DR DOS, FreeDOS, etc. There are two types of commands in DOS, internal and external. Internal commands are part of the command processor, whereas external commands exist as executable files. The entire operating system is small enough to fit on a floppy disk.

Booting

To run DOS on a computer, it should be the first program to be executed when the computer is switched on. This led to a problem for the designers: "How can DOS be loaded and executed when there is no DOS program running to load and execute *it*??!!". Well, just as the fictional Baron Munchausen managed to pull himself up by his own bootstraps, the computer manages this seemingly impossible trick, and the term "bootstrapping", or "booting up" is applied to this process.

Communicating with DOS

DOS is an entirely text based system. All it provides for the user is a prompt: "C:>" or "A:>", where the user can type in commands from the keyboard. The system is entirely case insensitive: so either "ForMAt C:" or "format c:" would erase your hard disk... The latter example is of course a small warning: with DOS comes power, you can very easily mess up your system if you use powerful commands in the wrong way. The commands you should be careful of are: "Format", "Recover", and "Del". All of these perform useful functions, when used correctly, and all the others are pretty much safe to use.

Working of DOS

DOS works within a file, directory and disk drive

structure. This means that all program and data files are named, and grouped together in named directories on disks. 'Directories' are just lists of files.

Naming of Files

While newer versions of DOS support longer filenames, the standard DOS filename format remains: 1-8 letter name, period, 3 letter extension eg:

`PROGRAM.EXE` `DATA.DAT` `LETTER.DOC`

The extension to a file's name is there to allow files of a similar type to be grouped together. Ie. all wordprocessor files might have the extension.DOC, while all picture files might have the extension.PIC While these extensions can be specified by the user, many programs have used them to differentiate between formats, and so they have gradually become standardised. For example you would expect a ".TXT" file to be a file containing unformatted text, or a ".BMP" file to be in a bit mapped graphics file format. To completely specify a file on your computer you must specify its drive and directory path, and its filename. However a file does not always have to be specified in this complete form: If it is in the current directory, then you can just enter its filename.

Naming Directories

Every disk drive has a root directory which can have subdirectories which are named in the same format as filenames, (though generally without any extension). The subdirectories can have subdirectories and so on. Eg: a floppy disk might contain the following directory structure:

- Pictures
- Holiday
- Italy
- France
- Family
- Pets
- Text
- Letters
- E-mail

A directory path name includes the disk drive and all subdirectories needed to specify a directory on a disk. The disk drive is specified by a single letter. Eg: The floppy disk drive is A and the hard disk drive is C.

The drive letter, is followed by a colon, the directory path names are separated by backward slashes (\), (*Not* forward slashes like internet addresses). Eg. In the above example "A:\PICTURES\HOLIDAY\FRANCE" would be more than likely to contain pictures of a few baguettes and onions.

Uses of DOS

When you type anything at the DOS prompt, and press enter, you are telling DOS to run a program. It will first look to see if there is an internal command program which has that name, and if it does not find one, then it will look to see if there is a file on disk with that name. If it finds an external file with the extension.COM (command), or.EXE (executable), then the program is loaded and run.

At this point DOS looses control of the computer until the program has ended.

However parts of it are still used by the programs as they are running, eg to load and save files etc.

Some very useful internal DOS commands:

- *A*: Change current directory path to the floppy disk drive
- *C*: Change current directory path to the hard disk drive
- *DIR*: Display current directory (show all files and sub-directories).
- *MD*: Make a new directory, eg: MD C:\E-MAIL
- *CD*: Change current directory, eg. CD C:\E-MAIL
- *COPY*: Copy file(s) from one place to another.
- *Del*: Delete/erase a file

Any other text on the input line after the file name, is passed to the program. This means that in the command "Copy help.txt help.bak", the text, "help.txt and help.bak" is passed to the copy program which will in this case use it to specify source and destination files for a copy.

WINDOWS OPERATING SYSTEM

Microsoft first started developing the Interface Manager (later renamed Microsoft Windows) in September 1981. While the first prototypes used Multiplan and Word-like menus at the bottom of the screen, the interface was modified in 1982 to utilize pull-down menus and dialogues, as used on the Xerox Star. On November 10, 1983, at the Plaza Hotel in New York City, Microsoft Corporation officially announced Microsoft Windows, a next-generation operating system that would supply a graphical user interface (GUI) and a multitasking environment for IBM computers. This was after the release of the Apple Lisa, and prior to Digital Research announcing GEM, and DESQ from Quarterdeck and the Amiga Workbench, or GEOS/GeoWorks Ensemble, IBM OS/2, NeXTstep or even DeskMate from Tandy. Windows assured an easy-to-use graphical interface, device-independent graphics and multitasking support. The development was held up several times, however, and the Windows 1.0 arrive at store shelves in November 1985. The selection of applications was thin, however, and Windows sales were moderate.

Windows 1.0 package, included: MS-DOS Executive, Calendar, Cardfile, Notepad, Terminal, Calculator, Clock, Reversi, Control Panel, PIF (Program Information File) Editor, Print Spooler, Clipboard, RAMDrive, Windows Write, Windows Paint.

Microsoft Windows version 1.0 was viewed as buggy, rough, and sluggish. This bumpy start was made sorrier by a threatened lawsuit from Apple Computers. In September 1985, Apple lawyers warned Bill Gates that Windows 1.0 infringed on Apple copyrights and patents, and that his corporation had stolen Apple's trade secrets. Microsoft Windows had similar drop-down menus, tiled windows and mouse support.

Bill Gates and his head counsel Bill Neukom, chose to make an offer to license features of Apple's operating system. Apple concurred and a contract was drawn up. The key to this is: Microsoft wrote the licensing agreement to include use of Apple features in Microsoft Windows version 1.0 and all future Microsoft software programs. As it turned out, this move by

Bill Gates was as intelligent as his decision to purchase QDOS from Seattle Computer Products and his persuading IBM to let Microsoft keep the licensing rights to MS-DOS.

Windows 1.0 fluttered on the market until January 1987, when a Windows-compatible program called Aldus PageMaker 1.0 was brought out. PageMaker was the first WYSIWYG desktop-publishing program for the PC. Later that year, Microsoft released a Windows-compatible spreadsheet called Excel. Other popular and functional software like Microsoft Word and Corel Draw helped advance Windows, yet, Microsoft recognized that Windows required further development. Microsoft Windows version 2.0 came out in December 1987, and evidenced somewhat more popular than its predecessor. A great deal of the popularity for Windows 2.0 came through its inclusion as a "run-time version" with Microsoft's new graphical applications, Excel and Word for Windows. They could be operated from MS-DOS, executing Windows for the length of their activity, and shutting down Windows upon exit.

Microsoft Windows incurred a major boost about this time when Aldus PageMaker came out in a Windows version, having previously run exclusively on Macintosh. Some computer historians date this, the introduction of a significant and non-Microsoft application for Windows, as the start of the success of Windows. Versions 2.0x used the real-mode memory model, which held it to a maximum of 1 megabyte of memory. In such a form, it could run under a different multitasker like DESQview, which used the 286 Protected Mode. Subsequently, two new versions were published: Windows/286 2.1 and Windows/386 2.1.Like preceding versions of Windows, Windows/286 2.1 used the real-mode memory model, but was the first version to support the HMA.

Windows/386 2.1 had a protected mode kernel with LIM-standard EMS emulation, the predecessor to XMS which would at last shift the topology of IBM PC computing. All Windows and DOS-based applications at the time were real mode, running over the protected mode kernel by using the virtual 8086 mode, which was new with the 80386 processor.

After Versions 2.0 and beyond were released, Apple began filing suit against IBM for various copyright infringements. In their defence, Microsoft claimed that their licensing agreement actually afforded them the rights to use Apple features. Apple claimed that Microsoft had encroached on 170 of their copyrights. After a four-year court case, Microsoft won. The courts stated that the licensing agreement gave Microsoft the rights to use all but nine of the copyrights, and Microsoft later convinced the courts that the other nine copyrights shouldn't be covered by copyright law. Bill Gates asserted that Apple had acquired ideas from the graphical user interface developed by Xerox for Xerox's Alto and Star computers.

FEATURES

Some individuals with disabilities require assistive technology (AT) in order to access computers. Hundreds of Windows AT third-party products are available, making it possible for almost anyone to use Windows applications, regardless of their disabilities. The Microsoft Windows operating systems also provides a core set of basic accessibility features and AT applications, which can be deployed on all computers in a computer lab or classroom without additional cost. These applications provide students with basic accessibility features from any workstation, maximizing the inclusiveness of the learning environment.

It should be noted that the AT applications that are bundled with Windows provide only a minimum level of accessibility, not the full set of features that many users require for equal access to the operating system, educational programs, and other software applications. Therefore, many educational entities deploy the standard set of Windows AT on all workstations by default, but addditionally 1) provide a small number of dedicated workstations that are equipped with commonly requested third party AT, and 2) are prepared to purchase and install additional AT as needed by specific students.

It should also be noted that the availability of AT does not itself guarantee accessibility. Software applications must be designed in a way that is compatible with AT and other accessibility features of the operating system. The following is a list of basic accessibility features that are included with Windows XP. Previous versions of Windows also included several of these same features.

Display and Readability

These features are designed to increase the visibility of items on the screen.

- Font style, colour, and size of items on the desktop—using the Display options, choose font colour, size and style combinations.
- Icon size—make icons larger for visibility, or smaller for increased screen space.
- Screen resolution—change pixel count to enlarge objects on screen.
- High contrast schemes—select colour combinations that are easier to see.
- Cursor width and blink rate—make the cursor easier to locate, or eliminate the distraction of its blinking.
- Microsoft Magnifier—enlarge portion of screen for better visibility.

Sounds and Speech

These features are designed to make computer sounds easier to hear or distinguish-or, visual alternatives to sound. Speech-to-text options are also available.

- Sound Volume—turn computer sound up or down.
- Sound Schemes—associate computer sounds with particular system events.
- ShowSounds—display captions for speech and sounds.
- SoundSentry—display visual warnings for system sounds.
- Notification—Get sound or visual cues when accessibility features are turned on or off.
- Text-to-Speech—Hear window command options and text read aloud.

Keyboard and Mouse

These features are designed to make the keyboard and mouse faster and easier to use.

Mouse Options:

- Double-Click Speed—choose how fast to click the mouse button to make a selection.
- ClickLock—highlight or drag without holding down the mouse button.
- Pointer Speed—set how fast the mouse pointer moves on screen.
- SnapTo—move the pointer to the default button in a dialog box.
- Cursor Blink Rate—choose how fast the cursor blinks—or, if it blinks at all.
- Pointer Trails—follow the pointer motion on screen.
- Hide Pointer While Typing—keep pointer from hiding text while typing.
- Show Location of Pointer—quickly reveal the pointer on screen.
- Reverse the function of the right and left mouse buttons—reverse actions controlled by the right and left mouse buttons.
- Pointer schemes—choose size and colour options for better visibility.

Keyboard Options

- Character Repeat Rate—set how quickly a character repeats when a key is struck.
- Dvorak Keyboard Layout—choose alternative keyboard layouts for people who type with one hand or finger.
- Sticky Keys—allow pressing one key at a time (rather than simultaneously) for key combinations.
- Filter Keys—ignore brief or repeated keystrokes and slow down the repeat rate.
- Toggle Keys—hear tones when pressing certain keys.
- MouseKeys—move the mouse pointer using the numerical keypad.

- Extra Keyboard Help—get ToolTips or other keyboard help in programs that provide it.

LINUX

FUNDAMENTAL

If you truly enjoy working with computers, Linux is the operating system of your dreams. It is more fun than any other computer operating system around. Linux is a computer hobbyist's paradise. However, the reason why Linux is truly revolutionary is that it is Open Software. Our science and technology work owing to the free availability of information, peer review, public critique, and the capablitiy to pick up ideas and modify or extend them. Open Software is an implementation of the scientific method into the field of software development. The freedom to pick-up, modify and extend, that comes with the Linux licence, offers a promise that the software development under Linux licence will continue in the way that science does.

The making of horseshoes, good glass, or measuring time were once closely guarded trade secrets. Science and technology exploded 500 years ago thanks to the sharing of knowledge by the means of printing, and thus breaking the monopoly of the few on the know-how. Why were the science and technology relatively stagnant before the printing era? Because the "trade secret" approach to growth has its limits: the development continues until the rate of learning equals the rate of forgetting. Moving the know-how to the public domain (printed on paper) shifted the position of the equilibrium to a higher level, which, after 500 years of turbulent development, we are still to achieve. For interested, I can present equations, borrowed from chemical equilibrium field, that describe this in a more formal way. The main point is that printing increased the audience, and allowed passing information across space and time.

In the early days of printing, many of those who dared to share were assassinated for revealing "trade secrets." Linux is for the computer age what Gutenberg was for writing.

Hopefully there will be no assassinations this time:-). Linux does clash, violently at times, with those who claim the "ownership" of information, trying to push time back 500 years.

Open Source Linux has also implications for computer security. Imagine a plane based on secret "scientific laws" and built to an unreviewed design, a plane at internals of which nobody but the manufacturer could inspect. Would you believe that this new, unique, completely proprietary plane, obviously built by clever and well-financed marketers in their basement, is any safer than one built in the open world, under the eyes of thousands of critical engineers and curious hobbyists with no association to the manufacturer? Then why would you trust a secret computer program? Open-source Linux is ideally suited for a mission-critical application—its security and power are based on robust solutions which are reviewed with no restrictions whatsoever, and continuously improved upon. Linux is quite different from MS Windows, so do not expect that if you can get around MS Windows, then Linux will be straightforward for you. You may need to learn. On the other hand, if you come from UNIX, Linux will be easy for you.

BENEFITS OF LINUX

Linux can give you:

- A modern, very stable, multi-user, multitasking environment on your inexpensive PC hardware, at no (or almost no) monetary cost for the software. Linux is a rich and powerful platform—don't think of it as a "poor people" operating system. Out-of-box Linux has as much capability as MS Windows NT with $5000 in software add-ons, is more stable, and requires less powerful hardware for comparable tasks.
- Standaɪd platform. Linux is VERY standard—it is essentially a POSIX compliant UNIX. (Yes, Linux is a best-of-the-breed UNIX. The word "UNIX" is not used in conjunction with Linux because "UNIX" is a registered trademark of "The Open Group".) Linux

includes all the tools and utilities typically associated with UNIX, plus more, significantly more than even the most expensive commercial UNIX implementations. To run Linux software, UNIX vendors these days implement "Linux compatiblity layers" into their platforms.

- Unsurpassed computing power, portability, flexibility, and customizibility. A Linux cluster recently (April 1999) beat a Cray supercomputer in a standard benchmark. Linux is most popular on Intel-based PCs (price of the hardware), but it runs very well on numerous other hardware platforms, from toy-like to mainframes. One distribution (Debian) expresses the idea like this: "Linux, The Universal Operating System." Linux can be customised to perform almost any computing task.
- Advanced graphical user interface. Linux uses a standard, network-transparent X-windowing system with a "window manager" (typically KDE or GNOME). The graphical desktop under Linux can be made to look like MS Windows (or probably ANY other graphical user interface of your choice).
- Dozens of excellent, free, general-interest desktop applications. These include a range of web browsers, e-mail programs, word processors, spreadsheets, bitmap and vector graphics programs, file managers, audio players, CD writers, some good games, etc.
- Thousands of free applets, tools, and smaller programs. "Small is beautiful" goes well with Linux philosophy. The small Linux tools and applets often work in tandem to perform more complex tasks.
- Hundreds of specialized applications built by researchers around the world (astronomy, information technology, chemistry, physics, engineering, linguistics, biology...). In many fields, Linux seems like "the only" operating system in existence (try to find out what your friend astronomer runs on her computer). The software in this category is typically

not very easy to use, but if you want the power, it is the best software that humanity has in these areas.

- Scores of top-of-the line commercial programs including all the big databases (*e.g.*, Oracle, Sybase, but no Microsoft's). Many (most?) of these are offered free for developers and for personal use.
- A truly great learning platform. If you are a parent, you should be really glad your daughter/son does Linux—s/he will surely learn something of lasting value. If you are a teacher, you should consider the installation of Linux at your school. "It is indeed a strange world when educators need to be convinced that sharing information, as opposed to concealing information, is a good thing". You select Linux if you care to provide education, not training. The better the university, the greater the chance their computer department uses Linux in teaching. For example, under Linux, you can immediately begin modifying and compiling for yourself a spreadsheet application which is in every bit as advanced and capable as MS Excel. Linux puts you right on the cutting edge (in technology, project management, QA, methodology of science). Many teachers won't use Linux in schools because they are lacking in computer education themselves.
- Excellent networking capability built into your operating system. You think you don't need a network? Once you try home networking, you will never be able to live without it! How about connecting the two or more computers that you have at home and sharing your hard drives, CDROM(s), sound card(s), modem, printer(s), etc.? How about browsing the net on two or more machines at the same time using a single Internet connection? How about playing a game with your son over your home network? Even your old 386 with Win3.11 may become useful again when connected to your Linux Pentium server and when it is able to use your network resources. All necessary

networking software comes with standard Linux, free, just setup is required. And it is not second-rate shareware--it is exactly the same software that runs most of the Internet (the Apache software runs more than 50% of all Internet web servers and Sendmail touches some 70% of all e-mail). The pleasure of home networking is something I was able to discover only owing to Linux.

- Connectivity to Microsoft, Novel, and Apple proprietary networking. Reading/writing to your DOS/MS Windows and other disk formats. This includes "transparent" use of data stored on the legacy MS Windows partition of your hard drive(s).
- State-of-the-art development platform with many best-of-the-kind programming languages and tools coming free with the operating system. Access to all the operating system source codes, should you require it, is also free. The "C" compiler that comes standard with Linux can compile code for more platforms than (probably) any other compiler on earth. Perl, Python, Guile, Tcl, Ruby, powerful "shell" scripting, and even assembler tools also come as standard with Linux.
- Freedom from viruses, "backdoors" to your computer, software manufacturer "features," invasion of privacy, forced upgrades, proprietary file formats, licensing and marketing schemes, product registration, high software prices, and pirating. How is this? Linux has no viruses worth mentioning because it is too secure an operating system for the viruses to spread with any degree of efficiency. The rest follows from the open-source and non-commercial nature of Linux: Linux evolved itself by "bazaar-like" mechanisms to encapsulate the best computing practices, code legibility and correctness, security, flexibility, usefulness, coolness, and performance.
- The operating platform that is guaranteed "here-to-

stay." Since Linux is not owned, it cannot possibly be put out of business. The Linux General Public License (GPL) insures that development/maintenance will be provided as long as there are Linux users. There are a great number of highly-educated Linux users and tens of thousands of actively developed projects.

- A platform which will technically develop at a rapid pace. This is insured by the modern, open-software development model which Linux implements: "build-on-the-back-of-the-previous-developer" and "peer-review-your-code" (as opposed to the anachronistic closed-software model: "always-start-from-scratch" and "nobody-will-see-my-code"). Even if the current "Linux hype" died out, Linux will develop as it did before the media hype started. Open source development does have its peculiarities: the development appears rather slow (vertically) but it proceeds on a very wide front, dangerous security bugs are fixed almost upon discovery, there are typically several alternatives for a program of similar functionality. Linux depth cannot be overestimated.

LINUX AND UNIX

Command-line-wise, almost none, although this has been changing (for better or worse). Linux has a much larger market appeal and following than any commercial UNIX. GUI-wise there are also no major differences—Linux, as most other UNIXes, uses an X-Windowing system.

The major differences:

- Linux is free, while many UNICES (this is supposed to be the plural of UNIX), are very expensive. The same for applications—many good applications are available on Linux free. Even the same commercial application (if you wanted to buy one) typically costs much more for a commercial UNIX than for Linux.
- Linux runs on many hardware platforms, the commodity Intel-x86/IBM-spec personal computers

being the most prominent. In contrast, a typical UNIX is proprietary-hardware-bonded (and this hardware tends to be much more expensive than a typical PC clone).

- With Linux, you are in charge of your computer, whereas on most UNICES you are typically confined to be an "l-user" (some administrators pronounce it "loser").
- Linux feels very much like DOS/Win in the late 80s/90s, but is much sturdier and richer, while a typical UNIX account feels like a mainframe from the 60s/70s.
- Some UNICES may be more mature in certain areas (for example, security, some engineering applications, better support of cutting-edge hardware). Linux is more for the average Joe who wants to run his own server or engineering workstation.

LINUX AND MS WINDOWS

Mouse-click-wise, almost none, once Linux is properly installed. Linux installation can be a challenge though, whereas MS Windows comes, most likely, pre-installed with your computer.

The major differences

Linux is free, whereas MS Windows costs money. Same for applications. If MS Windows or Office comes preinstalled with the computer it is unlikely it is free. Ask in the store to take it off your computer and you are likely to obtain a discount, at least in smaller stores.

- Linux file formats are free, so you can access them in a variety of ways. On MS Windows, the common practice is to make you lock your own data in secret formats that can only be accessed with tools leased to you at the vendor's price. How corrupt (or incompetent?) must be the politicians who lock our public records into these formats! "What we will get with Microsoft is a three-year lease on a health record we need to keep for 100 years" [http://news.bbc.co.uk/hi/english/health/newsid_1694000/1694372.stm].

- With Linux, you are unlikely to violate any licence agreement—all the software is happily yours. With MS Windows you likely already violate all kinds of licenses and you could be pronounced a computer pirate if only a smart lawyer was after you (don't worry, most likely none is after you).
- MS Windows tries to be the "lowest-common-denominator" operating system (for better or worse), whereas Linux is built for more sophisticated, feature-hungry computer users (for better or worse).
- MS Windows is based on DOS; Linux is based on UNIX. MS Windows Graphical User Interface (GUI) is based on Microsoft-owned specifications. Linux GUI is based on an industry-standard network-transparent X-Windowing system.
- Linux beats Windows hands down on network features, as a development platform, in data processing capabilities, and as a scientific workstation. MS Windows desktop has a more polished appearance, smoother general business applications, and many more games for kids (these are not better games though—Linux games tend to be more sophisticated).
- Linux is more feature-rich than you could imagine. Heard on the Internet: "Two big products came from the University of California: UNIX and LSD. And I don't think it's a coincidence." MS Windows is simpler.

LINUX IS A GOOD

The Linux community has repeatedly been labeled "religious zealots" by journalists whose well-established computer magazines received massive feedback after they had published highly unfair articles on Linux. So yes, the Linux community is numerous, literate, and willing to express its opinions. And many computer journalists/magazines know that Linux means less money for them (users pay less for their computing and the associated advertisement, while expecting more). Does this explain the "zealots"? Face it, you salespeople pretending to be journalists.

There is hardly any integrity left in the computing press. How many words on Linux did your PC Magazine (or any other IT magazine) publish by 1999-01-01? Wasn't Linux at least an interesting technology by that time? It surely was, yet you conspired to keep your readership in the dark, selling your journalistic integrity for a few dollars. And now, after Linux has surfaced in the mainstream (non-computer) media, you keep writing misleading articles about it saying "yah, but it will/cannot/may...." whatever (trying the "fear, uncertainty and doubt" tactics to kill it).

And adding "Microsoft is already...", continuing to write about the vapourware and the future paradise in the face of the increasingly stealthy, unstable, pricey, architecturally unsound computer platform, whose greatest achievement has been exhorting unheard-of-before money by denying inter-operatibility, and killing any existing or proposed standard (by "embracing" and then proprietary-extending it). Whom do you serve? Surely not your readers. You think "self-serving" is OK in business? How pathetic must your business be then! I always thought that business was a social contract in which we exchange good values, for a mutual benefit. As I read history, societies use to hang/guillotine/electrocute those members who really persisted in their self-serving business. Well, times have changed. A bit for the better, a bit for the worse:)) To be fair, there seems to be a number of hard-core devotees around any computer program/platform, and Linux might have accummulated a fair share of them. Oh, well, you may be religious about whatever you like.

LINUX AND DOS

LINUX AND MS-DOS

DOS was the first operating system I learned to use. I remember a test by my tutor in which one had to create a hierarchical set of directories. This probably sounds trivial to anyone familiar with graphical user interfaces, but then the scenario was very different. It even looks ancient by today's standards. Windows 95 hadn't been released at that time, and Linux was unheard of in India. I liked DOS much better than Windows 3.1, which looked quite flimsy and unstable, not to mention that it was a big memory hog. DOS is quite different from Linux in many ways. DOS does not provide any graphical user interface and you have to learn at least a dozen commands with its numerous options to do some basic tasks like copying a file or moving between the directories. Even a minor spelling mistake can result in a "Bad command or file name" error.

DOS does not support the concept of multi-users; each and every user has to customise the system according to his need every time he wants to work on it. It was also not a multitasking system. This meant that you could not check out the value of a calculation when typing a letter without closing that application first. DOS also does not have any in built security features. This was acceptable as long as you did not want a networking system. There was other variants of MS-DOS, like PC-DOS from IBM and some others, which tried to add the missing features. Some of the deficiencies have been resolved using third party utilities but basic limitations like the arcane 640kb-memory limit and single-tasking were not acceptable to many.

Now in case you are wondering why anyone would care to use DOS, I will point out some advantages. Basically DOS has had very different goals from that of Linux. It was a very cheap system (as far as cost is concerned) and it was quite usable with its minimalist set of features. It was a simple system to work with. There weren't too many complications to worry about if you didn't want to develop anything on it. It was arguably the world's most popular operating system and it had a comfortable number of applications for common tasks.

Files and Directories

The files in Linux can be very long, up-to 255 characters like Windows, and they do not always have extensions. The executable files are identified through an attribute rather than the extension. File extensions are less important to Linux than for DOS and Windows, since Linux usually identifies files by a unique identification code called the magic number that depends on the file type.

Linux shell

Several of the DOS commands have Linux equivalents. The Linux shell is similar to the DOS command line but is far more powerful, and I found that it was also more workable with features like colour highlighting and friendlier navigation capabilities, depending on the particular shell you are using. Most Linux distributions come with the Bash (Bourne Again SHell) as the default.

There are several others, like the Korn shell and the C shell. They are usually similar. It's recommended that you learn to work with one shell completely before trying out the others. Things usually get complicated if you want to run shell scripts, which are similar to batch files (files with the.bat extension) under DOS.

Running DOS Programs under Linux

There is a DOS emulator called dosemu www.dosemu.org for Linux that is capable of running DOS programs under the Linux operating system. This software is still under development; you may wish to try it out though. It is known to be fairly usable at least for some applications. If you are looking for Linux just to use DOS programs for free then try using FreeDOS www.freedos.org. That should be much better than Linux.

LINUX VS. WINDOWS

As I have said before Windows is more or less similar to Linux. When people are introduced to Linux they are at first intimidated by the system. It has different kinds of graphical interfaces and things don't always work as they are expected to. When users look at me in a puzzled manner I demonstrate in some easy ways how common tasks like changing the desktop wallpaper or playing a song is similar to Windows. The problem with this kind of approach is that the users complain very soon that Linux doesn't offer them much more than Windows does:-).

I agree with them to a certain extent on this. There are some limitations to what you can expect from an operating system. You just can't expect Linux to work like a 3D-shooter game or something. Of course, there are many differences in the shell, the choice of user interfaces and the philosophy and goals of the operating system. Linux is developed as a open system in which the source code of the core Linux system (kernel) is available for anyone for free but how this could affect the end user is difficult to explain initially.

The user interface is probably the first thing you notice when you begin to use the Linux system. Windows offers a single, monolithic user interface, which is more or less the same across all the versions. In contrast, Linux has two major desktop environments called KDE and Gnome. KDE has a built-in window manager, while Gnome is supported by many, such as Sawfish and Enlightenment.

The decision of choosing one among the desktop environments and windows managers is left to you. Some of them can run efficiently in a system with low amounts of memory and some of them are designed to look like a game console. KDE would be more similar to Windows, and Gnome with the Enlightenment window manager was fancy enough for me. Try out some of the popular ones before making the decision.

Versions of Windows

Windows has two major series, a desktop oriented series (Windows 9x) And a network oriented series Windows.There are also other versions like Windows CE for embedded systems.

Windows 9x series

Before Windows 95 was released, all versions of Windows until version 3.1 were graphical platforms on top of DOS. This offered limited capability for multitasking and the Program Manager interface was cluttered with no distinct hierarchy. Windows 95 was a 32-bit operating system and a major improvement in user interface with its "Desktop" concept adapted from the Macintosh user interface. It also offered limited compatibility with previous versions of Windows and DOS. Stability was also improved Windows 98 and Windows ME offered some more features though nothing major was added. The more recent version called Windows XP is considerably more stable due to incorporating the Windows 2000 kernel, and is comparatively friendlier and easier due to an attractive interface.

Windows NT Series

Windows NT is considerably stable but demands more resources. It supports the Intel architecture, and at one time the Digital alpha and MIPS processors, but I believe those have been dropped now. It managed to replace UNIX in small-scale networks due to the similarity to the popular Windows 95 interface. The latest incarnation called Windows 2000 provides a few more administrative utilities and services.

MEMORIES

The expensive nature of RAM spurred the creation of another type of computer memory called virtual memory. With virtual memory, a slow down in performance is observed only when you try to operate a program whose files are in the virtual memory. In essence, this slow down is only observed when shifting between programs. In this way, virtual memory often provides a cheaper alternative to RAM.

A third type of computer memory is cache. There are two types of cache. Primary cache, or level 1 cache, is built right into the central processing unit (CPU) and ensures instant availability of data that the CPU frequently needs. Secondary cache, or level 2 cache, is usually built on a memory chip, is located very close to the CPU, and has a direct connection to the CPU through a dedicated circuit. Secondary cache is bigger in capacity than primary cache. Cache basically speeds up the rate at which data moves from the main memory to the CPU. The registers form a fourth type of computer memory. These are units within the CPU that contain specific types of data, especially for the Arithmetic and Logic Unit (ALU). A final group of computer memory is called flash. This is a solid-state, rewritable type of memory. Examples of flash memory include BIOS and memory cards. Just like the RAM, they are electronic and not mechanical. They are also non-volatile, and are therefore suitable for digital cameras, mobile phones and other miniaturized computers

OVERVIEW

The system memory is the place where the computer holds current programs and data that are in use. There are various levels of computer memory (memory), including ROM, RAM, cache, page and graphics, each with specific objectives for system operation. This section focusses on the role of computer memory, and the technology behind it.

Although memory is used in many different forms around modern PC systems, it can be divided into two essential types: RAM and ROM. ROM, or Read Only Memory, is relatively small, but essential to how a computer works. ROM is always found on motherboards, but is increasingly found on graphics cards and some other expansion cards and peripherals. Generally speaking, ROM does not change. It forms the basic instruction set for operating the hardware in the system, and the data within remains intact even when the computer is shut down. It is possible to update ROM, but it's only done rarely, and at need. If ROM is damaged, the computer system simply cannot function.

RAM, or Random Access Memory, is "volatile." This means that it only holds data while power is present. RAM changes constantly as the system operates, providing the storage for all data required by the operating system and software. Because of the demands made by increasingly powerful operating systems and software, system RAM requirements have accelerated dramatically over time. For instance, at the turn of the millennium a typical computer may have only 128Mb of RAM in total, but in 2007 computers commonly ship with 2Gb of RAM installed, and may include graphics cards with their own additional 512Mb of RAM and more.

Clearly, modern computers have significantly more memory than the first PCs of the early 1980s, and this has had an effect on development of the PC's architecture. The trouble is, storing and retrieving data from a large block of memory is more time-consuming than from a small block. With a large amount of memory, the difference in time between a register access and a memory access is very great, and this has resulted in extra layers of cache in the storage hierarchy.

When accessing memory, a fast processor will demand a great deal from RAM. At worst, the CPU may have to waste clock cycles while it waits for data to be retrieved. Faster memory designs and motherboard buses can help, but since the 1990s "cache memory" has been employed as standard between the main memory and the processor. Not only this, CPU architecture has also evolved to include ever larger internal caches. The organization of data this way is immensely complex, and the system uses ingenious electronic controls to ensure that the data the processor needs next is already in cache, physically closer to the processor and ready for fast retrieval and manipulation.

CLASSIFICATION RAM

Random access memory or RAM most commonly refers to computer chips that temporarily store dynamic data to enhance computer performance. By storing frequently used or active files in random access memory, the computer can access the data faster than if it to retrieve it from the far-larger hard drive. Random access memory is also used in printers and other devices. Random access memory is volatile memory, meaning it loses its contents once power is cut. This is different from non-volatile memory such as hard disks and flash memory, which do not require a power source to retain data.

When a computer shuts down properly, all data located in random access memory is committed to permanent storage on the hard drive or flash drive. At the next boot-up, RAM begins to fill with programs automatically loaded at startup, and with files opened by the user. There are several different types of random access memory chips which come several to a "stick." A stick of RAM is a small circuit board shaped like a large stick of gum. Sticks of RAM fit into "banks" on the motherboard. Adding one or more sticks increases RAM storage and performance.

Random access memory is categorized by architecture and speed. As technology progresses, RAM chips become faster and employ new standards so that RAM must be matched to a compatible motherboard. The motherboard will only support certain types of random access memory, and it will also have a limit as to the amount of RAM it can support. For example, one motherboard may support dual-channel Synchronous Dynamic Random Access Memory (SDRAM), while an older motherboard might only support Single In-line Memory Modules (SIMMS) or Dual In-line Memory Modules (DIMMS).

Since random access memory can improve performance, the type and amount of RAM a motherboard will support becomes a major factor when considering a new computer. If there is a faster, better random access memory chip on the market, the buyer will want to consider purchasing a motherboard capable of using it. A year down the road, that 'new' RAM might be standard, while the buyer may be stuck with an old style motherboard. A new variety of non-volatile random access memory made with nanotubes or other technologies will likely be forthcoming in the near future. These RAM chips would retain data when powered down.

Memory, which is commonly referred to as RAM (Random Access Memory), is a temporary (Volatile) storage area utilized by the CPU. Before a program can be run, the program is loaded into the memory which allows the CPU direct access to the program. Memory is a necessity for any computer and it is recommend that you have at least 64MB of memory for your IBM or Macintosh.

Memory is commonly confused with Hard Drive Space. There are two types of memory; the first type of memory is the memory explained in the above paragraph, this memory is available in computer chips; the other type of memory is actually Hard Drive Space which is stored on the computer Hard Disk Drive. The Hard drive is actually a physical drive which contains several parts and is generally larger than the amount of memory found in your computer.

SINGLE IN-LINE MEMORY MODULE (SIMM)

A slender circuit board dedicated to storing memory chips. Each chip is capable of holding 8 to 9 chips per board, the ninth chip usually an error-checking chip (parity/non parity). The typical bus from the chip to the motherboard is 32-bits wide. When upgrading a Pentium motherboard you will be required to upgrade 2 of the same type of chips at the same time to accommodate the Pentium processor.

SPEED

Can determine the size amount of the chip by looking at the part number of each chip on the SIMM board. For 2-, 8- and 9-chip SIMMs, all the chips should have the same part numbers. Look at the number that ends with a dash and a digit such as "-7". This is the rate speed or nanoseconds of the chip. With "-7" this would indicate that the memory is 70ns.

SIZE

Look at the four digits to the left of this number; these often carry information about the number of bits in the chip. A 4256 indicates 256K bits arranged in sets of four, for a total of 1Mb. "1000" indicates 1MB of bits arranged in one set. With some types of memory, the last one or two digits may be changed to indicate different kinds of memory; there are 1MB chips that end with 4256, 4257, and 4258. In this case, round the last digits to an even 256 or thousand. Three-chip SIMMs will typically have two larger chips that are four times the capacity of the third chip (because 4 plus 4 plus 1 makes 9, which is the number of bits needed per byte including parity).

PARITY/NON PARITY

To determine if the SIMM is Parity/Non Parity, look for

x36/x9 which indicate that the chip is parity (Error checking). x36 is used with 72-pin SIMMs and x9 is for 30-pin SIMMs. If x32/x8 this would be an indication that the chip in Non Parity (Non Error checking) x32 is used with 72-pin SIMMs and x8 is used with 30-pin SIMMs. Another method: count the chips. If you see three or nine discrete chips, the SIMM probably includes a parity. If there are two or eight chips, the SIMM probably does not include parity bit. In this case, divide the number of bits by 8 to determine bytes.

SIMM Memory and Pentium Computers

When updating the computer's memory with a Pentium processor, ensure that you purchase two SIMMs rather than one. Such as if planning to upgrade to 32 MB of RAM that you use two 16 MB SIMMs rather than one. This must be done to allow the memory to work properly with the Pentium processor.

DUAL IN-LINE MEMORY MODULE (DIMM)

Type of Circuit board that holds memory chips. DIMMS have a 64-bit path because of the Pentium Processor requirements. Because of the new bit path, DIMMS can be installed one at a time un-like SIMMs which on a Pentium would require two be added.

Some of the Advantages DIMMs have over SIMMs

DIMMs have separate contacts on each side of the board, thereby providing twice as much data as a single SIMM.

The command address and control signals are buffered on the DIMMs. With heavy memory requirements this will reduce the loading effort of the memory.

STATIC RAM (SRAM)

Static RAM is a type of RAM that holds its data without external refresh, for as long as power is supplied to the circuit. This is contrasted to dynamic RAM (DRAM), which must be refreshed many times per second in order to hold its data contents.

SRAMs are used for specific applications within the PC, where their strengths outweigh their weaknesses compared to DRAM:

- *Simplicity*: SRAMs don't require external refresh circuitry or other work in order for them to keep their data intact.
- *Speed*: SRAM is faster than DRAM.

In contrast, SRAMs have the following weaknesses, compared to DRAMs:

- *Cost*: SRAM is, byte for byte, several times more expensive than DRAM.
- *Size*: SRAMs take up much more space than DRAMs (which is part of why the cost is higher).

These advantages and disadvantages taken together obviously show that performance-wise, SRAM is superior to DRAM, and we would use it exclusively if only we could do so economically. Unfortunately, 32 MB of SRAM would be prohibitively large and costly, which is why DRAM is used for system memory. SRAMs are used instead for level 1 cache and level 2 cache memory, for which it is perfectly suited; cache memory needs to be very fast, and not very large.

SRAM is manufactured in a way rather similar to how processors are: highly-integrated transistor patterns photo-etched into silicon. Each SRAM bit is comprised of between four and six transistors, which is why SRAM takes up much more space compared to DRAM, which uses only one (plus a capacitor). Because an SRAM chip is comprised of thousands or millions of identical cells, it is much easier to make than a CPU, which is a large die with a non-repetitive structure.

DYNAMIC RAM (DRAM)

Dynamic RAM is a type of RAM that only holds its data if it is continuously accessed by special logic called a refresh circuit. Many hundreds of times each second, this circuitry reads the contents of each memory cell, whether the memory cell is being used at that time by the computers or not. Due to the way in which the cells are constructed, the reading action itself refreshes the contents of the memory. If this is not done regularly, then the DRAM will lose its contents, even if it continues to have power supplied to it. This refreshing action is why the memory is called dynamic.

All PCs use DRAM for their main system memory, instead of SRAM, even though DRAMs are slower than SRAMs and require the overhead of the refresh circuitry. It may seem weird to want to make the computer's memory out of something that can only hold a value for a fraction of a second. In fact, DRAMs are both more complicated and slower than SRAMs.

The reason that DRAMs are used is simple: they are much cheaper and take up much less space, typically 1/4 the silicon area of SRAMs or less. To build a 64 MB core memory from SRAMs would be very expensive. The overhead of the refresh circuit is tolerated in order to allow the use of large amounts of inexpensive, compact memory. The refresh circuitry itself is almost never a problem; many years of using DRAM has caused the design of these circuits to be all but perfected.

DRAMs are smaller and less expensive than SRAMs because SRAMs are made from four to six transistors (or more) per bit, DRAMs use only one, plus a capacitor. The capacitor, when energized, holds an electrical charge if the bit contains a "1" or no charge if it contains a "0". The transistor is used to read the contents of the capacitor. The problem with capacitors is that they only hold a charge for a short period of time, and then it fades away.

These capacitors are tiny, so their charges fade particularly quickly. This is why the refresh circuitry is needed: to read the contents of every cell and refresh them with a fresh "charge" before the contents fade away and are lost. Refreshing is done by reading every "row" in the memory chip one row at a time; the process of reading the contents of each capacitor re-establishes the charge.

DRAM is manufactured using a similar process to how processors are: a silicon substrate is etched with the patterns that make the transistors and capacitors (and support structures) that comprise each bit. DRAM costs much less than a processor because it is a series of simple, repeated structures, so there isn't the complexity of making a single chip with several million individually-located transistors.

DDR-SDRAM

The DDR-SDRAM (Double Data Rate SDRAM) is a memory, based on the SDRAM technology, which doubles the transfer rate of the SDRAM using the same frequency. Data are read or written into memory based on a clock. Standard DRAM memories use a method known as SDR (Single Data Rate) involving reading or writing a piece of data at each leading edge.

The DDR doubles the frequency of reading/writing, with a clock at the same frequency, by sending data to each leading edge and to each trailing edge. DDR memories generally have a product name such as PCXXXX where "XXXX" represents the speed in Mo/s.

DDR2-SDRAM

DDR2 (or DDR-II) memory achieves speeds that are twice as high as those of the DDR with the same external fre.,uency. QDR (Quadruple Data Rate or quad-pumped) designates the reading and writing method used. DDR2 memory in fact uses two separate channels for reading and writing, so that it is able to send or receive twice as much data as the DDR. DDR2 also has more connectors than the classic DDR (240 for DDR2 compared with 184 for DDR).

OPERATION OF RNDOM ACESS MEMORY

The random access memory comprises hundreds of thousands of small capacitors that store loads. When loaded, the logical state of the capacitor is equal to 1, otherwise it is 0, meaning that each capacitor represents one memory bit. Given that the capacitors become discharged they must be constantly recharged (the exact term is refresh) at regular intervals, known as the refresh cycle. DRAM memories for example require refresh cycles of around 15 nanoseconds (ns). Each capacitor is coupled with a transistor (MOS-type) enabling "recovery" or amendment of the status of the capacitor. These transistors are arranged in the form of a table (matrix) thus we access a memory box (also called memory point) via a line and a column.

Each memory point is thus characterised by an address which corresponds to a row number and a column number. This access is not instant and the access time period is known as latency time. Consequently, time required for access to data in the memory is equal to cycle time plus latency time. Thus, for a DRAM memory, access time is 60 nanoseconds (35ns cycle time and 25ns latency time). On a computer, the cycle time corresponds to the opposite of the clock frequency; for example, for a computer with frequency of 200 MHz, cycle time is 5 ns (1/200*106)). Consequently a computer with high frequency using memories with access time much longer than the processor cycle time must perform wait states to access the memory. For a computer with frequency of 200 MHz using DRAM memories (and access time of 60ns), there are 11 wait states for a transfer cycle. The computer's performance decreases as the number of wait states increases, therefore we recommend the use of faster memories.

READ ONLY MEMORY

DEFINITION

ROM is an integrated-circuit memory chip that contains configuration data. ROM is commonly called firmware because its programming is fully embedded into the ROM chip. As such, ROM is a hardware and software in one. Because data is fully incorporated at the ROM chip's manufacture, data stored can neither be erased nor replaced. This means permanent and secure data storage. However, if a mistake is made in manufacture, a ROM chip becomes unusable. The most expensive stage of ROM manufacture, therefore, is creating the template. If a template is readily available, duplicating the ROM chip is very easy and affordable. A ROM chip is also non-volatile so data stored in it is not lost when power is turned off. There is a type of memory that stores data without electrical current; it is the ROM (Read Only Memory) or is sometimes called non-volatile memory as it is not erased when the system is switched off. This type of memory lets you stored the data needed to start up the computer. Indeed, this information cannot be stored on the hard disk since the disk parameters (vital for its initialisation) are part of these data which are essential for booting.

Different ROM-type memories contain these essential start-up data, i.e.:

- The BIOS is a programme for controlling the system's main input-output interfaces, hence the name BIOS ROM which is sometimes given to the read-only memory chip of the mother board which hosts it.
- The bootstrap loader: a programme for loading (random access) memory into the operating system and launching it. This generally seeks the operating system on the floppy drive then on the hard disk, which allows the operating system to be launched from a system floppy disk in the event of malfunction of the system installed on the hard disk.
- The CMOS Setup is the screen displayed when the computer starts up and which is used to amend the system parameters (often wrongly referred to as BIOS).
- The Power-On Self Test (POST), a programme that runs automatically when the system is booted, thus allowing the system to be tested (this is why the system "counts" the RAM at start-up).

Given that ROM are much slower than RAM memories (access time for a ROM is around 150 ns whereas for SDRAM it is around 10 ns), the instructions given in the ROM are sometimes copied to the RAM at start-up; this is known as shadowing, though is usually referred to as shadow memory). One major type of memory that is used in PCs is called read-only memory, or ROM for short. ROM is a type of memory that normally can only be read, as opposed to RAM which can be both read and written.

There are two main reasons that read-only memory is used for certain functions within the PC:

- *Permanence*: The values stored in ROM are always there, whether the power is on or not. A ROM can be removed from the PC, stored for an indefinite period of time, and then replaced, and the data it contains will still be there. For this reason, it is called non-volatile storage. A hard disk is also non-volatile, for the same reason, but regular RAM is not.

- *Security*: The fact that ROM cannot easily be modified provides a measure of security against accidental (or malicious) changes to its contents. You are not going to find viruses infecting true ROMs, for example; it's just not possible. (It's technically possible with erasable EPROMs, though in practice never seen.)

Read-only memory is most commonly used to store system-level programs that we want to have available to the PC at all times. The most common example is the system BIOS program, which is stored in a ROM called (amazingly enough) the system BIOS ROM. Having this in a permanent ROM means it is available when the power is turned on so that the PC can use it to boot up the system. Remember that when you first turn on the PC the system memory is empty, so there has to be something for the PC to use when it starts up. While the whole point of a ROM is supposed to be that the contents cannot be changed, there are times when being able to change the contents of a ROM can be very useful. There are several ROM variants that can be changed under certain circumstances; these can be thought of as "mostly read-only memory":^)

TYPES OF ROMS

There are types of ROMs with a description of their relative modifiability:

ROM

A regular ROM is constructed from hard-wired logic, encoded in the silicon itself, much the way that a processor is. It is designed to perform a specific function and cannot be changed. This is inflexible and so regular ROMs are only used generally for programs that are static (not changing often) and mass-produced. This product is analagous to a commercial software CD-ROM that you purchase in a store.

Programmable ROM (PROM)

This is a type of ROM that can be programmed using

special equipment; it can be written to, but only once. This is useful for companies that make their own ROMs from software they write, because when they change their code they can create new PROMs without requiring expensive equipment. This is similar to the way a CD-ROM recorder works by letting you "burn" programs onto blanks once and then letting you read from them many times. In fact, programming a PROM is also called burning, just like burning a CD-R, and it is comparable in terms of its flexibility.

Erasable Programmable ROM (EPROM)

An EPROM is a ROM that can be erased and reprogrammed. A little glass window is installed in the top of the ROM package, through which you can actually see the chip that holds the memory. Ultraviolet light of a specific frequency can be shined through this window for a specified period of time, which will erase the EPROM and allow it to be reprogrammed again. Obviously this is much more useful than a regular PROM, but it does require the erasing light. Continuing the "CD" analogy, this technology is analogous to a reusable CD-RW.

Electrically Erasable Programmable ROM (EEPROM)

The next level of erasability is the EEPROM, which can be erased under software control. This is the most flexible type of ROM, and is now commonly used for holding BIOS programs. When you hear reference to a "flash BIOS" or doing a BIOS upgrade by "flashing", this refers to reprogramming the BIOS EEPROM with a special software program. Here we are blurring the line a bit between what "read-only" really means, but remember that this rewriting is done maybe once a year or so, compared to real read-write memory (RAM) where rewriting is done often many times per second!

SECONDARY STORAGE DEVICES

DEFINITION

Storage Devices are the data storage devices that are used

in the computers to store the data. The computer has many types of data storage devices. Some of them can be classified as the removable data Storage Devices and the others as the non removable data Storage Devices. The data Storage Devices come in many sizes and shapes. And more over the technology used for the storage of the data over them is also altogether different. The storage devices are one of the most important components of the computer system. The memory is of two types; one is the primary memory and the other one is the secondary memory. The primary memory is the volatile memory and the secondary memory is the non volatile memory. The volatile memory is the kind of the memory that is erasable and the non volatile memory is the one where in the contents cannot be erased.

Basically when we talk about the data storage devices it is generally assumed to be the secondary memory. The secondary memory is used to store the data permanently in the computer. The secondary storage devices are usually as follows: hard disk drives-this is the most common type of storage device that is used in almost all the computer systems. The other ones include the floppy disk drives, the CD ROM, and the DVD ROM. The flash memory, the USB data card etc. The storage devices are used to record the data over any storage surface. The memories may also be of different types depending upon the architecture and the design like the optical data storage memory, magnetic media storage and the mechanical storage media etc and also the flash memory devices etc. The storage devices are actually defined as the peripheral unit which holds the data like the tape, disk, or flash memory card etc.

The most of the drives that are used for the purpose of data storage are fragile and the data can be easily corrupted in them. The data storage devices are the ones that are also used for the backup and the archiving of the data. The data storage devices were at a time in the past used to be too costly and expensive. But these days the data storage devices are becoming cheap day by day. Hence the data storage devices price is falling. So, we are in a position to get a storage device for a comparatively cheaper price than the earlier drive. The technology is improving a lot and now the memory storage capacity has gone up TB. The data in the storage devices can be in the form of the files, data bases, digital video and the audio etc. The storage devices that are called as the non volatile can store the data permanently until otherwise erased purposely. This is in the case of the hard disk drives or the floppy disk drives.

The other kinds of the storage media like for example the CD and the DVD can even have again two types of the storage; the first one is that in which the data once written cannot be erased. It is stored permanently over it. While the second type of the CD's or the DVD's are called as the rewritable; where in the data that is once written can be erased completely and the same storage device can be used again for storing the different data. The storage devices are used to record the data over any storage surface. The memories may also be of different types depending upon the architecture and the design like the optical data storage memory, magnetic media storage and the mechanical storage media etc and also the flash memory devices etc.

The storage devices are actually defined as the peripheral unit which holds the data like the tape, disk, or flash memory card etc. The most of the drives that are used for the purpose of data storage are fragile and the data can be easily corrupted in them. The data storage devices are the ones that are also used for the backup and the archiving of the data. The data storage devices were at a time in the past used to be too costly and expensive. But these days the data storage devices are becoming cheap day by day. Hence the data storage devices price is falling. So, we are in a position to get a storage device for a comparatively cheaper price than the earlier drive. The technology is improving a lot and now the memory storage capacity has gone up TB.

The data in the storage devices can be in the form of the files, databases, digital video and the audio etc. The storage devices that are called as the non volatile can store the data permanently until otherwise erased purposely. This is in the case of the hard disk drives or the floppy disk drives. The other kinds of the storage media like for example the CD and the DVD can even have again two types of the storage; the first one is that in which the data once written cannot be erased. It is stored permanently over it. While the second type of the CD's or the DVD's are called as the rewritable; where in the data that is once written can be erased completely and the same storage device can be used again for storing the different data.

TYPES OF STORAGE DEVICES

Removable Data Storage Devices

The Removable Storage Media are the types of storage devices that are used for the storage of the data. The main reason for using the removable storage media is the ease of portability. That is the ease with which the data can be transferred. The data is of importance and is necessary for the movement in some cases. Here the case of portability of the storage device comes into the picture. The removable storage media serves the same purpose. More over there are many application of the storage of the data over the removable media. The first and the foremost is the portability that is already discussed above. The next is the issue of the backup and archiving of the data that is important and also sensitive in nature. The backup of data is as important as the storage of data is important.

The CD and the DVD are key players in the removable storage types that are used for the purpose of backup and archiving of the data. The main reason for storing the data over the removable devices is that the data can be easily moved physically from one place to another at the time of any disaster or any other casualty. The floppy disk drive was the removable storage media that was used for the purpose of storing the data over the disk for the backup. This was the case in the 80's; but as the pace has increased in the technology the CD's and the DVD's had gained momentum for the purpose of providing backup to the data. The floppy disk drives that are available even today do not provide enough memory capacity. And now the concept of the flash memory devices is doing rounds for providing data transfer from place to another. There are some situations where in the normal data transfer through the networking is not possible. But as in the case of the removal storage media the data transfer can be easily done. Hence the main advantage regarding the removal storage media is the data transfer from the computers to the other computers where there is no existence of the network. The data transfer facility is important even in case; when the network actually exists but there is a failure of the network. In such situations the external data transfer is quite useful.

Also in some cases the data from one system is required to be used through the other system. Here the network connections are not at all possible. Hence the data has to be physically moved from one place to the other. The example for this may be the regular video or the audio. If it is so desired that the video or the audio is to be used through the mode of the large panel television; but the digital video or the audio is in the computer. Hence in such a situation it is not possible to connect the two different types of systems that are the computer and the television. In such a situation the removable data storage devices come into the play. The solution to this problem is that the digital video or the audio should be burned over the CD or the DVD in the format that is supported by the VCD player associated with the television. And after that is done the video could be used through the television. Similar is the case with the audio also. The removable storage media has one more example of the Zip drives.

Non Removable Data Storage Devices

The storage media is generally referred to the secondary memory devices such as the hard disk and the floppy disk drive, CD drive, DVD disk drive, USB drives and the flash memory devices and also to the Zip drives. But apart from the hard disk, none of them are the devices that are non removable in nature. It means that the hard disk is the only mentioned device that is considered as the Non-Removable Storage Media. All the rest are the removable storage media. Another example that can be used for the Non-Removable

Storage Media is the RAM. But it is a volatile memory that cannot be used for permanently storing the data. It is just the primary memory that is of utmost importance to the system but at the same time cannot be used for the backup or the archiving of the data.

The non removable storage media is fixed permanently in to the computer case and can also be used for the backup or the archiving of the data. The hard disk drives are the best suitable example for this type of storage media. It also important to mention here that the hard disk drive can also either be internal or the external disk drive. In the internal hard disk; the drive is fixed permanently to the computer case. Where as, in the case of the external disk drive the hard drive can be moved from one place to another. Such a drive has a hard casing made over the normal disk drive. It is made to with stand the shocks in case of any physical damage.

The external hard disk drive's case acts as shield and a shock absorber in case of any physical damage. The external hard drive is provided with a USB cable that is plugged into the computer case for the ease of usage. Hence this type of the external hard disk becomes the removal type of data storage. The discussion matters here only with the non removable storage media. Hence the internal hard disks and its types can be discussed elaborately. The internal hard disk drive is usually fixed in the computer case. The type of hard disk controller gives the name for the different types of the hard disks. The IDE hard disk is the normal hard disk that is used in the regular computers. The IDE controller is used for the purpose of providing connections to this type of the hard disk drive.

The SCSI controllers are used to provide the connections for the SCSI hard disk. The other technology that can be implemented by the internal hard disk drives is the RAID. The RAID is the Redundant Array of Independent (or Inexpensive) disks. In the regular cases the hard disk or mostly the internal hard disk is connected to the motherboard. The motherboard has the IDE connector where in the bus from the hard disk drive is to be plugged in. If two or more than two hard disk drives are used, then in such case the hard disk drive should clearly be specified as which one is used as the master drive and the other one should also clearly be specified as the slave. The hard disk drive has the jumper settings, by which it can be determined or specified. The internal hard disk is specifically used as the secondary memory. And most importantly the secondary memory that is used in the computer is the non removable storage media. The removal storage media is not used as the secondary memory.

SECONDARY STORAGE DEVICES

Secondary Storage refers to non-volatile data storage which is not directly accessible by the CPU and only accessible via primary storage devices using I/O (Input/Output) channels or device drivers. Typical examples of Secondary Storage are hard disks, floppy disks, optical storage devices (such as CD, DVD drives), magnetic tape data storage devices, RAM drives, and flash memory (such as USB sticks/keys.) The secondary storage helps in securing the data on media types and storage categories, as data is vulnerable to network attacks, administrative access and media theft. There are many organizations who are working with third parties and disaster recovery efforts. Often data goes offsite and is in the hands of employees that are not authorized to see critical company data. And storage consolidation opens the door to greater administrative access. All of these trends drive the need to ensure the data at rest is secure.

Secondary storage devices hold files that are not currently being used. For a file to be used it must first be copied to main memory first. After any modifications files must be saved to secondary storage. It is advisable to save your data files at the regular intervals as you work on them as data can be lost unexpectedly because of various reasons like interruption in power supply, memory management problems, freezing keyboard, etc. Compared to main memory, secondary memory is slower, bigger, and cheaper (per unit storage.) Any method for secondary storage must involve two physical parts: a peripheral device (the component of the computer which 'reads' in or 'writes' out the information to/from the system unit,) and an input/output medium, on which the information is actually stored. Diskettes and cassettes are types of media. The medium has to be 'in' a corresponding peripheral device for information transfer to take place. In most methods of secondary storage, this transfer is realised by passing the medium by a read/write head, which is capable of sensing/ writing information from/to that type of medium.

Secondary storage media may be removable (easily separable from the computer) like your diskettes, or fixed, like hard disks, which, for example, can be found in relatively expensive PCís. A fixed medium generally has much greater capacity (and is faster) compared to a removable one of the same type. On the other hand, by replacing your removable medium by another one when it is full, you can attain a virtually unlimited storage capacity. Another nice feature of removable media is that they allow backup copies of important material to be taken and kept away from the computer, so that they do not get corrupted if some disaster strikes the computer.

The act of retrieving pieces of stored information is called access. There may be two kinds of access to data stored as a sequence of items: Sequential access, where the items are traversed one by one from the beginning of the sequence to the desired one, and direct access (or random access), where any item can be accessed relatively independently of its location in the sequence. Different types of secondary memory media support one or more of these different methods, depending on their nature. Cassette tapes, for example, are sequential access media: You have to 'go through' the first 10 minutes if you want to listen to a piece which begins at the 11th minute of the tape. The most common type of secondary storage medium is the magnetic disk. Diskettes (small disks made of flexible plastic) and hard disks (made of rigid metal) are the two different kinds of magnetic disks. Magnetic disks are coated with a magnetizable substance, the spots on which mean '0' or '1', depending on whether they are magnetized or not. Each surface of the disk is subdivided into concentric rings called tracks. Disks with bigger capacity have more tracks than others. In larger computers, one stores the same amount of data in each track and keeps several disks mounted on a shaft on top of each other as a disk pack. The group of tracks which are at the same position in their respective disks on a disk pack is called the disk cylinder for that position. The associated peripheral device is called the disk unit.

At least one read-write head is assigned for each surface. The read-write heads are mounted on a device called the access mechanism, which positions them on the cylinder in which the appropriate data item is to be located. The time for the read-write head to move from its initial location to the appropriate track is called seek time. In larger computers, the shaft on which the disk is mounted continuously rotates at a great speed, and the time required for the relevant portion of the track to come near the head is called rotational delay. The time needed for the actual information transfer between head and disk is called data movement time. Disk access time is the sum of these three components. In larger computers, the read/write head never touches the disk.

Diskettes, on the other hand, rotate only when a read/write is taking place. Furthermore, the head actually touches the diskette. Diskettes usually come in one of two diameters: 3.5 inches or 5.25 inches. 3.5-inch diskettes are products of a newer technology and can store more than 5.25-inch diskettes. Different types of computers employ different methods of data organization on a diskette. For this reason, a new diskette has to be formatted before it is used on a particular computer. Formatting a disk involves designating parts of each track as individually addressable (directly accessible) sectors. Each diskette contains a file directory, in which the names, lengths and starting addresses of the files (collections of related data) stored on it are listed. People with many files to store in the same disk are encouraged to use a tree-like directory structure in which related files are kept in separate subdirectories.

If a computer system has enough main memory and a program designed to read/write data from/to a disk is to be executed, one can transfer the contents of the disk to main memory and then use a method called disk emulation (or RAM disk) to 'trick' the computer into thinking that it is accessing the disk, while it actually deals with the much faster main memory. An older type of secondary storage medium is magnetic tape. Characters of data are represented in byte form across the tracks which go along the length of the tape.

Other types of secondary storage media include mass storage units, which are combinations of spools of magnetic tape that can be automatically retrieved from a huge 'library' and read to disk. These store enormous amounts of information and do not require the intervention of a human operator, note that some disk packs and tapes need this kind of intervention. Optical disks employ a relatively new technology. They use laser beams for the read/write operations. Most optical disks are of the CD-ROM (Compact Disk/Read-Only Memory) type; whose vendor-determined contents cannot be changed by the user. Because of their great capacity, these are used for storing multimedia (*i.e.* mixed text, graphics, sound, etc.) applications of great size. Their speed is low, compared to magnetic hard disks. As secondary storage media can be damaged and files on them become corrupted, it is suggested to make back-up copies of valuable files on a regular basis. Lots of people skip the last but very important step in the backup procedure-check that the backup copy of files is not damaged.

TYPES OF SECONDARY STORAGE DEVICES

It is important to know the difference between secondary storage and a computer's main memory. Secondary storage is also called auxiliary storage and is used to store data and programs when they are not being processed. Secondary storage is more permanent than main memory, as data and programs are retained when the power is turned off. The needs of secondary storage can vary greatly between users. A personal computer might only require 20,000 bytes of secondary storage but large companies, such as banks, may require secondary storage devices that can store billions of characters. Because of such a variety of needs, a variety of storage devices are available. The two most common types of secondary storage are magnetic tapes and magnetic disks.

Magnetic Tape Storage

Magnetic tape is a one-half inch or one-quarter inch ribbon of plastic material on which data is recorded. The tape drive is an input/output device that reads, writes and erases data on tapes. Magnetic tapes are erasable, reusable and durable. They are made to store large quantities of data inexpensively and therefore are often used for backup. Magnetic tape is not suitable for data files that are revised or updated often because it stores data sequentially.

Magnetic Disk Storage

Magnetic disks are the most widely used storage medium for computers. A magnetic disk offers high storage capacity, reliability, and the capacity to directly access stored data. Magnetic disks hold more data in a small place and attain faster data access speeds.

Types of magnetic disks include diskettes, hard disks, and removable disk cartridges. Diskettes and hard disks are magnetic media; that is, they are based on a technology of representing data as magnetized spots on the disk with a magnetized spot representing a 1 bit and the absence of such a spot representing a 0 bit. Reading data from the disk means converting the magnetized data to electrical impulses that can be sent to the processor. Writing data to disk is the opposite: sending electrical impulses from the processor to be converted to magnetized spots on the disk. The surface of each disk has concentric tracks on it. The number of tracks per surface varies with the particular type of disk.

Diskettes

Made of flexible Mylar, a diskette can record data as magnetized spots on tracks on its surface. Diskettes became popular along with the personal computer. The older diskette, 5-1/4 inches in diameter, is still in use, but newer computers use the 3-1/2 inch diskette. The 3-1/2 inch diskette has the protection of a hard plastic jacket, a size to fit conveniently in a shirt pocket or purse, and the capacity to hold significantly more data than a 5-1/4 inch diskette. Diskettes offer particular advantages, which, as you will see, are not readily available with hard disk:

Portability

Diskettes easily transport data from one computer to another. Workers, for example, carry their files from office computer to home computer and back on a diskette instead of in a briefcase. Students use the campus computers but keep their files on their own diskettes.

New Software

Although, for convenience, software packages are kept on hard disk, new software out of the box may come on diskettes (new software also may come on CD-ROM disks, which we will discuss shortly). The end of the diskettes useful life-time may be upon us. In 1998 Macintosh introduced its new computer, the IMAC, without a floppy disk drive. Alternatives such as Zip disks (discussed later), or transferring data via networks are making the low-capacity diskette become obsolete.

The diskette was introduced in the early 1970s by IBM as a new type of secondary storage. Originally they were eight inches in diameter and were thin and flexible which gave them the name floppy disks, or floppies. Diskettes are used as the principle medium of secondary storage for personal computers. They are available in two different sizes: 3 1/2 inch and 5 1/4 inch.

Storage Capacity

The amount of data you can store on a diskette depends on the recording density and the number of tracks on the diskette. The recording density is the number of bits (G) that can be recorded on one inch of track on the diskette, or bits per inch (bpi). The second factor that influences the amount of data stored on a diskette is the number of tracks on which the data can be stored or tracks per inch (tpi). Commonly used diskettes are referred to as either double-density or high-density (single-density diskettes are no longer used). Double-density diskettes (DD) can store 360K for a 5 1/4 inch diskette and 720K for a 3 1/2 inch diskette. High-density diskettes (HD) can store 1.2 megabytes (G) on a 5 1/4 inch diskette and 1.44 megabytes on a 3 1/2 inch diskette.

Care of Diskettes

You should keep diskettes away from heat, cold, magnetic fields (including telephones) and contaminated environments such as dust, smoke, or salt air. Also keep them away from food and do not touch the disk surface.

Hard Disks

A hard disk is a metal platter coated with magnetic oxide that can be magnetized to represent data. Hard disks come in a variety of sizes. Hard disk for mainframes and minicomputers may be as large as 14 inches in diameter. Several disks can be assembled into a disk pack. There are different types of disk packs, with the number of platters varying by model. Each disk in the pack has top and bottom surfaces on which to record data. Many disk devices, however, do not record data on the top of the top platter or on the bottom of the bottom platter.

A disk drive is a machine that allows data to be read from a disk or written on a disk. A disk pack is mounted on a disk drive that is a separate unit connected to the computer. Large computers have dozens or ever hundreds of disk drives. In a disk pack all disks rotate at the same time although only one disk is being read or written on at any one time. The mechanism for reading or writing data on a disk is an access arm; it moves a read/write head into position over a particular track. The read/write head on the end of the access arm hovers just above the track but does not actually touch the surface. When a read/write head does accidentally touch the disk surface, this is called a head crash and all data is destroyed. Data can also be destroyed if a read/write head encounters even minuscule foreign matter on the disk surface. A disk pack has a series of access arms that slip in between the disks in the pack. Two read/write heads are on each arm, one facing up for the surface above it and one facing down for the surface below it. However, only one read/write head can operate at any one time. In some disk drives the access arms can be retracted; then the disk pack can be removed from the drive. Most disk packs, however, combine the disks, access arms, and read/write heads in a sealed module called a Winchester disk. Winchester disk assemblies are put together in clean rooms so even microscopic dust particles do not get on the disk surface. Hard disks for personal computers are 5-1/4 inch or 3-1/2 inch disks in sealed modules and even gigabytes are not unusual. Hard disk capacity for personal computers has soared in recent years; capacities of hundreds of megabytes are common and gigabytes are not unusual. Although an individual probably cannot imagine generating enough output-letters, budgets, reports, and so forth-to fill a hard disk, software packages take up a lot of space and can make a dent rather quickly.

Furthermore, graphics images and audio and video files require large file capacities. Perhaps more important than capacity, however, is the convenience of speed. Personal computer users find accessing files on a hard disk is significantly faster and thus more convenient than accessing files on a diskette. Hard disks provide larger and faster secondary storage capabilities than diskettes. Usually hard disks are permanently mounted inside the computer and are not removable like diskettes. On minicomputers (G) and mainframes (G), hard disks are often called fixed disks. They are also called direct-access storage devices (DASD). Most personal computers have two to four disk drives. The input/output device that transfers data to and from the hard disk is the hard disk drive.

Hard Disk Storage Capacity

Like diskettes, hard disks must be formatted before they can store information. The storage capacity for hard drives is measured in megabytes. Common sizes for personal computers range from 100MB to 500MB of storage. Each 10MB of storage is equivalent to approximately 5,000 printed pages (with approximately 2,000 characters per page).

Hard Disks in Groups

A concept of using several small disks that work together as a unit is called a redundant array of inexpensive disks, or simply RAID. The group of connected disks operates as if it were just one large disk, but it speeds up reading and writing by having multiple access paths. The data file for, say, aircraft factory tools, may be spread across several disks; thus, if the computer is used to look up tools for several workers, the computer need not read the data in turn but instead read them at the same time in parallel. Furthermore, data security is improved because if a disk fails, the disk system can reconstruct data on an extra disk; thus, computer operations can continue uninterrupted. This is significant data insurance.

How Data Is Organized on a Disk

There is more than one way of physically organizing data on a disk. The methods we will consider here are the sector method and the cylinder method.

The Sector Method

In the sector method each track is divided into sectors that hold a specific number of characters. Data on the track is accessed by referring to the surface number, track number, and sector number where the data is stored. The sector method is used for diskettes as well as disk packs.

Zone Recording

The fact that a disk is circular presents a problem: The distances around the tracks on the outside of the disk are greater than that of the tracks or the inside. A given amount of data that takes up 1 inch of a track on the inside of a disk might be spread over several inches on a track near the outside of a disk. This means that the tracks on the outside are not storing data as efficiently.

Zone recording involves dividing a disk into zones to take advantage of the storage available on all tracks, by assigning more sectors to tracks in outer zones than to those in inner zones. Since each sector on the disk holds the same amount of data, more sectors mean more data storage than if all tracks had the same number of sectors.

The Cylinder Method

A way to organize data on a disk pack is the cylinder method. The organization in this case is vertical. The purpose is to reduce the time it takes to move the access arms of a disk pack into position. Once the access arms are in position, they are in the same vertical position on all disk surfaces. To appreciate this, suppose you had an empty disk pack on which you wished to record data. You might be tempted to record the data horizontally-to start with the first surface, fill track 000, then fill track 001, track 002, and so on, and then move to the second surface and again fill tracks 000, 001, 002, and so forth. Each new track and new surface, however, would require movement of the access arms, a relatively slow mechanical process.

Recording the data vertically, on the other hand, substantially reduces access arm movement. The data is recorded on the tracks that can be accessed by one positioning of the access arms-that is, on one cylinder. To visualize cylinder organization, pretend a cylindrically shaped item, such as a tin can, were figuratively dropped straight down through all the disks in the disk pack. All the tracks thus encountered, in the same position on each disk surface, comprise a cylinder. The cylinder method, then, means all tracks of a certain cylinder on a disk pack are lined up one beneath the other, and all the vertical tracks of one cylinder are accessible by the read/write heads with one positioning of the access arms mechanism. Tracks within a cylinder are numbered according to this vertical perspective: A 20-surface disk pack contains cylinder tracks numbered 0 through 19, top to bottom.

Removable Storage: Zip Disks

Personal computer users, who never seem to have enough hard disk storage space, may turn to a removable hard disk cartridge. Once full, a removable hard disk cartridge can be replaced with a fresh one. In effect, a removable cartridge is as portable as a diskette, but the disk cartridge holds much more data. Removable units also are important to businesses concerned with security, because the units can be used during business hours but hidden away during off hours. A disadvantage of a removable hard disk is that it takes longer to access data than a built-in hard drive.

The most popular removable disk media is the Zip drive as shown in Figure Over 100's of millions have been sold, making it the de facto standard. The disk cartridges look like a floppy disk, but are slightly bigger in all dimensions. Older Zip disks hold 100MB, newer ones hold 250MB and cost $8-$10 a piece (Floppies hold 1.4MB and cost around $2). The drive sells for around $80-$125. Many new PCs come with Zip drives built in addition to floppy drives. Zip disks are a great way to store large files and software programs.

Disk Cartridges

Removable disk cartridges are another form of disk storage for personal computers. They offer the storage and fast access of hard disks and the portability of diskettes. They are often used when security is an issue since, when you are done using the computer, the disk cartridge can be removed and locked up leaving no data on the computer.

Backup

Backup means creating a copy of important programs and data. To backup diskettes, copy the data from one to the other. Diskettes are frequently used to backup important files on hard drives of personal computers.

Data Recovery

There does exist certain software programs that, under special circumstances, can recover data and programs that have been "lost." Often your operating system (G) will be able to do this, or applications such as Norton Utilities.

Optical Disk Storage

The explosive growth in storage needs has driven the

computer industry to provide cheaper, more compact, and more versatile storage devices with greater capacity. This demanding shopping list is a description of the optical disk, like a CD. The technology works like this: A laser hits a layer of metallic material spread over the surface of a disk. When data is being entered, heat from the laser produces tiny spots on the disk surface. To read the data, the laser scans the disk, and a lens picks up different light reflections from the various spots. Optical storage technology is categorized according to its read/write capability. Read-only media are recorded on by the manufacturer and can be read from but not written to by the user. Such a disk cannot, obviously, be used for your files, but manufacturers can use it to supply software. Applications software packages sometimes include a dozen diskettes or more; all these could fit on one optical disk with plenty of room to spare. The most prominent optical technology is the CD-ROM, for compact disk read-only memory.

CD-ROM has a major advantage over other optical disk designs: The disk format is identical to that of audio compact disks, so the same dust-free manufacturing plants that are now stamping out digital versions of Mozart or Mary Chapin Carpenter can easily convert to producing anything from software to an encyclopedia. Furthermore, CD-ROM storage is large-up to 660 megabytes per disk, the equivalent of over 400 3-1/2 inch diskettes. When buying a computer the speed of the CD-ROM drive is advertised using an "X" factor, like 12X, or 24X. This indicates the speed at which the CD can transfer data to the CPU-the higher the X factor, the faster the CD. Modern computers now offer a write CD drive or, CD-RW as an option. CD-RW is a write-once, read-many media. With a CD-RW drive, you can create your own CDs. This offers an inexpensive, convenient, safe way to store large volumes of data such as favourite songs, photographs, etc.

DVDs

Digital Versatile Disk (DVD) drives are now widely available in computers as well as home entertainment centers. DVD-ROM drives can read data, such as stored commercial videos for playing. DVD-RW allow DVDs to be created on a computer. The DVD is a flat disk, the size of a CD-4.7 inches diameter and.05 inches thick. Data are stored in a small indentation in a spiral track, just like in the CD. DVD disks are read by a laser beam of shorter wave-length than used by the CD ROM drives. This allows for smaller indentations and increased storage capacity.

The data layer is only half as thick as in the CD-ROM. This opens the possibility to write data in two layers. The outer gold layer is semi transparent, to allow reading of the underlying silver layer. The laser beam is set to two different intensities, strongest for reading the underlying silver layer. A 4.7 GB side of a DVD can hold 135 minutes top quality video with 6 track stereo. This requires a transmission rate of 4692 bits per second. The 17 GB disk holds 200 hours top quality music recording. DVD movies are made in two "codes." Region one is USA and Canada, while Europe and Asia is region two. When you play movies, your hardware (MPEG decoder. MGEG is the data coding for movies similar to JPEG for pictures.) must match the DVD region. The movies are made in two formats, each with their own coding. The DVD drives come in 2X, 4X, etc. versions, like the CD-ROM's.

The DVD drives will not replace the magnetic hard disks. The hard disks are being improved as rapidly as DVD, and they definitely offer the fastest seek time and transmission rate (currently 5-10 MB/second). No optic media can keep up with this. But the DVD will undoubtedly gain a place as the successor to the CD ROM and is playing an important role in the blending of computers and entertainment centers.

Magnetic Tape Storage

We saved magnetic tape storage for last because it has taken a subordinate role in storage technology. Magnetic tape looks like the tape used in music cassettes plastic tape with a magnetic coating. As in other magnetic media, data is stored as extremely small magnetic spots. Tapes come in a number of forms, including l/2-inch-wide tape wound on a reel, l/4-inch-wide tape in data cartridges and cassettes, and tapes that look like ordinary music cassettes but are designed to store data instead of music. The amount of data on a tape is expressed in terms of density, which is the number of characters per inch (cpi) or bytes per inch (bpi) that can be stored on the tape. The highest-capacity tape is the digital audio tape, or DAT, which uses a different method of recording data. Using a method called helical scan recording, DAT wraps around a rotating read/write head that spins vertically as it moves. This places the data in diagonal bands that run across the tape rather than down its length. This method produces high density and faster access to data.

Two reels are used, a supply reel and a take-up reel. The supply reel, which has the tape with data on it or on which data will be recorded, is the reel that is changed. The take-up reel always stays with the magnetic tape unit. Many cartridges and cassettes have the supply and take-up reels built into the same case. Tape now has a limited role because disk has proved the superior storage medium. Disk data is quite reliable, especially within a sealed module. Furthermore, as we will see, disk data can be accessed directly, as opposed to data on tape, which can be accessed only by passing by all the data ahead of it on the tape. Consequently, the primary role of tape today is as an inexpensive backup medium.

Backup Systems

Although a hard disk is an extremely reliable device, a hard disk drive is subject to electromechanical failures that cause loss of data. Furthermore, data files, particularly those accessed by several users, are subject to errors introduced by users. There is also the possibility of errors introduced by software. With any method of data storage, a backup system a way of storing data in more than one place to protect it from damage and errors is vital. As we have already noted, magnetic tape is used primarily for backup purposes. For personal computer users, an easy and inexpensive way to back up a hard disk file is to simply copy it to a diskette whenever it is updated. But this is not practical for a system with many files or many users.

Personal computer users have the option of purchasing their own tape backup system, to be used on a regular basis for copying all data from hard disk to a high-capacity tape. Data thus saved can be restored to the hard disk later if needed. A key advantage of a tape backup system is that it can copy the entire hard disk in minutes, saving you the trouble of swapping diskettes in and out of the machine. A rule of thumb among computer professionals is to estimate disk needs generously and then double that amount. But estimating future needs is rarely easy. Many users, therefore, make later adjustments like adding a removable hard disk cartridge to accommodate expanding storage needs.

BENEFITS OF SECONDARY STORAGE DEVICES

Secondary storage, sometimes called auxiliary storage, is storage separate from the computer itself, where you can store software and data on a semi permanent basis. Secondary storage is necessary because memory, or primary storage, can be used only temporarily. If you are sharing your computer, you must yield memory to someone else after your program runs; if you are not sharing your computer, your programs and data will disappear from memory when you turn off the computer. However, you probably want to store the data you have used or the information you have derived from processing; that is why secondary storage is needed. Furthermore, memory is limited in size, whereas secondary storage media can store as much data as necessary.

- *Capacity*: Organizations may store the equivalent of a roomful of data on sets of disks that take up less space than a breadbox. A simple diskette for a personal computer holds the equivalent of 500 printed pages, or one book. An optical disk can hold the equivalent of approximately 400 books.
- *Reliability*: Data in secondary storage is basically safe, since secondary storage is physically reliable. Also, it is more difficult for unscrupulous people to tamper with data on disk than data stored on paper in a file cabinet.

- *Convenience*: With the help of a computer, authorized people can locate and access data quickly.
- *Cost*: Together the three previous benefits indicate significant savings in storage costs. It is less expensive to store data on tape or disk (the principal means of secondary storage) than to buy and house filing cabinets. Data that is reliable and safe is less expensive to maintain than data subject to errors. But the greatest savings can be found in the speed and convenience of filing and retrieving data.

These benefits apply to all the various secondary storage devices but, as you will see, some devices are better than others. We begin with a look at the various storage media, including those used for personal computers, and then consider what it takes to get data organized and processed.

3

Internet Applications

GLOBAL NETWORK

Every computer that is connected to the Internet is considered a part of that network. This means even your home computer. It's all a matter of degrees, you connect to your ISP's network, then your ISP connects to a larger network and so on. At the top of the tree is the high-capacity backbones, all of these interconnect at 'Network Access Points' 'NAPs' at important regions around the world. The entire Internet is based on agreements between these backbone providers who set in place all the fibre optics lines and other technical aspects of the Internet. The first high speed backbone was created by the 'National Science Foundation' in 1987.

The Internet was first created by the Advanced Research Projects Agency (ARPA) of the U.S. government in 1960's, and was first known as the ARPANet. At this stage the Internet's first computers were at academic and government institutions. They were mainly used for accessing files and to send e-mail. From 1983 onwards the Internet as we know it today started to form with the introduction of the communication protocol TCP/IP to ARPANet.

Since 1983 the Internet has accommodated alot of changes and continues to keep developing. The last two decades has seen the Internet accommodate such things as network LANs and ATM and frame switched services. The Internet continues to evolve with it becoming available on mobile phones and pagers and possibly on televisions in the future. The underpinnings of the Internet are formed by the global interconnection of hundreds of thousands of otherwise independent computers, communications entities and information systems. What makes this interconnection possible is the use of a set of communication standards, procedures and formats in common among the networks and the various devices and computational facilities connected to them. The procedures by which computers communicate with each other are called "protocols." While this infrastructure is steadily evolving to include new capabilities, the protocols initially used by the Internet are called the "TCP/IP" protocols, named after the two protocols that formed the principal basis for Internet operation.

On top of this infrastructure is an emerging set of architectural concepts and data structures for heterogeneous information systems that renders the Internet a truly global information system. In essence, the Internet is an architecture, although many people confuse it with its implementation. When the Internet is looked at as an architecture, it manifests two different abstractions. One abstraction deals with communications connectivity, packet delivery and a variety of end-end communication services. The other abstraction deals with the Internet as an information system, independent of its underlying communications infrastructure, which allows creation, storage and access to a wide range of information resources, including digital objects and related services at various levels of abstraction.

Interconnecting computers is an inherently digital problem. Computers process and exchange digital information, meaning that they use a discrete mathematical "binary" or "two-valued" language of 1s and 0s. For communication purposes, such information is mapped into continuous electrical or optical waveforms. The use of digital signaling allows accurate regeneration and reliable recovery of the underlying bits. We use the terms "computer," "computer resources" and "computation" to mean not only traditional computers, but also devices that can be controlled digitally over a network, information resources such as mobile programs and other computational capabilities.

The telephone network started out with operators who manually connected telephones to each other through "patch panels" that accepted patch cords from each telephone line and electrically connected them to one another through the panel, which operated, in effect, like a switch. The result was called circuit switching, since at its conclusion, an electrical circuit was made between the calling telephone and the called telephone. Conventional circuit switching, which was developed to handle telephone calls, is inappropriate for connecting computers because it makes limited use of the telecommunication facilities and takes too long to set up connections. Although reliable enough for voice communication, the circuit-switched voice network had difficulty delivering digital information without errors. For digital communications, packet switching is a better choice, because it is far better suited to the typically "burst" communication style of computers. Computers that communicate typically send out brief but intense bursts of data, then remain silent for a while before sending out the next burst. These bursts are communicated as packets, which are very much like electronic postcards. The postcards, in reality packets, are relayed from computer to computer until they reach their destination.

The special computers that perform this forwarding function are called variously "packet switches" or "routers" and form the equivalent of many bucket brigades spanning continents and oceans, moving buckets of electronic postcards from one computer to another. Together these routers and the communication links between them form the underpinnings of the Internet. Without packet switching, the Internet would not exist, as we now know it. Going back to the postcard analogy, postcards can get lost. They can be delivered out of order, and they can be delayed by varying amounts. The same is true of Internet packets, which, on the Internet, can even be duplicated. The Internet Protocol is the postcard layer of the Internet. The next higher layer of protocol, TCP, takes care of re-sending the "postcards" to recover packets that might have been lost, and putting packets back in order if they have become disordered in transit.

Of course, packet switching is about a billion times faster than the postal service or a bucket brigade would be. It also has to operate over many different communications systems, or substrata. The authors designed the basic architecture to be so simple and undemanding that it could work with most communication services. Many organizations, including commercial ones, carried out research using the TCP/IP protocols in the 1970s. E-mail was steadily used over the nascent Internet during that time and to the present. It was not until 1994 that the general public began to be aware of the Internet by way of the World Wide Web application, particularly after Netscape Communications was formed and released its browser and associated server software.

Thus, the evolution of the Internet was based on two technologies and a research dream. The technologies were packet switching and computer technology, which, in turn, drew upon the underlying technologies of digital communications and semiconductors.

The research dream was to share information and computational resources. But that is simply the technical side of the story. Equally important in many ways were the other dimensions that enabled the Internet to come into existence and flourish. This aspect of the story starts with cooperation and far-sightedness in the U.S. Government, which is often derided for lack of foresight but is a real hero in this story.

It leads on to the enthusiasm of private sector interests to build upon the government funded developments to expand the Internet and make it available to the general public. Perhaps most important, it is fueled by the development of the personal computer industry and significant changes in the telecommunications industry in the 1980s, not the least of which was the decision to open the long distance market to competition. The role of workstations, the Unix operating system and local area networking (especially the Ethernet) are themes contributing to the spread of Internet technology in the 1980s into the research and academic community from which the Internet industry eventually emerged. Many individuals have been involved in the development and evolution of the Internet covering a span of almost four decades if one goes back to the early writings on the subject of computer networking by Kleinrock, Licklider, Baran, Roberts, and Davies. The ARPANET, described below, was the first wide-area computer network.

The NSFNET, which followed more than a decade later under the leadership of Erich Bloch, Gordon Bell, Bill Wulf and Steve Wolff, brought computer networking into the mainstream of the research and education communities. It is not our intent here to attempt to attribute credit to all those whose contributions were central to this story, although we mention a few of the key players

ROLE OF DARPA

Modern computer networking technologies emerged in the early 1970s. In 1969, The U.S. Defence Advanced Research Projects Agency (variously called ARPA and DARPA), an agency within the Department of Defence, commissioned a wide-area computer network called the ARPANET. This network made use of the new packet switching concepts for interconnecting computers and initially linked computers at universities and other research institutions in the United States and in selected NATO countries. At that time, the ARPANET was essentially the only realistic wide-area computer network in existence, with a base of several dozen organizations, perhaps twice that number of computers and numerous researchers at those sites. The program was led at DARPA by Larry Roberts. The packet switches were built by Bolt Beranek and Newman (BBN), a DARPA contractor. Others directly involved in the ARPANET activity included the authors, Len Kleinrock, Frank Heart, Howard Frank, Steve Crocker, Jon Postel and many many others in the ARPA research community.

Back then, the methods of internetworking (that is interconnecting computer networks) were primitive or non-existent. Two organizations could interwork technically by agreeing to use common equipment, but not every organization was interested in this approach. Absent that, there was jury-rigging, special case development and not much else. Each of these networks stood on its own with essentially no interaction between them-a far cry from today's Internet.

In the early 1970s, ARPA began to explore two alternative applications of packet switching technology based on the use of synchronous satellites (SATNET) and ground-based packet radio (PRNET). The decision by Kahn to link these two networks and the ARPANET as separate and independent networks resulted in the creation of the Internet program and the subsequent collaboration with Cerf. These two systems differed in significant ways from the ARPANET so as to take advantage of the broadcast and wireless aspects of radio communications.

The strategy that had been adopted for SATNET originally was to embed the SATNET software into an ARPANET packet switch, and interwork the two networks through memory-to-memory transfers within the packet switch. This approach, in place at the time, was to make SATNET an "embedded" network within the ARPANET; users of the network would not even need to know of its existence. The technical team at Bolt Beranek and Newman (BBN), having built the ARPANET switches and now building the SATNET software, could easily produce the necessary patches to glue the programs together in the same machine.

Indeed, this is what they were under contract with DARPA to provide. By embedding each new network into the ARPANET, a seamless internetworked capability was possible, but with no realistic possibility of unleashing the entrepreneurial networking spirit that has manifest itself in modern day Internet developments. A new approach was in order.

The Packet Radio (PRNET) program had not yet gotten underway so there was ample opportunity to change the approach there. In addition, up until then, the SATNET program was only an equipment development activity. No commitments had been obtained for the use of actual satellites or ground stations to access them. Indeed, since there was no domestic satellite industry in the U.S. then, the only two viable alternatives were the use of Intelsat or military satellites. The time for a change in strategy, if it was to be made, was then.

ARCHITECTURE

The authors created architecture for interconnecting independent networks that could then be federated into a seamless whole without changing any of the underlying networks. This was the genesis of the Internet, as we know it today. In order to work properly, the architecture required a global addressing mechanism (or Internet address) to enable computers on any network to reference and communicate with computers on any other network in the federation. Internet addresses fill essentially the same role as telephone numbers do in telephone networks. The design of the Internet assumed first that the individual networks could not be changed to accommodate new architectural requirements; but this was largely a pragmatic assumption to facilitate progress.

The networks also had varying degrees of reliability and speed. Host computers would have to be able to put disordered packets back into the correct order and discard duplicate packets that had been generated along the way. This was a major change from the virtual circuit-like service provided by ARPANET and by then contemporary commercial data networking services such as Tymnet and Telenet. In these networks, the underlying network took responsibility for keeping all information in order and for re-sending any data that might have been lost. The Internet design made the computers responsible for tending to these network problems. A key architectural construct was the introduction of gateways (now called routers) between the networks to handle the disparities such as different data rates, packet sizes, error conditions, and interface specifications. The gateways would also check the destination Internet addresses of each packet to determine the gateway to which it should be forwarded.

These functions would be combined with certain end-end functions to produce the reliable communication from source to destination. A draft paper by the authors describing this approach was given at a meeting of the International Network Working Group in 1973 in Sussex, England and the final paper was subsequently published by the Institute for Electrical and Electronics Engineers, the leading professional society for the electrical engineering profession, in its Transactions on Communications in May, 1974. DARPA contracted with Cerf's group at Stanford to carry out the initial detailed design of the TCP software and, shortly thereafter, with BBN and University College London to build independent implementations of the TCP protocol (as it was then called-it was later split into TCP and IP) for different machines. BBN also had a contract to build a prototype version of the gateway.

These three sites collaborated in the development and testing of the initial protocols on different machines. Cerf, then a professor at Stanford, provided the day-to-day leadership in the initial TCP software design and testing. BBN deployed the gateways between the ARPANET and the PRNET and also with SATNET. During this period, under Kahn's overall leadership at DARPA, the initial feasibility of the Internet Architecture was demonstrated. The TCP/IP protocol suite was developed and refined over a period of four more years and, in 1980, it was adopted as a standard by the U.S. Department of Defence. On January 1, 1983 the ARPANET converted to TCP/IP as its standard host protocol. Gateways (or routers) were used to pass packets to and from host computers on "local area networks." Refinement and extension of these protocols and many others associated with them continues to this day by way of the Internet Engineering Task Force.

RUNNING THE INTERNET

The Domain Name System

The Internet evolved as an experimental system during the 1970s and early 1980s. It then flourished after the TCP/IP protocols were made mandatory on the ARPANET and other networks in January 1983; these protocols thus became the standard for many other networks as well. Indeed, the Internet grew so rapidly that the existing mechanisms for associating the names of host computers (*e.g.* UCLA, USC-ISI) to Internet addresses (known as IP addresses) were about to be stretched beyond acceptable engineering limits. Most of the applications in the Internet referred to the target computers by name.

These names had to be translated into Internet addresses before the lower level protocols could be activated to support the application. For a time, a group at SRI International in Menlo Park, CA, called the Network Information Center (NIC), maintained a simple, machine-readable list of names and associated Internet addresses which was made available on the net. Hosts on the Internet would simply copy this list, usually daily, so as to maintain a local copy of the table. This list was called the "host.txt" file (since it was simply a text file). The list served the function in the Internet that directory services (*e.g.* 411 or 703-555-1212) do in the US telephone system-the translation of a name into an address. As the Internet grew, it became harder and harder for the NIC to keep the list current. Anticipating that this problem would only get worse as the network expanded, researchers at USC Information Sciences Institute launched an effort to design a more distributed way of providing this same information. The end result was the Domain Name System (DNS) which allowed hundreds of thousands of "name servers" to maintain small portions of a global database of information associating IP addresses with the names of computers on the Internet.

The naming structure was hierarchical in character. For example, all host computers associated with educational institutions would have names like "stanford.edu" or "ucla.edu". Specific hosts would have names like "cs.ucla.edu" to refer to a computer in the computer science department of UCLA, for example. A special set of computers called "root servers" maintained information about the names and addresses of other servers that contained more detailed name/ address associations. Under this system, for example, the host name "UCLA" became "UCLA.EDU" because it was operated by an educational institution, while the host computer for "BBN" became "BBN.COM" because it was a commercial organization. Top-level domain names also were created for every country: United Kingdom names would end in ".UK," while the ending ".FR" was created for the names of France. The Domain Name System (DNS) was and continues to be a major element of the Internet architecture, which contributes to its scalability.

It also contributes to controversy over trademarks and general rules for the creation and use of domain names, creation of new top-level domains and the like. At the same time, other resolution schemes exist as well. One of the authors (Kahn) has been involved in the development of a different kind of standard identification and resolution scheme that, for example, is being used as the base technology by book publishers to identify books on the Internet by adapting various identification schemes for use in the Internet environment. For example, International Standard Book Numbers (ISBNs) can be used as part of the identifiers. The identifiers then resolve to state information about the referenced books, such as location information (*e.g.* multiple sites) on the Internet that is used to access the books or to order them. These developments are taking place in parallel with the more traditional means of managing Internet resources. They offer an alternative to the existing Domain Name System with enhanced functionality.

The growth of Web servers and users of the Web has been remarkable, but some people are confused about the relationship between the World Wide Web and the Internet. The Internet is the global information system that includes communication capabilities and many high level applications. The Web is one such application.

The existing connectivity of the Internet made it possible for users and servers all over the world to participate in this activity. Electronic mail is another important application. As of today, over 60 million computers take part in the Internet and about 3.6 million web sites were estimated to be accessible on the net. Virtually every user of the net has access to electronic mail and web browsing capability. E-mail remains a critically important application for most users of the Internet, and these two functions largely dominate the use of the Internet for most users.

INTERNET STANDARDS PROCESS

Internet standards were once the output of research activity sponsored by DARPA. The principal investigators on the internetting research effort essentially determined what technical features of the TCP/IP protocols would become common. The initial work in this area started with the joint effort of the two authors, continued in Cerf's group at Stanford, and soon thereafter was joined by engineers and scientists at BBN and University College London.

This informal arrangement has changed with time and details can be found elsewhere. At present, the standards efforts for Internet are carried out primarily under the auspices of the Internet Society (ISOC). The Internet Engineering Task Force (IETF) operates under the leadership of its Internet Engineering Steering Group (IESG), which is populated by appointees approved by the Internet Architecture Board (IAB) which is, itself, now part of the Internet Society. The IETF comprises over one hundred working groups categorized and managed by Area Directors specializing in specific categories. There are other bodies with considerable interest in Internet standards or in standards that must interwork with the Internet.

Examples include the International Telecommunications Union Telecommunicationsstandards group (ITU-T), the International Institute of Electrical and Electronic Engineers (IEEE) local area network standards group (IEEE 801), the Organization for International Standardization (ISO), the American National Standards Institute (ANSI), the World Wide Web Consortium (W3C), and many others. As Internet access and services are provided by existing media such as telephone, cable and broadcast, interactions with standards bodies and legal structures formed to deal with these media will become an increasingly complex matter. The intertwining of interests is simultaneously fascinating and complicated, and has increased the need for thoughtful cooperation among many interested parties.

MANAGING THE INTERNET

Perhaps the least understood aspect of the Internet is its

management. In recent years, this subject has become the subject of intense commercial and international interest, involving multiple governments and commercial organizations, and recently congressional hearings. At issue is how the Internet will be managed in the future, and, in the process, what oversight mechanisms will insure that the public interest is adequately served. In the 1970s, managing the Internet was easy. Since few people knew about the Internet, decisions about almost everything of real policy concern were made in the offices of DARPA. It became clear in the late 1970s, however, that more community involvement in the decision-making processes was essential. In 1979, DARPA formed the Internet Configuration Control Board (ICCB) to insure that knowledgeable members of the technical community discussed critical issues, educated people outside of DARPA about the issues, and helped others to implement the TCP/IP protocols and gateway functions. At the time, there were no companies that offered turnkey solutions to getting on the Internet.

It would be another five years or so before companies like Cisco Systems were formed, and while there were no PCs yet, the only workstations available were specially built and their software was not generally configured for use with external networks; they were certainly considered expensive at the time. In 1983, the small group of roughly twelve ICCB members was reconstituted (with some substitutions) as the Internet Activities Board (IAB), and about ten "Task Forces" were established under it to address issues in specific technical areas. The attendees at Internet Working Group meetings were invited to become members of as many of the task forces as they wished.

The management of the Domain Name System offers a kind of microcosm of issues now frequently associated with overall management of the Internet's operation and evolution. Someone had to take responsibility for overseeing the system's general operation. In particular, top-level domain names had to be selected, along with persons or organizations to manage each of them. Rules for the allocation of Internet addresses had to be established. DARPA had previously asked the late Jon Postel of the USC Information Sciences Institute to take on numerous functions related to administration of names, addresses and protocol related matters. With time, Postel assumed further responsibilities in this general area on his own, and DARPA, which was supporting the effort, gave its tacit approval. This activity was generally referred to as the Internet Assigned Numbers Authority (IANA). In time, Postel became the arbitrator of all controversial matters concerning names and addresses until his untimely death in October 1998.

It is helpful to consider separately the problem of managing the domain name space and the Internet address space. These two vital elements of the Internet architecture have rather different characteristics that colour the management problems they generate. Domain names have semantics that numbers may not imply; and thus a means of determining who can use what names is needed. As a result, speculators on Internet names often claim large numbers of them without intent to use them other than to resell them later. Alternate resolution mechanisms, if widely adopted, could significantly change the landscape here. The rapid growth of the Internet has triggered the design of a new and larger address space (the so-called IP version 6 address space); today's Internet uses IP version 4. However, little momentum has yet developed to deploy IPv6 widely. Despite concerns to the contrary, the IPv4 address space will not be depleted for some time. Further, the use of Dynamic Host Configuration Protocol (DHCP) to dynamically assign IP addresses has also cut down on demand for dedicated IP addresses. Nevertheless, there is growing recognition in the Internet technical community that expansion of the address space is needed, as is the development of transition schemes that allow interoperation between IPv4 and IPv6 while migrating to IPv6.

In 1998, the Internet Corporation for Assigned Names and Numbers (ICANN) was formed as a private sector, non-profit, organization to oversee the orderly progression in use of Internet names and numbers, as well as certain protocol related matters that required oversight. The birth of this organization, which was selected by the Department of Commerce for this function, has been difficult, embodying as it does many of the inherent conflicts in resolving discrepancies in this arena. However, there is a clear need for an oversight mechanism for Internet domain names and numbers, separate from their day-to-day management. Many questions about Internet management remain. They may also prove difficult to resolve quickly. Of specific concern is what role the U.S. government and indeed governments around the world need to play in its continuing operation and evolution. This is clearly a subject for another time.

ADVANTAGES OF INTERNET

There are many advantages of using the Internet, such as:

Global Audience

Content published on the World Wide Web is immediately available to a global audience of users. This makes the World Wide Web a very cost-effective medium to publish information. Reaching more than 190 countries.

Operates 24 hours and 365 days

You don't need to wait until resources are available to conduct business. From a consumer's perspective as well as a provider's business can be consummated at any time. The fact that the Internet is operational at all times makes it the most efficient business machine to date.

Relatively Inexpensive

It is relatively inexpensive to publish information on the Internet. At a fraction of the cost to publish information by traditional methods, various organizations and individuals can now distribute information to millions of users. It costs only a few thousand dollars to establish an Internet presence and publish content on the Internet.

Product Advertising

You can use the World Wide Web to advertise various

products. Before purchasing a product, customers will be able to look up various product specification sheets and find out additional information. You can use the multimedia capabilities of the World Wide Web to make available not only various product specification sheets but also audio files, images, and even video clips of products in action.

The beauty of the Web is that it allows customers to explore products in as much detail as they desire. If the client just wants a general overview, he or she can look at the advertising information. For those wanting more in depth information, you can provide white papers and product descriptions for download. The Web allows a business to provide timely information, you can simply place the information on the Web page and it is available immediately for your customers.

Distribute Product Catalogs

The World Wide Web is a very effective medium for distributing product catalogs. In the old days, putting together a product catalog used to be very costly in terms of time and money needed to publish and distribute it. The World Wide Web changes all this by allowing content developers to put together a sales catalog and make it available to millions of users immediately. Furthermore, unlike printed product catalogs that are usually updated around once a month, product catalogs on the World Wide Web can be updated as needed to respond to various changing market conditions.

Online Surveys

Traditional methods of performing surveys are often relatively slow and expensive compared to online surveys conducted on the Internet. For example, in order to fill out various needs of customers or what they would like to see in a future product, it's often necessary to compile a list of address and mail a questionnaire to many customers. The success of such an attempt is not always guaranteed and can be very costly in terms of mailing the questionnaires and entering responses to a databases and analysing it.

On the other hand, you can use the World Wide Web to automate the whole process. For example, you can set up a CGI script to conduct online surveys. Results of such a survey can be automatically updated to a database. This database can then be used to keep a pulse on various opinions and needs of customers.

Announcements

With the World Wide Web, you can distribute various announcements to millions of users in a timely manner. Because there is virtually no time lag from the time it takes to publish information to making the information available to users, the Web is an ideal medium to publicize announcements.

As more people discover the virtues of the Web and get connected to the Internet, the Web will become the medium of choice for many organizations and individuals to publicize various announcements.

Provide Technical Support

You can also use Web site to provide technical support to users. Because Web pages can be updated immediately with new information, various technical support literature can be immediately modified in light of new findings and developments. This can be accomplished without having to distribute changes to all users affected by any changes using traditional mediums of information distribution, which are often quite costly compared to the World Wide Web.

Create Online Discussion Forums

By using applications such as WebBoard, it's possible to set up online discussion forums on the Web.

Obtain Customer Feedback

The interactive nature of the World Wide Web is ideal for obtaining customer feedback. You can easily set up a CGI script to obtain customer feedback about a product or service. Because customer feedback submitted by customers can be read immediately, it's possible to respond to various customer concerns in a timely manner, increasing customer satisfaction and quality of customer service.

Immediate Distribution of Information

When information is added to a Web site, it's immediately available for browsing by millions of Internet users. The World Wide Web is an ideal medium of information distribution because it takes away the time lag associated with publishing content and actually making it available to users

Easy Integration with Internal Information Systems

Internet information systems deployed on the Internet can be easily integrated with internal information systems managed with office productivity applications such as Microsoft Office.

Powerful Content Publishing Tools

A new breed of Internet aware applications will start emerging in software stores by the time you read this. These applications will enable users to develop content for the World Wide Web by simply saving as an HTML file. In addition to software developers making existing applications Internet aware, various new, powerful, and easy-to use Internet content publishing applications are also being developed. These applications will make the task of publishing content on the Internet even easier. Most of these applications are developed for Windows users.

Multimedia

The capability to incorporate multimedia into Web pages is a major advantage of using World Wide Web to publish information. For example, many Web sites use sounds and video clips to make the content easier and more interesting to browse.

Formatting Capabilities

Content published on the World Wide Web can be richly formatted by using various HTML tags and graphic formats.

The capability to do this is a major reason for the success of the World Wide Web. In addition to using HTML tags and various multimedia formats in Web pages, various interactive controls can also be added to a web page. This capability allows Web site content developers to create "active" Web sites. For example, before a user sends some information to a Web server for processing, a VBScript or JavaScript subroutine can be used to verify information typed in by the user. Various formatting capabilities, along with technologies such as Java and VBScript, make the World Wide Web a richly interactive medium that you can use to distribute information to millions of users.

DISADVANTAGES OF INTERNET

Many fear the Internet because of its disadvantages. They claim to not use the Internet because they are afraid of the possible consequences or are simply not interested. People who have yet connected to the Internet claim they are not missing anything. Today's technological society must realise, it is up to them to protect themselves on the Internet.

Children using the Internet has become a big concern. Most parents do not realise the dangers involved when their children log onto the Internet. When children are online, they can easily be lured into something dangerous. When children talk to others online, they do not realise they could actually be talking to a harmful person. In addition, children may also receive pornography online by mistake; therefore, causing concern among parents everywhere.

Whether surfing the Web, reading newsgroups, or using e-mail, children can be exposed to extremely inappropriate material. Pornographic sites tend to make sure they are the first sites to be listed in any search area. Some critics say that parents are responsible for their own children on the Internet because there are available services to protect children. To keep children safe, parents and teachers must be aware of the dangers. They must actively guide and guard their children online.There are a number of tools available today that may help keep the Internet environment safer for children.

Musicians are also concerned with disadvantages to the Net such as, accessibility and freedom. They are upset because the Internet provides their music online at no charge to consumers. File-sharing software, such Kazaa, Emule and may others provides copyrighted songs to all Internet users. The main concern is-the music is free! Musicians feel "they are not getting paid for their work". It is almost impossible to close down all file-sharing services; there are too many of them to count.

Another major disadvantage of the Internet is privacy. Electronic messages sent over the Internet can be easily snooped and tracked, revealing who is talking to whom and what they are talking about. As people surf the Internet, they are constantly giving information to web sites. People should become aware that the collection, selling, or sharing of the information they provide online increases the chances that their information will fall into the wrong hands. When giving personal information on the Internet, people should make sure the Web site is protected with a recognizable security symbol. On the other hand, this does not mean they are fully protected because anyone may obtain a user's information.

Today, not only are humans getting viruses, but computers are also. Computers are mainly getting these viruses from the Internet; yet, viruses may also be transmitted through floppy disks. However, people should mainly be concerned about receiving viruses from the Internet. Some of these dangerous viruses destroy the computer's entire hard drive, meaning that the user can no longer access the computer. Virus protection is highly recommended

In conclusion, today's society is in the middle of a technological boom. People can either choose to take advantage of this era, or simply let it pass them by. The Internet is a very powerful tool. It has many advantages; however, people need to be extremely aware of the disadvantages as well.

4

Computer Network

NETWORK

A network is simply a collection of computers or other hardware devices that are connected together, either physically or logically, using special hardware and software to allow them to exchange information and cooperate. Networking is the term that describes the processes involved in designing, implementing, upgrading, managing and otherwise working with networks and network technologies. Networks are used for an incredible array of different purposes. In fact, the definitions above are so simple for the specific reason that networks can be used so broadly, and can allow such a wide variety of tasks to be accomplished. While most people learning about networking focus on the interconnection of PCs and other "true" computers, you use various types of networks every day. Each time you pick up a phone, use a credit card at a store, get cash from an ATM machine, or even plug in an electrical appliance, you are using some type of network.

In fact, the definition can even be expanded beyond the world of technology altogether: I'm sure you've heard the term "networking" used to describe the process of finding an employer or employee by talking to friends and associates. In this case too, the idea is that independent units are connected together to share information and cooperate.

The widespread networking of personal computers is a relatively new phenomenon. For the first decade or so of their existence, PCs were very much "islands unto themselves", and were rarely connected together. In the early 1990s, PC networking began to grow in popularity as businesses realised the advantages that networking could provide. By the late 1990s, networking in homes with two or more PCs started to really take off as well.

This interconnection of small devices represents, in a way, a return to the "good old days" of mainframe computers. Before computers were small and personal, they were large and centralized machines that were shared by many users operating remote terminals. While having all of the computer power in one place had many disadvantages, one benefit was that all users were connected because they shared the central computer. Individualized PCs took away that advantage, in favour of the benefits of independence. Networking attempts to move computing into the middle ground, providing PC users with the best of both worlds: the independence and flexibility of personal computers, and the connectivity and resource sharing of mainframes. in fact, networking is today considered so vital that it's hard to conceive of an organization with two or more computers that would not want to connect them together!

TYPES OF NETWORKING

The word "networking" strikes fear into legions of otherwise intrepid job hunters. It conjures up one of three images: calling everyone in your address book to see whether anyone knows anyone who may know anyone who may give you an informational interview, attending club meetings with other job hunters or having your friends come up with ideas and contacts instead of advising you to get out there and network. But there is no need to fear because there are many different types of networking techniques you can use to help with your job search and references.

Obviously number three doesn't always work. But the other two aren't so appealing either. Who enjoys calling total strangers and asking them to meet with you when there's nothing in it for them? If they're successful in what they do-and why else would you want to meet with them?-they're likely to be busy doing it.

STRONG-CONTACT NETWORKS-

Structured explicitly to pass business referrals among members, they allow only one member per profession. Strong-contact networks are particularly good for developing in-depth relationships because you see the same members week after week and pass referrals as a part of each meeting.

CASUAL-CONTACT NETWORKS-

Bring businesspeople together in a less-structured context than strong-contact networks, but for many they are a primary source of referrals; membership is not limited by profession. These groups are good for developing breadth in your network, but deep, long-lasting relationships can be formed as well.

SERVICE ORGANIZATIONS-

Associations that exist to provide and support humanitarian efforts and good works in the community and larger venues. They also bring people together in settings that facilitate referral and knowledge networking. Like casual-contact groups, they help you add breadth and diversity to your network.

PROFESSIONAL ASSOCIATIONS--

Established to exchange information and ideas among those in a given industry, as well as to promote and support that industry. These networks often include direct competitors, but they also provide contacts in related, non-competing businesses as well.

SOCIAL/BUSINESS ORGANIZATIONS

Combine social activities with business networking and can provide a variety of networking opportunities; many tend to resemble singles bars.

WOMEN'S NETWORKING GROUPS-

Still important networking organizations, but are slowly disappearing as women enter the business mainstream, especially as professionals, entrepreneurs, and small-business owners.

ONLINE NETWORKS-

A new phenomenon covering a wide range of interests.

TYPES OF COMPUTER NETWORKS

A computer network is two or more computers connected together using a telecommunication system for the purpose of communication and sharing resources". Ask any computer network expert to simplify this definition to you and you will start a debate on how it should not be just two computers but three. Simply put a network is a means of communication between computers. Within a given network, computers can send files, e-mails and other correspondence to each other. Even things like instant messaging, is set up within a computer's network.

There are two basic types of computer Networks:

LAN

LAN or Local Area Network is the most common kind of network set up. There are two ways to connect a LAN network. The simplest and easiest way is the peer-to-peer connection network. This is when two or more computers are directly connected to each other. For example if there were four computers in the network, computer 1 would be connected to computer 2, computer 2 would be connected to computer 3 and computer 3 would be connected to computer 4. This means each computer is dependent on the other. And if there were a network problem with any one computer, all of them would be affected. The other type if the client server connection. This is the type of connection where all the computers in a given network are connected to one central computer. This is a more complicated network but one that is much more efficient that peer-to-peer.

A local area network, or LAN, is a network of connected computers in a room, building, or set of buildings. Local area networks have been around since the beginning of computer use. A LAN is defined as a user network whereby data is sent at high rates between people located relatively close to each other. LANs do not usually make use of leased communication lines, but only means of communication that are provided by the installer of the network. The Internet is a wide area network, or WAN, which is distinct from a LAN. In contrast to the term Internet, local area networks are often called intranets, though sometimes this term refers to a cluster of LANs associated with a particular company or organization but not connected to the larger Internet. A local area network uses a hub or router to connect computers together. The means of communication is the omnipresent Ethernet cable or wireless wi-fi technology. These technologies offer data transfer rates running between 10 to 10000 Mbit/s.

Larger, more important LANs have redundant lines or other backup protocols. In networked computers, the most popular communication protocol is TCP/IP. Smaller LANs may be temporary and used between friends to play computer games over the network. Over a network, users can share files, view files, make changes to data on other computers if permitted, play movies or music on multiple computers at once, chat with instant messaging, send e-mails to each other, play games, and so on. All the advantages of the Internet apply, although they only include others on the LAN, and the data transfer rates are high. Perhaps the most frequently employed use of a LAN is to connect users to the Internet with only one connected router. In modern times, we use broadband cable or DSL modems to connect to the Internet, and it would be clumsy to have a modem associated with every computer, so we simply plug the modem into a router and link the router to computers with Ethernet cables. Configuring a LAN can be intimidating at first, but contemporary operating systems have programs that do most of the necessary configurations automatically, so setting up a local area network is pretty easy.

A local area network (LAN) supplies networking capability to a group of computers in close proximity to each other such as in an office building, a school, or a home. A LAN is useful for sharing resources like files, printers, games or other applications. A LAN in turn often connects to other LANs, and to the Internet or other WAN. Most local area networks are built with relatively inexpensive hardware such as Ethernet cables, network adapters, and hubs. Wireless LAN and other more advanced LAN hardware options also exist.

Examples

The most common type of local area network is an Ethernet LAN. The smallest home LAN can have exactly two computers; a large LAN can accommodate many thousands of computers. Many LANs are divided into logical groups called subnets. An Internet Protocol (IP) "Class A" LAN can in theory accommodate more than 16 million devices organized into subnets.

The High Performance Network

The HPN is used for the exchange of large amounts of operational data. Two Force10 E600 Routers, interconnected via 4-way 10-Gigabit Ethernet aggregated links, provide connectivity between the High Performance Computing Facility (HPCF) and the Data-Handling System (DHS). The HPCF network nodes are connected via 10-Gigabit Ethernet and all DHS nodes via Gigabit Ethernet aggregated links.

The General Purpose Network

The GPN is used for all other traffic. It has at its core two Foundry BigIron RX-16 routers and at the edge seven Foundry Super-X switches. The core routers are interconnected via 4-way 10-Gigabit Ethernet aggregated links and have multiple Gigabit Ethernet uplinks to the edge routers. The core also includes two further Super-X switches that are dual-attached to the RX-16s via 10-Gigabit Ethernet.

The GPN provides connectivity to:

- The HPCF, the DHS and additional servers via Gigabit Ethernet ports in the core.
- The user desktops and laptops via Gigabit Ethernet ports on the edge switches.
- The firewalls (for the Wide Area Network and the Demilitarized Zone (DMZ) via Gigabit Ethernet ports in the core. The DMZ includes ECaccess, web servers, the mail gateway and DNS (Domain Name Servers).

The Hardware

Both the Force10 E600 chassis are populated with 24 10-Gigabit-Ethernet and 144 Gigabit Ethernet ports. For resiliency there are four power supplies, two CPU modules and nine switching fabric modules. Both the RX-16 chassis are populated with 8 10-Gigabit Ethernet ports and 144 Gigabit Ethernet ports. For resiliency there are seven power supplies, two CPU modules and four switching fabric modules. The Super-X chassis each contain up to 156 Gigabit Ethernet ports and dual power-supplies.

WAN

Definition

The wide area network, often referred to as a WAN, is a communications network that makes use of existing technology to connect local computer networks into a larger working network that may cover both national and international locations. This is in contrast to both the local area network and the metropolitan area network, which provides communication within a restricted geographic area. Here is how the wide area network functions, and why it is so important to communications today.

The concept of linking one computer network with another is often desirable, especially for businesses that operate a number of facilities. Beginning with the local area network and going up to the wide area network, this is most easily accomplished by using existing telephony technology. Essentially, fibre optics are used to create the link between networks located in different facilities.

Often, this means using standard phone lines, referred to as POTS, or employing PSTN (public switched telephone network) technology. During the 1990s, a third option, that of ISDN (integrated services digital network) solutions for creation a wide area network gained a great deal of popularity, mainly because the concept made it more cost effective to extend the network beyond national boundaries. With coverage in a broad area, a wide area network allows companies to make use of common resources in order to operate. For example, many retail drugstores make use of a wide area network as part of their support to customers who fill prescriptions with one of their stores. Once in the common customer database for the pharmacy, the client is free to fill a prescription at any of the company's locations, even while vacationing in another state. Companies also make good use of the wide area network as well. Internal functions such as sales, production and development, marketing and accounting can also be shared with authorized locations through this sort of broad area network application. The concept of a wide area network as a means of taking individual location based computer networks and using them to create a unified computer network for the entire corporation means that employees can work from just about anywhere. Should one facility be damaged or rendered inaccessible due to natural disaster, employees simply move to another location where they can access the unified network, and keep on working.

Overview

WAN or Wide Area Network is when several LANs or independent computers are connected to a single, wider network. The Internet is the perfect example of WAN. E-mails, Chat Rooms and IMs all connect to the WAN of the Internet. WAN is much more complex and requires connecting devices or hubs from all over the world.

The term Wide Area Network (WAN) usually refers to a network which covers a large geographical area, and use communications circuits to connect the intermediate nodes. A major factor impacting WAN design and performance is a requirement that they lease communications circuits from telephone companies or other communications carriers. Transmission rates are typically 2 Mbps, 34 Mbps, 45 Mbps, 155 Mbps, 625 Mbps (or sometimes considerably more).

Numerous WANs have been constructed, including public packet networks, large corporate networks, military networks, banking networks, stock brokerage networks, and airline reservation networks. Some WANs are very extensive, spanning the globe, but most do not provide true global coverage. Organizations supporting WANs using the Internet Protocol are known as Network Service Providers (NSPs). These form the core of the Internet.

Wide Area Networks, or WANs, connect a geographically diverse group of computers within a state, country, or even across several states or countries. WANs typically are connected by telephone lines, other types of communication lines, or radio waves. Quite often, smaller local area networks (LANs) are linked together to form a WAN. This is accomplished via dedicated private lines, leased from telecommunications firms like Sprint and AT&T, or by Switched Multi-Megabit Data Services (SMDS) technology, developed in 1995 to eliminate the need for a leased line. WAN technology has been refined over a period of several decades. It first emerged in the mid-twentieth century with the advent of networks like ARPAnet. Developed in 1969 by the Department of Defence, ARPAnet and several other networks eventually evolved into the Internet, the largest WAN in the world. The packet switching technology most commonly used with WANs surfaced in the 1960s, and standard packet switching protocol, known as X.25, was developed in 1976. To increase network speed, packet switching allows for the parceling of data into smaller chunks, known as packets, prior to transmission.

These packets can travel independently via alternate routes, and they are reassembled once they reach their target. Although X.25 remained the most popular WAN packet switching protocol for years, other packet switching protocols used with increasing frequency by WAN developers and administrators include the Internet standard, Transmission Control Protocol/Internet Protocol (TCP/IP), and Frame Relay, used most often by WANs connected via high speed T-1 and T-3 lines. WANs are used for a variety of purposes. A corporation with offices in several locations may use a WAN to form an intranet. Quite often, the individual offices will use their own LANs for things like internal messaging, data processing functions, and hardware and software sharing. When these LANs are joined together to form a WAN, similar data sharing and messaging capabilities become possible across a much broader geographic area. Businesses wanting to link up with their suppliers or distributors may create a WAN as a means of establishing an extranet.

For example, an extranet could provide a sales representative with electronic access to information in about the time it might take to deliver a product, or the availability of a product. Some WANs bring together various types of communications, such as data, video, and voice. Some organizations, including companies, universities, research centers, hospitals, and libraries, use WANs to connect to the Internet. By connecting the NSP WANs together using links at Internet Packet Interchanges (sometimes called "peering points") a global communication infrastructure is formed. NSPs do not generally handle individual customer accounts (except for the major corporate customers), but instead deal with intermediate organizations whom they can charge for high capacity communications.

They generally have an agreement to exchange certain volumes of data at a certain "quality of service" with other NSPs. So practically any NSP can reach any other NSP, but may require the use of one or more other NSP networks to reach the required destination. NSPs vary in terms of the transit delay, transmission rate, and connectivity offered. The characteristics of the transmission facilities lead to an emphasis on efficiency of communications techniques in the design of WANs. Controlling the volume of traffic and avoiding excessive delays is important. Since the topologies of WANs are likely to be more complex than those of LANs, routing algorithms also receive more emphasis. Many WANs also implement sophisticated monitoring procedures to account for which users consume the network resources. The size of a network is limited due to size and distance constraints. However networks may be connected over a high-speed communications link (called a WAN link) to link them together and thus becomes a WAN.

WAN links are usually:

- Dial up connection

- Dedicated connection-It is a permanent full time connection. When a dedicated connection is used, the cable is leased rather than a part of the cable bandwidth and the user has exclusive use.
- Switched network-Several users share the same line or the bandwidth of the line.

There are two types of switched networks:

- Circuit switching-This is a temporary connection between two points such as dial-up or ISDN.
- Packet switching-This is a connection between multiple points. It breaks data down into small packets to be sent across the network.

A virtual circuit can improve performance by establishing a set path for data transmission. This will shave some overhead of a packet switching network. A variant of packet switching is called cell-switching where the data is broken into small cells with a fixed length.

WAN CONNECTION TECHNOLOGIES

- X.25-This is a set of protocols developed by the CCITT/ITU which specifies how to connect computer devices over an internet work. These protocols use a great deal of error checking for use over unreliable telephone lines. They establish a virtual communication circuit. It uses a store and forward method which can cause about a half second delay in data reception when two way communications are used. Their speed is about 64Kbps. Normally X.25 is used on packed switching PDNs (Public Data Networks). A line must be leased from the LAN to a PDN to connect to an X.25 network. A PAD (packet assembler/disassembler) or an X.25 interface is used on a computer to connect to the X.25 network. CCITT is an abbreviation for International Telegraph and Telephone Consultative Committee. The ITU is the International Telecommunication Union.
- Frame Relay-devices at both sides of the connection handle Error checking. Frame relay uses frames of

varying length and it operates at the data link layer of the OSI model. A permanent virtual circuit (PVC) is established between two points on the network. Frame relay speed is between 56Kbps and 1.544Mbps. Frame relay networks provide a high-speed connection up to 1.544Mbps using variable-length packet switching over digital fibre-optic media. Frame relay does not store data and has less error checking than X.25.

- Switched Multi-megabit Data Service (SMDS)-Uses fixed length cell switching and runs at speeds of 1.533 to 45Mbps. It provides no error checking and assumes devices at both ends provide error checking.
- Telephone connections
  - Dial up
  - Leased lines-These are dedicated analog lines or digital lines. Dedicated digital lines are called digital data service (DDS) lines. A modem is used to connect to analog lines, and a Channel Service Unit/Data Service Unit or Digital Service Unit(CSU/DSU) is used to connect to digital lines. The DSU connects to the LAN and the CSU connects to the line.
  - T Carrier lines-Multiplexors are used to allow several channels on one line. The T1 line is basic T Carrier service. The available channels may be used separately for data or voice transmissions or they may be combined for more transmission bandwidth. The 64Kbps data transmission rate is referred to as DS-0 (Digital Signal level 0) and a full T1 line is referred to as DS-1.

Signal	System	Total Kbps	Channels	Number of equivalent T1 lines
DS-1	T1	1544	24	1
DS-2	T2	6312	96	4
DS-3	T3	44736	672	28
DS-4	T4	274760	4032	3668

- T1 and T3 lines are the most common lines in use today. T1 and T2 lines can use standard copper wire. T3 and T4 lines require fibre-optic cable or other high-speed media. These lines may be leased partially called fractional T1 or fractional T3, which means a customer, can lease a certain number of channels on the line. A CSU/ DSU and a bridge or router is required to connect to a T1 line.
- Integrated Services Digital Network (ISDN)-Comes in two types and converts analog signals to digital for transmission. It is a dial up service

* Basic Rate ISDN (BRI)-Two 64Kbps B-channels with one 16Kbps D channel. The D-channel is used tor call control and setup.
* Primary Rate ISDN (PRI)-23 B-channels and one D channel.
* A device resembling a modem (called an ISDN modem) is used to connect to ISDN. The computer and telephone line are plugged into it.
  - Switched-56-A switched line similar to a leased line where customers pay for the time they use the line. Speed is 56Kbps. It is not dedicated and will not work to connect a WAN.
* Asynchronous Transfer Mode (ATM)-May be used over a variety of media with both baseband and broadband systems.

It is used for audio, video, and data. It uses fixed length data packets of 53 8 bit bytes called cell switching. 5 bytes contain header information. The cell contains path information that the packet is to use. It uses hardware devices to perform the switching of the data. Speeds from 155Mbps to 622 Mbps are achieved. Error checking is done at the receiving device, not by ATM. A permanent virtual connection or circuit (PVC) is established.

It may also use a switched virtual circuit (SVC). Service classes:

* Constant bit rate for data.
* Variable bit rate for audio or video.

- Connection less for data.
- Connection oriented for data.

ATM can be embedded in other protocols such as ATM-25, T1, T3, OC-1, OC-3, OC-12, and OC-48.

Some ATM technologies include:

- ATM-25-25Mbps speed.
- STS-3-155Mbps on fibre or category 5 cable.
- STS-12-620 Mbps on fibre cable for campus wide network.
- STS-48-2.2 Gbps on fibre cable on a MAN.
- STS-192-8.8 Gbps on fibre cable on intercity long distance. Phone companies normally use this.

Synchronous Optical Network (SONET)-A physical layer standard that defines voice, data, and video delivery methods over fibre optic media. It defines data rates in terms of optical carrier (OC) levels. The transmission rate of OC-1 is 51.8 Mbps. Each level runs at a multiple of the first. The OC-5 data rate is 5 times 51.8 Mbps which is 259 Mbps. SONET also defines synchronous transport signals (STS) for copper media which use the same speed scale of OC levels. STS-3 runs at the same speed of OC-3. Mesh or ring topology is used to support SONET. SONET uses multiplexing. The ITU has incorporated SONET into their Synchronous Digital Hierarchy (SDH) recommendations.

TOPOLOGIES

DEFINITION

Network topology refers to the way that your computer network is arranged. The network can have a physical or a logical topology. The physical topology describes the layout of computers and where the workstations are positioned. The logical network topology describes how the information flows through the network.

Choosing your physical topology is important because if it is not chosen correctly, this could cause your network to not operate properly. There are several terms that describe the type of physical topology that a network can have. The most common topologies are bus, ring, star, and mesh. In a bus topology, all of the computers are attached to a single cable using terminators. The terminators work to absorb the energy from the signals in the network. The bus topology is easy to install, but it is not reliable because a single default can bring down your network.

In a ring topology, each computer is connected directly to two other computers on the network. As with a bus topology, a single fault can disrupt a ring network. This type of network does have advantages, however, and does not require a network server. In a star topology, each computer is connected using its own separate cable. This set up is more reliable than a bus topology because its design makes it fault tolerant and susceptible to errors. The information on the network is transmitted from one system to another and the data flows in one single direction. The topology is expensive to maintain and is not reliable because removing one computer can disrupt your entire network.

In a mesh topology, a path is present from one computer to another computer in the network. The mesh topology is usually used in internet structure. The mesh topology can be complicated to construct because it has multiple connection between locations.

For every computer that you have you will need at least one and a half connections for each one. This contributes to the expensive structure. In choosing a network topology, understand that each one has its advantages and disadvantages. Research each one and see which one fits within your budget and which one fits your network layout. Also consider the amount of maintenance required in each topology.

When setting up a network at home, consider a network topology that is simple and easy to maintain. You will also want a topology that is inexpensive to set up. If you are choosing a topology for a business, you will want to consider a topology that is reliable and resistant to errors. Your customers will need a network that is free of downtime; therefore, be sure that your topology is one that withstands disruption.

NETWORKING TOPOLOGIES

BUS TOPOLOGY

A bus topology is a method of transmission on networks that uses a common vehicle for transmissions and thus it is categorized as shared communication. Imagine a bus picking up various people from one stop and dropping of people as it travels and then picking a few more. That is what happens in a bus network exactly. A bus network uses a multi-drop transmission medium, all node on the network share a common bus and thus share communication. This allows only one device to transmit at a time. A distributed access protocol determines which station is to transmit. Data frames contain source and destination addresses, where each station monitors the bus and copies frames addressed to itself.

A bus topology connects each computer (nodes) to a single segment trunk (a communication line, typically coax cable, that is referred to as the 'bus'. The signal travels from one end of the bus to the other. A terminator is required at each to absorb the signal so as it does not reflect back across the bus. A media access method called CSMA/MA is used to handle the collision that occur when two signals placed on the wire at the same time. The bus topology is passive. In other words, the computers on the bus simply 'listen' for a signal; they are not responsible for moving the signal along.

However in a Bus topology only one device is allowed to transmit at a given point of time. The DAP or the Distribute Access Protocol has the information about which station has to transmit the data. The data that is being transmitted have frames that will have the source name and the network address.

Function of Bus Topology

The bus topology connects each computer on the network into something called the segment trunk. A bus is usually referred to a cable that connects end to end and this is used to transmit the signals from one end to the other end. At every end a terminator is placed so that it understands in which direction the data is traveling and also the terminator is used to absorb the signals. If the terminator does not absorb the signal then the same signal is reflected back to the bus confusing the whole data flow. The bus is considered to be a passive network because the computers are largely dependant on the signal that is being transmitted. The advantage of the Bus network is that if one computer fails in the network the others are still not affected and they continue to work. Bus network is very simple and easy to set up. If there is an urgent need to set up a network and perhaps be used on a short term basis then the Bus network is the best possibility. Bus networks use the least amount of cable to set up making it cost effective.

Limitations

In the bus network you will need a network connection in order to determine if the data is being transferred between two nodes. If the data transfer rate is high then the Bus network does not perform very well because the data travels in a stream and cannot be overloaded. The bus network is a bit challenging when you have to troubleshoot the problems. Bus networks are not suitable as large networks as there are limitations to the number of nodes you can set up for one single cable. As the number of computers increase in the network the data transfer rate goes down accordingly and noticeably.

RING TOPOLOGY

Definition

A ring topology is a network topology or circuit arrangement in which each network device is attached along the same signal path to two other devices, forming a path in the shape of a ring. Each device in the network that is also referred to as node handles every message that flows through the ring. Each node in the ring has a unique address. Since in a ring topology there is only one pathway between any two nodes, ring networks are generally disrupted by the failure of a single link.

The redundant topologies are used to eliminate network downtime caused by a single point of failure. All networks need redundancy for enhanced reliability. Network reliability is achieved through reliable equipment and network designs that are tolerant to failures and faults. The FDDI networks overcome the disruption in the network by sending data on a clockwise and a counterclockwise ring. In case there is a break in data flow,the data is wrapped back onto the complementary ring before it reaches the end of the cable thereby maintaining a path to every node within the complementary ring.

Ring network connects computers in a circle of point-to-point connections, with no central server, such as a series of desktop computers in an office. Each node handles its own applications and also shares resources over the entire network. If one node becomes inoperative, the other nodes are still able to maintain contact with one another. Such a network is best for decentralized systems in which no priorities are required

Under the network, a signal is transferred sequentially via a "token" fro one station to the next. When a station wants to transmit, it "grabs" the token, attaches data and an address to it, and then sends it around the ring. The token travels along the ring until it reaches the destination address. The receiving computer acknowledges receipt with a return message to the sender. The sender then releases the token for the token for use by another computer.

Each station on the ring has equal access but only one station can talk at a time. To allow an orderly access to the ring, a single electronic token passes from one computer to the next around the ring as seen in (token ring). A computer can only transmit data when it capture the token. In a true ring topology, if a single computer or section of cable fails, there is an interruption in the signal. The entire network becomes inaccessible. Network disruption can also occur when computers are added or removed from the network, making it an impractical network design in environments where there is constant change to the network.

Ring networks are most commonly wired in a star configuration. In a Token Ring network, a multistation access unit (MSAU) is equivalent to a hub or switch on an Ethernet network. The MSAU performs the token circulation internally.

To create the complete ring, the ring in (RI) port on each MSAU is connected to the ring out (RO) port on another MSAU. The last MSAU in the ring is then connected to the first, to complete the ring.

TOKEN RING TOPOLOGY

Unlike Ethernet, Token Ring uses a ring topology whereby the data is sent from one machine to the next and so on around the ring until it ends up back where it started. It also uses a token passing protocol which means that a machine can only use the network when it has control of the Token, this ensures that there are no collisions because only one machine can use the network at any given time.

At the start, a free Token is circulating on the ring, this is a data frame which to all intents and purposes is an empty vessel for transporting data. To use the network, a machine first has to capture the free Token and replace the data with its own message. The packet of data is then sent to machine who reads the address, realises it is not its own, so passes it on to machine Machine does the same and passes the Token on to machine. This time it is the correct address and so number reads the message. It cannot, however, release a free Token on to the ring, it must first send the message back to number with an acknowledgement to say that it has received the data (represented by the purple flashing screen).

The receipt is then sent to machine who checks the address, realises that it is not its own and so forwards it on to the next machine in the ring, number.Machine does the same and forwards the data to number, who sent the original message. Machin erecognizes the address, reads the acknowledgement from number (represented by the purple flashing screen) and then releases the free Token back on to the ring ready for the next machine to use.

That's the basics of Token Ring and it shows how data is sent, received and acknowledged, but Token Ring also has a built in management and recovery system which makes it very fault tolerant. Below is a brief outline of Token Ring's self maintenance system.

Token Ring Self Maintenance

When a Token Ring network starts up, the machines all take part in a negotiation to decide who will control the ring, or become the 'Active Monitor' to give it its proper title. This is won by the machine with the highest MAC address who is participating in the contention procedure, and all other machines become 'Standby Monitors'. The job of the Active Monitor is to make sure that none of the machines are causing problems on the network, and to re-establish the ring after a break or an error has occurred. The Active Monitor performs Ring Polling every seven seconds and ring purges when there appears to be a problem. The ring polling allows all machines on the network to find out who is participating in the ring and to learn the address of their Nearest Active Upstream Neighbour (NAUN). Ring purges reset the ring after an interruption or loss of data is reported.

Each machine knows the address of its Nearest Active Upstream Neighbour. This is an important function in a Token Ring as it updates the information required to re-establish itself when machines enter or leave the ring. When a machine enters the ring it performs a lobe test to verify that its own connection is working properly, if it passes, it sends a voltage to the hub which operates a relay to insert it into the ring. If a problem occurs anywhere on the ring, the machine that is immediately after the fault will cease to receive signals. If this situation continues for a short period of time it initiates a recovery procedure which assumes that its NAUN is at fault, the outcome of this procedure either removes its neighbour from the ring or it removes itself.

Token Ring Operation using a Hub

A Token Ring hub simply changes the topology from a physical ring to a star wired ring. The Token still circulates around the network and is still controlled in the same manner, however, using a hub or a switch greatly improves reliability because the hub can automatically bypass any ports that are disconnected or have a cabling fault. Further advancements have been made in recent years with regard to Token Ring technology, such as early Token release and Token Ring switching but as this site is primarily concerned with cabling issues we will not go into any more detail here.

STAR TOPOLOGY

Star topology is the most commonly used physical technology in Ethernets LANS, when installed, the star topology resembles spokes I n a bicycle wheel. The star topology is made up of a central connection point that is a device such as a hub, switch, or router, where all the cabling segments meet. Each host in the network is connected to the central devices with its own cables although a physical star topology costs more to implement than the physical bus topology, the advantage of star topology make it worth the additional cost. Because each host it connected to the central device with its own cable, when that cable has a problem, only that host is affected, the rest of the network remains operational this benefit is extremely important and is why virtually every newly designed Ethernet a central connection point might be desirable for security or restricted access, but this is also a main disadvantage of a star topology.if the central device fails, the whole network become disconnected.when a star network is expanded to include an additional networking device that is connected for the main networking device, it is called an extended star topology.

Description

Data on a star network passes through the hub or concentrator before continuing to its destination. The hub or concentrator manages and controls all functions of the network. It also acts as a repeater for the data flow.

This configuration is common with twisted pair cable; however, it can also be used with coaxial cable or fibre optic cable. Devices typically connect to the hub with Unshielded Twisted Pair (UTP) Ethernet cables also known as RJ45 cables. Compared to the bus topology, a star network generally requires more cable, but a failure in any star network cable will only take down one computer's network access and not the entire LAN. (If the hub fails, however, the entire network also fails.)

Star topology has the following advantages:

- Easy to manage
- Easy to locate problems (cable/workstations)
- Easier to expand than a bus or ring topology
- Easy to Install and Wire
- No disruptions to the network then connecting or removing devices.
- Easy to detect faults and to remove parts.

Star topology has following disadvantages:

- It is susceptible to a single point of failure be it the server or hub/switch
- With Increased devices and traffic can make the network slow
- Requires more Cable Length.
- If the hub or concentrator fails, nodes attached are disabled.
- More expensive than linear bus topologies because of the cost of the concentrators.

TREE TOPOLOGY

Among all the Network Topologies we can derive that the Tree Topology is a combination of the bus and the Star Topology.

The tree like structure allows you to have many servers on the network and you can branch out the network in many ways. This is particularly helpful for colleges, universities and schools so that each of the branches can identify the relevant systems in their own network and yet connect to the big network in some way.

A Tree Structure suits best when the network is widely spread and vastly divided into many branches. Like any other topologies, the Tree Topology has its advantages and disadvantages. A Tree Network may not suit small networks and it may be a waste of cable to use it for small networks. Tree Topology has some limitations and the configuration should suit those limitations.

Benefits

A Tree Topology is supported by many network vendors ad even hardware vendors. A point to point connection is possible with Tree Networks. All the computers have access to the larger and their immediate networks. Best topology for branched out networks.

Limitations

In a Network Topology the length of the network depends on the type of cable that is being used. The Tree Topology network is entirely dependant on the trunk which is the main backbone of the network. If that has to fail then the entire network would fail. Since the Tree Topology network is big it is difficult to configure and can get complicated after a certain point.

The Tree Topology follows a hierarchical pattern where each level is connected to the next higher level in a symmetrical pattern. Each level in the hierarchy follows a certain pattern in connecting the nodes. Like the top most level might have only one node or two nodes and the following level in the hierarchy might have few more nodes which work on the point to point connectivity and the third level also has asymmetrical node to node pattern and each of these levels are connected to the root level in the hierarchy. Think of a tree that branches out in various directions and all these branches need the roots and the tree trunk to survive. A Tree Structured network is very similar to this and that is why it is called the Tree Topology.

Features

There will be at least three levels of hierarchy in the Tree Network Topology and they all work based on the root node. The Tree Topology has two kinds of topology integral in it, the star and the linear way of connecting to nodes. The Tree Topology functions by taking into account the total number of nodes present in the network. It does not matter how many nodes are there on each level. Nodes can be added to any level of the hierarchy and there are no limitations a far as the total number of nodes do not exceed. The higher levels in the hierarchy are expected to perform more functions than the lower levels in the network.

Advantages of a Tree Topology

- Point-to-point wiring for individual segments.
- Supported by several hardware and software venders.

Disadvantages of a Tree Topology

- Overall length of each segment is limited by the type of cabling used.
- If the backbone line breaks, the entire segment goes down.
- More difficult to configure and wire than other topologies.

MESH TOPOLOGY

A type of network setup where each of the computers and network devices are interconnected with one another, allowing for most transmissions to be distributed, even if one of the connections go down. This type of topology is not commonly used for most computer networks as it is difficult and expensive to have redundant connection to every computer. However, this type of topology is commonly used for wireless networks.

The mesh topology incorporates a unique network design in which each computer on the network connects to every other, creating a point-to-point connection between every device on the network. The purpose of the mesh design is to provide a high level of redundancy. If one network cable fails, the data always has an alternative path to get to its destination. Further, the cabling costs associated with the mesh topology can be high, and troubleshooting a failed cable can be tricky. Because of this, the mesh topology is rarely used. A variation on a true mesh topology is the hybrid mesh. It creates a redundant point-to-point network connection between only specific network devices.

Wireless Mesh Networks

Wireless Mesh Networks work based on the radio frequencies and was originally developed by the army to be able to communicate. The reliability factor is high in any kind of Mesh Network.

There are three types of wireless Mesh Topologies:

- Fixed Wireless Connections
- Peer to Peer or Adhoc Networks
- Node to Node

Fixed Mesh Networks

The fixed Mesh Networks will work only in the specified location and they are not mobile networks. They are meant to be used in a limited surrounding with boundaries. The location of nodes in affixed Mesh Network is all pre determined and they are not interchangeable. The fixed Mesh Network does not work on line of sight like the other types of Mesh Networks. The total number of hops in a fixed Mesh Network is usually fixed and also short. There may not be many nodes as this kind of Mesh Networks exist within an office or building. More often than not the data travels ion a specific direction.

Peer to Peer Mobile Networks

In a peer to peer mobile network the individual devices connect to each other using the Mesh Network. The peer does not require connecting to the main node and they can still communicate from one device to another device by taking the shortest possible data transfer route. However many experts believe that in the peer to peer Mesh Networks the problems with scalability in terms of time taken for data transfer is questionable. The device has to know to transmit the data in the most optimal path and the entire data transfer or depends on this single factor. If the device is incapable then the whole purpose of using it in a peer to peer connection is lost.

E-MAIL

DEFINITION

E-mail is simply the shortened form of electronic mail, a

protocol for receiving, sending and storing electronic messages. E-mail has gained popularity with the spread of the Internet. In many cases, e-mail has become the preferred method of communication. Though there is some degree of uncertainty as to when e-mail was invented, the father of the modern version is generally regarded to be American Ray Tomlinson. Before Tomlinson, messages could be sent between users but only those connected to the same computer. They could not be targeted to a particular individual. Tomlinson devised a way to address e-mail to certain users and thus was credited for one of the most important communication inventions in the 20th century. Tomlinson's idea was to identify the name of the user and the computer at which they were located. As a result, the basic formula for addressing an e-mail was username@usercomputer. This standard has not changed over the years, other than the user computer now commonly being replaced by the name of an e-mail provider. In many cases, this is the same as the user's Internet service provider.

The influence of e-mail cannot be overstated. The United States Postal Service, for example, notes that it handles 212 billion pieces of mail per year. Many sources have nearly that many e-mails being sent back and forth every single day. In other words, e-mail handles more than 300 times the amount of mail of the largest postal system in the world. In many cases, users receive, send and store e-mail based on one of two standards, SMTP or POP. SMTP stands for simple message transfer protocol. POP stands for Post Office Protocol. Though there is some amount of confusion over what these two protocols mean, the explanation is rather simple. POP is a protocol for storage of e-mail. SMTP is a protocol for sending and receiving.

WORKING WITH E MAIL

In reality, sending your message off into the network cloud is a bit like sending Little Red Riding Hood into the deep dark woods. You never know what might happen. In this diagram, the sender is a human being using their company account to send an e-mail to someone at a different company.

Step A: Sender Creates and Sends an E-mail

The originating sender creates an e-mail in their Mail User Agent (MUA) and clicks 'Send'. The MUA is the application the originating sender uses to compose and read e-mail, such as Eudora, Outlook, etc.

Step B: Sender's MDA/MTA Routes the E-mail

The sender's MUA transfers the e-mail to a Mail Delivery Agent (MDA). Frequently, the sender's MTA also handles the responsibilities of an MDA. Several of the most common MTAs do this, including sendmail and qmail (which Kavi uses).

Step C: Network Cloud

An e-mail can encounter a network cloud within a large company or ISP, or the largest network cloud in existence: the Internet. The network cloud may encompass a multitude of mail servers, DNS servers, routers, lions, tigers, bears (wolves!) and other devices and services too numerous to mention.

These are prone to be slow when processing an unusually heavy load, temporarily unable to receive an e-mail when taken down for maintenance, and sometimes may not have identified themselves properly to the Internet through the Domain Name System (DNS) so that other MTAs in the network cloud are unable to deliver mail as addressed. These devices may be protected by firewalls, spam filters and malware detection software that may bounce or even delete an e-mail. When an e-mail is deleted by this kind of software, it tends to fail silently, so the sender is given no information about where or when the delivery failure occurred.

E-mail service providers and other companies that process a large volume of e-mail often have their own, private network clouds. These organizations commonly have multiple mail servers, and route all e-mail through a central gateway server (*i.e.,* mail hub) that redistributes mail to whichever MTA is available. E-mail on these secondary MTAs must usually wait for the primary MTA (*i.e.,* the designated host for that domain) to become available, at which time the secondary mail server will transfer its messages to the primary MTA.

Step D: E-mail Queue

The e-mail in the diagram is addressed to someone at another company, so it enters an e-mail queue with other outgoing e-mail messages. If there is a high volume of mail in the queue-either because there are many messages or the messages are unusually large, or both-the message will be delayed in the queue until the MTA processes the messages ahead of it.

Step E: MTA to MTA Transfer

When transferring an e-mail, the sending MTA handles all aspects of mail delivery until the message has been either accepted or rejected by the receiving MTA. As the e-mail clears the queue, it enters the Internet network cloud, where it is routed along a host-to-host chain of servers. Each MTA in the Internet network cloud needs to "stop and ask directions" from the Domain Name System (DNS) in order to identify the next MTA in the delivery chain. The exact route depends partly on server availability and mostly on which MTA can be found to accept e-mail for the domain specified in the address.

Most e-mail takes a path that is dependent on server availability, so a pair of messages originating from the same host and addressed to the same receiving host could take different paths. These days, it's mostly spammers that specify any part of the path, deliberately routing their message through a series of relay servers in an attempt to obscure the true origin of the message. To find the recipient's IP address and mailbox, the MTA must drill down through the Domain Name System (DNS), which consists of a set of servers distributed across the Internet. Beginning with the root nameservers at the top-level domain (.tld), then domain nameservers that handle requests for domains within that.tld, and eventually to nameservers that know about the local domain.

DNS Resolution and Transfer Process

- There are 13 root servers serving the top-level domains (*e.g.*.org.com.edu.gov.net, etc.). These root servers refer requests for a given domain to the root name servers that handle requests for that tld. In practice, this step is seldom necessary.

- The MTA can bypass this step because it has already knows which domain name servers handle requests for these.tlds. It asks the appropriate DNS server which Mail Exchange (MX) servers have knowledge of the subdomain or local host in the e-mail address. The DNS server responds with an MX record: a prioritized list of MX servers for this domain.
  An MX server is really an MTA wearing a different hat, just like a person who holds two jobs with different job titles (or three, if the MTA also handles the responsibilities of an MDA). To the DNS server, the server that accepts messages is an MX server. When is transferring messages, it is called an MTA.
- The MTA contacts the MX servers on the MX record in order of priority until it finds the designated host for that address domain.
- The sending MTA asks if the host accepts messages for the recipient's username
- *Step F*: Firewalls, Spam and Virus Filters

The transfer process described in the last step is somewhat simplified. An e-mail may be transferred to more than one MTA within a network cloud and is likely to be passed to at least one firewall before it reaches it's destination. An e-mail encountering a firewall may be tested by spam and virus filters before it is allowed to pass inside the firewall. These filters test to see if the message qualifies as spam or malware. If the message contains malware, the file is usually quarantined and the sender is notified. If the message is identified as spam, it will probably be deleted without notifying the sender.

Spam is difficult to detect because it can assume so many different forms, so spam filters test on a broad set of criteria and tend to misclassify a significant number of messages as spam, particularly messages from mailing lists. When an e-mail from a list or other automated source seems to have vanished somewhere in the network cloud, the culprit is usually a spam filter at the receiver's ISP or company. This explained in greater detail in Virus Scanning and Spam Blocking.

Delivery

In the diagram, the e-mail makes it past the hazards of the spam trap...er...filter, and is accepted for delivery by the receiver's MTA. The MTA calls a local MDA to deliver the mail to the correct mailbox, where it will sit until it is retrieved by the recipient's MUA.

RFCs

Documents that define e-mail standards are called "Request For Comments (RFCs)", and are available on the Internet through the Internet Engineering Task Force (IETF) website. There are many RFCs and they form a somewhat complex, interlocking set of standards, but they are a font of information for anyone interested in gaining a deeper understanding of e-mail.

5

Learning Applications

LEARNING CURVES

The learning curve describes the empirical relationships between output quantities and quantities of certain inputs (mainly directlabor hours) where learning inducement improvement is present. It portrays the concept that the cumulative average unit cost decreases systematically by a common percentage each time the volume of production increases geometrically (that is, increases by doubling). The phenomenon is helpful in the investigation of the cost behavioural patterns, cost estimation, and decision making in general. In effect the forecasting of labour input and its impact on various economic decisions has been a laborious and time—consuming job. The learning curve is intended to make such forecasting easier, quicker, and much more accurate.

In brief, learning curves are applicable to all the aspects of production planning and control where there are tasks subject to improvement. A schematic representation of how learning curves can influence the use of production resources. Synonyms for the learning curve include the manufacturing progress function, cost-quantity relationship, cost curve, product acceleration curve, improvement curve, performance curve, experience curve, and efficiency curve.

THEORY

The learning curve was first recognized in the aircraft industry, where any reduction in the considerable number of direct-labour hours needed for assembly work is quickly recognized and formalized. However, the learning curve was not translated into an empirical theory curve until 1925, when it was observed in a military manufacturing operation. Some eleven years later, T. P. Wright disclosed the results of empirical tests of the learning curve. He observed that on the average, when output doubled in the aircraft industry, the labour requirements decreased by about 20 per cent; in other words, there was an 80 per cent learning factor. Interest in such a discovery applied to a wartime situation; the U.S. Defence Department commissioned the Stanford Research Institute to study the direct-labour input required for aircraft production in a number of firms.

The resulting learning curves had a common characteristic: An 80 per cent improvement rate. From 1909, when the first Model T Ford was produced, until 1926, productivity improved along an 86 per cent learning curve. Evidence of improvement over sixteen years and on sixteen million items was found in a human-paced operation that involved assembling candy boxes. The learning continued for the production of tens of millions of units in a machine-paced operation. The learning curve theory is based on a simple principle of human nature: People learn from experience. As workers repeat a task, they become more efficient at it. The net result is a reduced use of direct-labour hours per unit. This improvement can be regular enough to follow a predictable pattern that should apply to any task or job in any industry.

The early literature considered the learning improvement possible only in labour-intensive, discontinuous forms of manufacture, such as airframe assembly. It was later proved, however, that the improvement could take place in continuous and capital-intensive forms of manufacture. Industries where the learning phenomenon is applicable include the petroleum, refining, and basic chemical industries. Finally, learning was found to exist in process-oriented contexts as well as in job-order production, and in mature phases of production as well as in start-up phases. Industries in which the learning curve phenomenon was found applicable include machine-intensive manufacturing (steel mills and glass, paper, and electrical products), automotive assembly, apparel manufacture, large musical instruments and electromechanical assembly, housing construction, machine tools, petroleum refining, clerical operations, printing and typesetting, machine shop processes, electronic (radar), and electrical manufacture.

As an example of the learning phenomenon, assume that the average labour hours required per unit are reduced by 30 per cent as the quantity produced doubles. If the first unit takes 100 hours, then the average for 2 units is 70 hours (0.7 × 100 hours), or a total of 140 hours for 2 units. Therefore, the time required to complete the second unit equals 40 hours (140-100). Continuing this line of reasoning, 4 units would require an average of 49 hours per unit (0.7 × 70 hours), and a total of 196 hours (4 × 49 hours) for all 4 units. The third and fourth units require 56 hours (196 hours required for 4 units minus 140 hours required for 2 units).

The basic doctrine of the learning curve can be summarized as follows:

- *Where there is life, there can be learning:* The more complex the life, the greater the rate of learning. Man-paced operations are more susceptible to learning or can give greater rates of progress than machine-paced operations. The rate of learning can be sufficiently regular to be predictive. Operations can develop trends which are characteristic of themselves. Projecting such established trends is more valid than assuming a level performance or no learning. What factors account for the learning curve phenomenon? *It is appropriate to distinguish between the impact of two factors*:
  - The learning in the literal sense on the part of the workers, and
  - Other factors, including management innovation. Although these factors operate together, the presence of a consistent behaviour indicates that of the various factors, learning in the literal sense is the predominant influence. The non learning factors, such as new machinery, time studies, or

design changes, do bring some labour savings; however, they will probably have an irregular effect on the learning curve. Furthermore, the learning factors will be subject to two conditions:

- The predisposition of an operation to an improvement, and
- The extent to which the predisposition is used.

On one hand, the predisposition to an improvement is related to the human content of an operation. It is reflected in the ratio of assembly (human content) to machine work. In assembly work there are relatively large possibilities for learning; in machine work the improvement is. Constrained by the fact that the machines cannot "learn" to run any faster.

The following rates are often employed as possible benchmarks:

- 75% assembly labour, 25% machine labour: 80% curve
- 50% assembly labour, 50% machine labour: 85% curve
- 25% assembly labour, 75% machine labour: 90% curve

On the other hand, the extent to which the predisposition is used may depend on the following two factors:

- *The effect of faith*: A positive attitude towards the possibility of learning can reinforce progress. Winfred B. Hirschmann states: "If progress is believed possible, it will likely be sought; and if it is looked for, there is some possibility of finding it. Conversely, if improvements are considered unlikely, there will be little urge to seek them. A defeatist philosophy can be engendered which so debilitates an effort that it helps to produce the very condition it assumes." The presence of open-ended expectations. The absence of "ceiling psychology" may create a predisposition to learning and permit improvement to continue. Some companies obtain more rapid progress when the workers are not informed of the target rate.

Learning Curve

Since the discovery of the learning curve and the publication in 1936 of the first article formulating the theory of learning curves, various geometric versions have been proposed.

The more well known are these:

- The log-linear model
- Pegels's exponential function
- Levy's adaptation function
- The Stanford-B model
- DeJong's learning formula with an incompressibility factor

The S-curve: Glover's learning formula with a work commencement factor Common to all these models, however, is the need to estimate these two basic parameters: Input resources associated with the production of the first unit The learning curve characteristic or some measure of the rate reduction These various models are described next. It is, however, appropriate to note that the log-linear model has been and still is, by far, the most useful model. The other models are described because they have been found and may be found in the future to be applicable to some manufacturing experiences.

The Log-Linear Model: The log-linear model or constant percentage model basically states that the improvement in productivity is fairly constant as output increases.

- γ = KXn where,
- γ = the number of direct-labour hours required to produce the xth unit,
- K = the number of direct-labour hours required to produce the first unit,
- X = the cumulative unit number,
- n = log ∏/log 2 = learning index,
- ∏ = the learning rate,
- 1-Õ = the progress ratio.

Assume that a company's rate of learning, like the aircraft industry's, is 80 per cent. On an arithmetic chart with linear coordinates, the relationship between the cumulative average direct-labour hours and the cumulative units of production is portrayed by a curve showing a rapid decline that trails off. The same curve on a logarithmic chart will follow a straight declining rate. The portrayal of the learning phenomenon as a straight line is generally preferred for practical reasons.

Pegels's Exponential Function

As an alternative to the power function formulation of the log-linear model, various authors proposed models based on exponential functions. As an example, Pegels proposed an alternative algebraic function, an exponential-type function, to complement or replace the power function approach. The functions are expressed as follows:

The marginal cost per unit index for the xth unit, M·C(x) is as follows:

$$MC(x) = aax-1 +b$$

where α, β, and a are empirically based parameters.

By integrating across x yields TC(x) which is the total cost index up to the xth unit in terms of the marginal cost per unit index, in other words where α, β, and a are empirically based parameters, and C is a constant to be derived after the parameters have been derived. In fact, the constant C can be derived by letting *MC* (1) = *TC*(1) = *AC*(1) which yields

The average cost AC(x) of the first x units produced in marginal cost index terms or cumulative average cost can be derived as follows: The main assumption in the exponential function formulation is that the marginal cost of the first unit, MC(1) = y0, is assumed to be known and will be set equal to the index value of one. In other words, y0 = α +β = 1.00.

In comparing the merits of his model to the other power function models, Pegels concluded as follows: The proposed exponential model is only slightly more difficult to apply than the common power function model. Although there are three parameters to be estimated, one of these, ß, is based on subjective estimates or historically based subjective estimates. The other two parameters, *a* and *b*, can be as readily determined as the two power function parameters. Since the exponential function is based on a zero-to-one marginal cost index, applying the exponential function requires slightly more training and care.

In addition, the basic power function has the disadvantage of showing both marginal and average costs decreasing with increasing output, while in the exponential function the marginal cost becomes constant after a certain number of units produced.

Levy's Adaptation Function

Levy cites two shortcomings of the log-linear model—namely, it does not recognize the leveling off of production rate, and it does not give insight into factors that may influence learning. The new type of learning function which he proposes is particularly useful in showing how a firm can adapt itself to the learning process and isolate the variables which influence learning. Levy's function has the following form: MC = [1/β-(1/β-xb/a)C-cx]-1 where MC = marginal cost, a and b are the parameters that are analogous to the power function parameters, C is a third parameter to be estimated, and ß is the production index for the first unit. The function of the parameter C is to flatten the curve for large values of x. In other words, Levy's learning function reaches a plateau and does not continue to decrease or increase as does the power function.

Stanford-B Model

The search for something other than the log-linear model stems from the fact that the linear model does not always provide the best fit in all situations. A Stanford study found that the linear formulations of the learning curve may be inappropriate for some World War II data. Instead the following equation, usually referred to as the Stanford-B formula or the learning formula with a B-factor, was found to be more representative:

$$y = a(X + B)n$$

where

y = Direct-man hours required for cumulative unit number x,

a = constant, equivalent to the cost of the first unit when B = 0,

n = Exponent describes slope of the asymptote (-0.5 is a typical value),

B = Constant which may be expressed as the number of units theoretically produced prior to the first unit acceptance, or the equivalent units of experience available at the start of a manufacturing process (1 < B < 10 and 4 is a typical value).

The Stanford study found that n for 29 cases ranged between-0.397 and-0.599 (66.1% and 75.9% slopes) with a mean value of-0.499. In fact, the Boeing Company found that the Stanford-B model was the best for the manufacturing of the Boeing 707 if it is modified to incorporate design differences for special customers' requirements. The modified progress curve developed suffers, however, from the following limitations: It assumes that the learning experienced on any component is fully retained, no matter how much time elapses before the same work is repeated. Modifying the assumption will lead to a more cumbersome formulation and has not been attempted.

- When the number of versions in a family of airplanes gets large, the computations become extensive. The difficulty is relieved if attention is restricted to a smaller number of versions in a combination with the version to be estimated. These will be ones which share the most work with this version and contribute the most experience.

The Stanford-B model includes as a main feature the B factor which measures design differences or complexities beyond the control of management know-how or the amount of engineering or retooling. Another explanation is that the Stanford-B model accounts for previous learning retained by using a scale of displacement B.

Note that setting $n = 0.5$, the Stanford-B model yields a unit learning curve equation as follows: With B = 0, the same equation becomes y = ax-0.5 which is equivalent to a 70.7 per cent linear unit time reduction curve. A typical learning curve of the Stanford-B type is asymptotic to a straight line with slope n and approaches such a line over its entire length as B approaches zero. The main result of the B factor is that the curve tends to follow a convex shape in the early part of a programme.

There is at least one known attempt at evaluating the superiority of the Stanford curve over the conventional log-linear curve. Hoffman used the same data used by the Stanford Research Institute and concludes that there is little basis for choice between the two curves in spite of the fact that in several cases the inclusion of parameter B did result in smaller sums of squared deviations.

DeJong's Learning Formula with an Incompressibility Factor

DeJong proposed a version of the power function which suggests parameters to be assigned for the proportion of manual activity in a given task. When the activities are mainly controlled by manual operations, the time is compressible as successive units are completed. If machine time was dominant in the cycle of activities, the time will be less compressible as the number of units increases.

Accordingly, DeJong introduced an incompressibility factor M in the log-linear model to take into account the man-machine ratio and the asymptotic behaviour of the curve when it approaches a limit of unit time as the number of units increases. This model generates, then, two components: a fixed component which is set equal to the irreducible portion of the task and a variable component which is subject to learning. It has the following form: MC = a [M + (1-M)/Xn] where*MC* = marginal time for the xth unit,*a* and *n* are parameters analogous to the power function,*M* is the factor of incompressibility.

The incompressibility factor suggested by DeJong is often 0.25 for manually dominated activities and 0.50 for machine-dominated activities. When *M* is zero, the DeJong formulation becomes the log-linear model, which would happen in a situation of a completely manual situation. In a machine-dominated situation, *M* approaches 1, and the expected unit time is a constant, thus *MC* = *a*.

A set of curves for various values of *M*, for all of which the learning exponent is *n* = 0.32. The incompressibility factor indicates the inability to reduce production time as the number of cycles is repeated. A completely machine-dominated operation would be unlikely to improve and thus possess high incompressibility. In addition, the model demonstrates a practical limit to the amount of learning or improvement. The curve ultimately approaches a plateau as the number of units increases.

The S-Curve

Another curve useful when the data "miss" the straight learning curve is the somewhat S-shaped curve. For example, Carr proposed an S-type function which was based on the assumption of a gradual startup. An S-type function has the shape of the cumulative normal distribution function for the start-up curve and the shape of an operating characteristics function for the learning curve.

Several factors appear to contribute to this pattern:

- The early stages of production are a time of partial experimentation by all personnel. Various approaches are tried in learning to use prescribed tooling and methods, which preclude rapid improvement. Further, last minute changes in design and materials sometimes hit during this period, and these prevent the solidification of techniques necessary for rapid learning or initial low cost.
- As corrections are made to toolings and methods, a rapid reduction in cost is possible for some time. For our assembly operation, the learning slope often reaches 50 per cent during the period, compared with a norm of 75 per cent.

3. Finally, however, the "water" has been taken out of the costs and we settle down to a more routine activity—the slope activity. The slope of learning now proceeds somewhat more slowly than average, say at 80 per cent for assembly.

Because the Stanford-B may better fit the early part of the curve and the DeJong model the latter part, one approach may be to combine these two models to obtain an S-curve such as:

$$MC = a [M + (1\text{-}M) (x + B)n].$$

To solve this equation, however, assumptions have to be made to preselect the incompressibility M and equivalent experience units B and a to solve for a value of n. In other words, values for any of the unknown can be determined given a logical pre selection of the other three independent variables. Another procedure for the determination of the coefficients of the Scurve is to look at it as a smooth "cubic curve." In such a case the model log MC = A + B(log x) + C(log X2) + D(log X3) represents the cubic curve on a log-log plot. The fitting of a cubic curve to actual time can then be accomplished by the use of any polynomial fit programme from the available computer library statistical routines.

LEARNING FORMULA

In contrast to other theories which were based on an analysis of the output of complete factories, Glover examined studies of the gain in speed skill of individuals before extending the model to complete departments of companies. A model derived for the learning of individuals in experimental psychology was found applicable to learning of all kinds in industry. It is expressed as follows: where yi and xi are interchangeable in the sense that either may represent time or quantity, C is a commencement factor, a is the time of the first cycle, and n is the index of the curve = 1 + b. If "y is used to represent the total elapsed time, then xi will normally be unity, that is,

The model differs from the conventional power function of the introduction of the work commencement factor C. The rationale for such adjustment is stated as follows: The nature of logarithmic scales tends to exaggerate any early deviation from the straight line, and it is not surprising that, if only a few cycles of practice can upset a laboratory experiment, lack of understanding of the importance of recording exact times in industry can cause a curve to be obtained instead of a straight line.

The "work commencement" factor C in the model is, in effect, a factor of ignorance concerning the commencement of a job. As has been stated, there is reason to think that when C is not zero, the data relating to the time of commencement may be inaccurate. The reader may synthesize such inaccuracies by taking data which is known to yield a straight line relationship and introduce a fictitious constant error into either the time or practice scales.

The learning curve is a well-accepted model in the production and managerial accounting literature. Although various mathematical models have been suggested as descriptive of the phenomenon, only one—the constant-percentage or log-linear model—is widely used and discussed in the managerial accounting literature. The log-linear model basically states that the improvement in productivity is fairly constant as output increases. A basic knowledge of the working of these models is important for an efficient implementation in actual managerial situations.

GENERAL MODEL

The learning phenomenon based on the constant-percentage model is generally expressed by the mathematical function,

$$(Y, I_* \text{ or } M) = ax$$

where the right side of the function is defined as,

a = the number of direct-labour hours required to produce the first unit of output, where

r = the rate of learning or improvement represented by the constant percentage decrease in hours,

f = the factor increase in output (usually discussed in terms of 2).

As can be seen from the formulae, the dependent variable is represented by either Y, I_* or M. This is due to the existence of three types of learning curve models which differ in their definition of the dependent variable. They are the average time model, the marginal time model, and the individual unit-time model. They may be defined as follows: The average time model specifies that the new cumulative average time per unit (Y) will decrease by a constant percentage (r) as the cumulative production doubles.

The marginal time model specifies that the new marginal time per unit (M) will decrease by a constant percentage (r) as cumulative production doubles. The individual unit-time model specifies that the new individual time per unit (I_*) will decrease by a constant percentage (r) as cumulative production doubles. In what follows I will explain each of these models, present a synthesis of the three models, provide guidance for the choice of one of these models, and elaborate on the relationships between the percentage of learning and the b parameter (the learning exponent).

The Individual Unit-Time Model

As stated earlier, the individual unit model specifies that the new individual time per unit (I_*) will decrease by a constant percentage (r) as cumulative production doubles. More precisely, the basic formulae for the individual unit-time or unit-time curve specifies that the new individual time per unit (I_*) will decrease by a constant percentage (r) as cumulative production doubles. Besides the individual time, the models provide formulae for the total time or total curve, the average time or average curve, and the marginal time or marginal curve.

Distinguishing among the Three Forms of the Constant Percentage Learning Curve Model

The three models differ in their definition of the dependent variable (the left side of the equation) which is subject to the learning phenomena.

- In the average time model, the dependent variable is the new cumulative average time per unit Y.
- In the unit time model, the dependent variable is the individual time per unit, I_*
- In the marginal time model, the dependent variable is the marginal time per unit, M_{**}

It is important to determine which is the correct dependent variable which is subject to the learning phenomena because it dictates the types of formulae to be used. The formulae for the three types of models

Which Model to Use

The process being studied determines whether the average time, the marginal time, or the individual unit time should be used.

The procedure consists of the following steps:

- Collecting average time, marginal time, and

individual unit-time information and cumulative output information.

- Plotting the information on a log-log graph and the line providing the best visual fit between, on one hand, the average time, the managerial time, or the individual time information and, on the other hand, the cumulative output defines the model to be used.
- To be more exact in determining whether the average time, marginal time, or individual unit time applies, perform a logarithmic linear regression of either one of the possible dependent variables with the output, that is, log (time, average, total, or individual unit) = log *a* + *b* log (cumulative units).

The model which provides the best statistical fit in terms of the highest coefficient of determination, *R*, should be used as the right model for the observed learning phenomenon.

Relationships between Percentage of Learning and Parameter b

To simplify the computations necessary in the applications of the learning curve, the relationships between the percentage of learning (*r*) and the exponent (*b*) can be established for all possible values of *r*. In general, the relationship is computed as *b* = log 2/log 2. For example, for 2 = 70 per cent, *b* =-0.51457. This relationship for all values of *r* ranging from 51 through 97, and it can be used as an expedient way to find the appropriate value of *b*.

FORMULAE FOR DETERMINING THE SLOPE

The average time model of the log-linear model is represented by the formula *Y* = *ax*. If production doubles, then the formula becomes *Y* = *a*(2*x*). Given that learning (r%) takes place when production doubles, then. If we take the logarithm of both sides and solve for b, then we obtain For example, the slope b for a 50 per cent curve is

COST ESTIMATION

The learning curve can be used in cost estimation. Cost

estimation when cumulative costs are known and when the learning phenomenon is in effect consists of estimating the coefficients of the learning curve from past data using the logarithmic linear equation log Y = log a-b log x. In one method, the regression analysis of the logarithmic data on y and x using the least-squares method will provide a regression line. Its slope coefficient, exponent, or learning constant can be determined using the least-squares method as follows: where N = number of observations for which cost and hours are available, XY = product of log y and log x, X = log of the cumulative production, Y = log of the cumulative labour hours.

For a first example, suppose you were provided the data disclosing only the first three columns: column,

- For the weeks, column.
- For total production, column.
- For direct-labour hours. On the basis of these data two new columns are added: column.
- For cumulative units completed and column.
- For cumulative direct-labour hours. The data for columns and
- Are then plotted on a log-log graph. If the scatter diagram indicates the presence of a learning phenomenon, then we need to determine the following information to insert in the formula for the slope coefficient: Inserting the correct values in the formula yields. Next the learning rate,
- Can be determined as follows: b = log 2/log 2 or log r = b log 2 =-0.267(0.3010) =-0.080367 r = 83.3%

The other method of finding the learning rate is the doubling approach. Basically, it reads the gain time over any doubled quantity. The learning factor can be expressed as the ratio between the time taken to produce Z units and the cumulative time to produce 2Z units.

If double quantities are not available, use instead the following formula:Using the, the learning rate may be computed as follows. If the time to produce 10 units is 174 hours and the cumulative time for 20 units is 290 hours, the learning factor is equal to (290/20 ÷ (174/10) × 100% = 83.3%.

After determining the learning rate using either the regression approach or the doubling approach, any of the computational formulae can be used to compute the average cumulative labour hours, unit labour hours, total labour hours, or marginal hours required to produce a specific number of units. The results of these computations. Finally, assuming the rate of learning will continue beyond total estimated production of 80 units, the learning curve can be used to make cost estimates.

WARRANTY

The learning phenomenon has been used in both the areas of warranty maintenance and estimating the size of a maintenance force. In the area of warranty maintenance, Kneip suggested that a progress function exists in the relationship of a product's maintenance requirement to cumulative production. Whereas in the conventional application of the learning phenomenon, the dependent variable (cost *r* labour time) is a production efficiency variable, in the maintenance progress function, the dependent variable is a quality, reliability, and serviceability characteristic.

The results of regression analysis on two products showed that the maintenance progress function exists, that it relates warranty period maintenance to cumulative production, and that the relationship is logarithmic. Kneip also made the following interesting note: Progress in a product's maintenance requirement is thus a characteristic of the organization, dependent upon both its structure and personnel, as well as the nature of the product. It cannot be overemphasized that progress is neither automatic nor self-perpetuating, but is the result of continual effort towards improvement.

Furthermore, its use as a management control device involves the possibility of actually impeding progress that might otherwise have been attained through the selection of a progress rate too slow to provide challenging objectives. The selection of the progress rate is a critical decision in the application of the function. In the area of maintenance force, Clarke used the learning phenomenon to predict the required size of a plant's maintenance force.

WORK-ACCIDENT EXPERIENCE

Work-accident is an unfortunate but recurring event in all types of human endeavors. Public data on the subject are available in most industries. Among those industries which collect, tabulate, and publish the work-accident experience of its member firms is the American Petroleum Industry. In that industry "disabling injury" and the computation of injury experience are accomplished on the basis of USASI Standard Z16.1. One of the statistics defined by that standard is this:

The assumption taken in the foundation of the standard is that in every unit of time some constant number of exposures occurs and is some multiple of the duration. Greenberg argued that the method was misleading and that the denomination of the standard should be in units of production rather than in units of time, especially in light of evidence that the incidence of accidents was highly negatively correlated with productivity.

He also found that accident experience follows a learning curve pattern, showing a decreasing trend in accident sequence as productivity increases. In fact, using mining industry data, Greenberg showed again in another study that mining accidents also conformed to a learning model. Such accident-experience learning curves may be used to evaluate the effectiveness of a safety programme and to open new possibilities in the analysis and prevention of accident occurrence.

STANDARD COSTS AND EFFICIENCY VARIANCE ANALYSIS

A standard cost is a forecast of what costs should be used as a basis of cost control and as a measure of productive efficiency when ultimately compared with actual costs. In a traditional labour variance analysis, where standard costs are compared to actual costs, the standard cost is assumed to be a constant amount per unit of output. The analysis proceeds generally by dichotomizing the difference between the actual cost and the flexible budget into wage rate and efficiency variances as follows: WRV = H (r-r) EV = r (H-H) where WRV

= wage rate variance, EV = efficiency variance, H = actual labour hours, r = actual wage rate per hour, r = standard wage rate per hour, H = standard labour hours.This traditional labour variance analysis rests in the assumption that no learning phenomenon is affecting labour usage and that it is realistic to assume that standard labour is constant over the total production of the period.If learning was present, then the assumption of constant standard cost is unrealistic and the traditional labour variance analysis inapplicable.

In such a case, it would be preferable to consider one of two possible approaches:

- One approach would be to use "moving standard costs" rather than "constant standard costs." The moving standard costs would be computed on the basis of the relevant learning curve formulae.
- A second approach would be to dichotomize the traditional labour efficiency variance into
  - Labour efficiency variance due to learning, and
  - A labour efficiency variance due to factors other than the learning factors.

To illustrate the three possible approaches, the traditional and the two approaches incorporating the learning effect, let's use this example: The XYZ Company makes personal computers. Its engineering department has determined that 800 direct-labour hours are necessary to assemble the first unit of a new model and that an 80 per cent learning phenomenon is present in the assembling process.

The standard direct-labour rate per hour is $20. During the month of January, 10 personal computers were assembled in 800 hours. The actual direct-labour rate per hour is $75. Discussion of the three approaches to labour variance analysis follows:

NO LEARNING EFFECT

Under this approach the traditional labour variance analysis consists of computing a labour rate variance and a labour efficiency variance based on a standard labour hours per unit of 100. It will be computed as follows:

LEARNING EFFECT WITH STANDARDS

The standard labour hours per unit is adjusted to take into account the learning effect resulting in the use of a moving standard cost. In such case, the standard direct-labour hours allowed for actual production of 20 personal computers is derived using the learning curve formulae as follows: Therefore, the analysis can now proceed as follows: As can be seen by the analysis, the labour efficiency variance is $79,800 unfavourable taking the learning effect into account rather than $4,000 favourable effect in the traditional approach.

TOTAL CONSIDERATION

In this case the traditional labour efficiency variance is dichotomized into both a labour efficiency variance due to the learning effect and a labour efficiency variance due to factors other than the learning factors. This approach shows the whole picture by disclosing the pure efficiency variance due to the nonlearning factors and the learning efficiency variance due to the learning effect. This approach should allow for a better analysis and effective control of labour cost.

External Reporting

External reporting may be affected by the learning phenomenon. It may be suggested that the cost savings due to the learning effect should be abstracted from the profit so actual increased productivity can be examined rather than productivity due to a repetition of tasks. A more important problem is the distortion of profit that can occur when production costs follow the learning curve phenomenon if two conditions exist:

- The contract(s) cover two or more periods, and
- The unit price is based on a cumulative average cost permit.

To correct for the possible misstatement of profit, that a cost allocation model based on the learning phenomenon will disclose the relationships between efforts and accomplishments better than the conventional method. To illustrate the problem of profit misstatement and how to correct it with the learning curve allocation model, let us use the data shown in Let us also assume that 40 units are sold in 19 × 1, and 120 units are sold in 19 × 2; the unit selling price is $50 per unit in both years; the factory overhead and the direct-labour cost are each incurred at the rate of $5 per direct-labour hour; and the material cost is $1 per unit.

The income statements for both years under the conventional method of matching actual costs with revenues and the learning curve allocation model. Under the conventional method the company shows a loss of $608 the first year followed by a profit (net income) of $1,168 in the second year; the learning curve cost allocation model shows a profit of $140 in the first year and a profit of $420 the second year. Notice that the total profit for the two years is $560 under both methods. To avoid such reporting differences which may adversely affect the market image of the firm, Morse proposed the following reporting system: As production takes place, any excess of the projected cost of each unit over the expected average cost of all anticipated production is charged to a deferred production expense account, and inventory is charged with an amount equal to the expected average unit cost of all anticipated production. When the projected unit cost is less than the expected average unit cost of all anticipated production, this difference is deducted from the deferred production expense account, and inventory is charged with an amount equal to the expected average unit cost of all anticipated production. As production takes place, any differences between actual and projected costs are written off as a period variance unless a change in a parameter of the model occurs.

Cost Reduction

Finding ways to reduce costs sometimes may be crucial to firms and is a necessity most of the time. The learning phenomenon and the learning curve offer opportunities for cost reduction programs in general and in the preproduction planning and the product redesign areas in particular.In the preproduction planning stage, the type of learning curve to be used subsequently may be affected by the level and content of organizational planning. More precisely, the more preplanning that is done in all aspects associated with the launching of a new product, the lower the cost of the initial unit. With the cost of the initial unit being the starting point of the learning phenomenon, the lower it is through effective preproduction planning, the greater the savings generated by the resulting learning curve.

Various studies, including an empirical one, have pinpointed the impact of preproduction planning on the time taken to produce the first unit and the dynamic rate resulting during the course of production. Other authors have emphasized the importance of proper preproduction planning undertaken at the initial stages to lessen the scope of improvement during the course of production, which results in a flatter function, lying considerably below one which depicts a smaller amount of preproduction planning. Bhada identifies the following factors which influence initial cost and production time, indirectly affecting the dynamic rate:

- Anticipated duration of the production run.
- Estimated rate of output.
- The type of tooling utilized.

The degree of detail presented by engineering specifications. Effort expanded on settling problems regarding manufacturing design and inspection procedures. The degree of coordination achieved between different functions within the organization. The importance given to proper working methods, planning and shop organization. The influence of experience gained on similar product and processes. The impact of preproduction planning was even demonstrated in an experiment investigating the impact of types of organization structures on complex problem solving. Note: "Groups with higher initial performance (a values) demonstrated relatively smaller indices of performance improvement than groups that began with relatively lower initial performance."

In the same vein, Abernathy and Baloff examined the supply-demand imbalances during the preproduction stage and suggested that effective and proper planning at the production marketing phase would help prevent costly imbalances because the rate of increase in productivity was different from the rate of increase in sales.

In the redesigning state of a product, the learning curve may also be used to reduce the cost and help estimate the engineering effort required to do the job. More explicitly, it can be applied to the engineering effort in repeated design passes directed towards the reduction of total cost of the first unit. Bruns presented a two-dimensional model relating the curve of the manufacturing learning improvement to the engineering learning improvement curve. Bruns shows that the unit cost depends on the engineering design as well as a manufacturing cost factor and uses the model to determine how many engineering design passes are needed to drive the product cost down to some predetermined target. The model allows reconciliation of the various approaches to new-product development where, on one side, researchers and scientists are attempting to build the first unit of some useful object at any cost, and, on the other side, engineers are trying to reduce cost while meeting given requirements. Bruns concludes:

In any event, whether engineering learning improvement is applied objectively or intuitively, this procedure warns the manager that the engineering effort to achieve a goal can vary widely, and may be beyond the range of interest or capability. New materials, processes, or designs and new personnel suggest possible reduction of costs through redesign. Conversely, experienced people and a steady technology suggest that great cost progress at small expense should not be expected.

Price Estimation

The learning curve is a study tool that can help managers understand and predict trends in cost. As such it can also be used to develop price strategies aimed at controlling market share and profitability. During phase A of, the dominant producer creates a price umbrella by keeping the price constant (or showing little decline), which may attract more producers. During phase B the price declines as a result of a price war where aggressive competitors strive for dominance. Finally, during phase C the price war is over, and a more stable and competitive situation is established among the price war survivors. The weak producers may have been eliminated or have differentiated their product.

Given that the cost function (Y) follows the pattern Y = KXb, the dominant producer may adopt a parallel stable pattern for the price function: Y1 = K1Xb, where Y1 is the average price and K1 the price of the first unit. This may discourage the entry of competitors. Although initial margins are small, final margins are usually greater.

Basically prices are set using the learning curve as an anchor. They are set at low levels with slim margins but which will generate higher sales volume and profits. The preemptive pricing strategy was successfully used by the so-called trusts of the late nineteenth century. The strategy consists of deferring the rewards and using the low prices generated on the basis of the learning curve to create a shakeout in the industry. Preemptive pricing is not successful in those situations where there is a constant need for product model changes or new-product introductions.

The following features were found to be important for an effective use of preemptive pricing:

- The expected product life is long.
- The product is standardized, like a commodity, with little risk that consumer tastes will suddenly turn against it.
- The expected growth of the market is rapid.
- The apparent slope of the learning curve is steeper, since the learning curve in that instance can constitute a substantial barrier to the entry of other firms into-the industry.
- The product is not patent protected.
- The company is not particularly strapped for cash.

A price umbrella at a high price followed by a sudden price shakeout. It is an aggressive strategy aimed at eventual industry shakeout and "brutal" elimination of competitors. Although other price patterns may exist, the predictive ability of the learning curve can be generally used as a determinant in estimating the number of labour hours required for production. This facilitates the seller's pricing of the output, of course. Thus, given a knowledge of prime costs, the labour hours determined from the learning curve can be used as an allocation base for other indirect costs. Furthermore, the buyer, aware of the learning characteristics of the seller's costs, may be willing initially to pay a higher price that is to be reduced as the supplier's production increases and its costs begin declining.

Capital Budgeting

For most companies capital budgeting is a very serious and precarious proposition, and any reduction in the uncertainty of the potential cash flow is desirable. First, in a capital budgeting situation the company is likely to be at the top of its learning curve; hence, it can derive significant labour and time savings estimates from the curve. Second, the greater the proposition of labour assembly time, the more likely the curve will explain cost behaviour. Third, the more planning the company does, the more useful will be the predictive aspects of learning curves.

As an example of the application of the learning curve, let's assume the following fictional example of the XYZ Company which is considering the investment of $50,000 in equipment having a five-year expected life and no salvage value. The investment is expected to generate a cumulative expected demand of 200 units composed of 25, 40, 60, 40, and 35 units per year for the respective five years. The required minimum rate of return is 20 per cent.

The engineering estimation led to the following costs for 200 units of production: direct material, $500; direct labour ($5 per hour for an average per unit of 100 hours), $500; variable factory overhead (50% of direct labour), $250; variable selling and administration (10% of the sales price of $2,500 per unit), $250. The total fixed costs are estimated to be $5,000 per year. Based on these data the capital budgeting analysis will proceed. It shows that a net present value in favour of production equals $6,739. The XYZ Company has, however, determined that an 80 per cent learning rate is applicable to both labour and variable overhead. It concluded that the capital budgeting analysis should instead include the correct time required as determined by the learning curve.

POSSIBLE LIMITATIONS

INFLUENCE OF CAUSAL FACTORS

Common to all the learning curve models is the need to estimate these two basic parameters:

- Input resources associated with the production of the first unit, and
- The learning curve characteristic or some measure of the rate reduction.

The exact determination of these two parameters is essential to the validity of the use of the learning curve. There are, however, factors which may affect the exact determination of these parameters. Hammer, for example, alluded to the fact that the incurring of more effort in the preproduction stage would lower the initial cost while the incurring of more resources during the production stage would increase the learning rate and cost reduction as production accumulates. Conway and Schultz attempted to categorize the factors which influence cost initially and during production.

All these factors suggest that to be useful the determination of the first piece cost of any item should be made far in advance of production.The production factors which will influence learning subsequently include the following:

- Tooling—changes during production, method of increasing capacity for increasing demand (replication or redesign of production method).
- Methods—changes during production, work simplification and similar programs, operator originated changes, method of capacity increase.
- Design Changes—degree to which manufacturing and product designs are changed to allow minor economies, specification and inspection changes as experience is gained.

- Management—improved planning, scheduling and supervision to encourage progress, increase effectiveness, diminish delays and idle time.
- Volume Changes—changes in rate or anticipated duration of production which affect other factors and decisions.
- Quality Improvements—the gradual reduction of re-work and repair operations, the reduction of scrap losses.
- Incentive Pay Plans—manner in which administered, when installed.
- Operator Learning—degree to which operations decrease time utilized in execution of a specific task.

All these factors affect the determination of the basic parameters of the learning curve and may cause the learning relationship computed to differ under various circumstances. The last factor, operator learning, has been considered by some writers to be the most important causal factor in those cases where the operator can contribute improvements in task method.

Others maintain that in most cases the tooling, flow, and methods changes are the most significant causal factors of the learning phenomenon. They result more from management effort than operator learning. A more reasoned position is that the learning curve depends equally on both factors. More precisely, this position is supported by McCampbell and McQueen, who maintain that the function is based on the following:

- The human element (man's ability to learn and improve and the elimination of direct thought-process activities through repetition).
- The natural process of methods improvements and his foreman.
- More efficient material handling, transportation, pallet moving, and so forth.
- Less percentage owed to scrap, rejection, and re-works.

MEASUREMENT AND AGGREGATION PROBLEMS

In trying to determine the parameters of the learning

curves in industrial situations, the cost analyst should beware of various measurement problems reported in the literature and in practice.

Some of these problems follow:

- The accuracy of the industrial data may be in doubt in most firms which use individual incentives such as piece rates for wage payment and control purposes. In effect such situations may create an environment in which output is restricted, actual times are seldom accurately recorded, and considerable doubt exists as to the validity of operator times charged to direct versus indirect labour accounts.
- The determination of the production count may be difficult because such factors as varying lot sizes, varying lead times, and varying schedules distort the association between costs and production quantities.
- The learning curve is generally determined for an aggregation rather than individual operations. What items to aggregate to determine the learning curve is a difficult and serious question. The aggregation may be determined following the organization of the facility and the method of production or following the inherent characteristics of operations performed and the components of the product or operation. The problems of what to aggregate may be exacerbated by the mechanics of aggregation when product is produced at different times in different lots.

NARROW UNDERSTANDING

One of the deficiencies in the learning curve literature is the narrow understanding of the causes and existence of the learning curve. The causes and existence of the learning phenomenon have been typically associated with clearing, or adaptation on the part of direct-labour workers, especially those involved in assembly. In general the contribution of engineers and indirect labour to the learning curve phenomenon has been ignored. In short, the learning phenomenon has been limited to direct labour, manual adaptation to repetitive tasks and has eliminated the machine-paced or machine-intensive manufacture. Some authors have considered the generality of the learning phenomenon and criticized the narrow understanding of the causes and existence of the learning curve. For example Baloff states: "However, the emphasis on direct-labour learning as the primary cause of the learning phenomenon and the implications for machine-intensive manufacture that have been drawn from it appear to have very limited applicability."

What Baloff was alluding to is the generally accepted thesis in a variety of machine-intensive industries that a distinct learning phenomenon occurs during the start-up or debugging of new products and new production processes. An example of the learning phenomenon in the debugging of automated processes was provided by Bright. This learning or debugging is not necessarily the result of an improvement in direct labour but more likely in direct labour, indirect labour, and technical personnel.

In these cases, it is more the effort of engineers and other indirect labour employees that generated the learning in the start-up or debugging. According to Baloff, this learning includes "such cognitive activities as redesigning the product or process, altering raw-material and end-product quality specifications, evolving more effective maintenance procedures and finding the proper operating (balance) of a manufacturing process."

PRACTICES IN ESTIMATION OF PARAMETERS

One of the major deficiencies in the learning curve literature is the dubious practice in the estimation of the *b* parameter in the learning curve model. As one may see by a cursory review of major cost account textbooks, it is the practice to simplify the parameter estimation problem by assuming that the *b* parameter retain the same constant value from start-up to start-up, *i.e.*, "empirical parameter value." Baloff calling for more empirical investigation to shake the tenacity of this unfortunate assumption states:

This is not meant to eschew the role of empirical investigation, however, for it is clear that the generalization of the learning curve techniques will ultimately depend on empirical demonstration of the phenomenon in a variety of contents. Empiricism can make a further contribution in scrutinizing such dubious practices as the constant *b* parameter value and "interminable progress" assumptions that have plagued past applications of the learning curve. In fact, evidence of the instability of the b parameter has been reported by Alchian in different airframe start-ups during World War II, Asher for a number of other postwar airframe start-ups, Conway and Schultz in the electronics industry, and Hirsh in the start-ups of machine tools.

SEPARATING THE WHEAT FROM THE CHAFF

The learning curve may be used by management as an artificial device to secure contracts and justify their cost estimates. In other words management may estimate their labour requirements with a false learning curve presumably based on empirical performance. If the contract is accepted, the learning curve-based estimates are used to prove its own existence. In other words the reduced labour became cursed by budgetary action more than by improved productivity through learning.

This artificial technique may be produced by:

- Increasing the labour content of the first unit or setting it at a very high point,
- Fluctuating labour classifications by frequently shifting the designation of workers between "direct" or "support/indirect" and hence reducing the labour content on a specific unit,
- Using manufacturing methods and tooling changes to create a reduction in the labour content, and
- Using at the start of the process small manufacturing lot sizes resulting in a high labour content for the first unit. These are some of the factors which obscure the true significance of the learning curve by causing it to reflect budgetary-and management-directed

> influence more than the increased productivity resulting from skill acquired in reflective operations. These factors which obscure the true significance of the learning phenomenon have been mostly noted to last in the aerospace industry. That industry is conducive to the use of the learning curve as an artificial device because of specific conditions in that industry that are outlined as follows: Profit is a negotiated element, dependent on cost. There is little direct incentive to reduce cost, and there is incentive to maintain a high cost level.

The basic product starts the production cycle with relatively little definition, thus requiring much rework, modification and delays and an abundance of manpower to cope with those problems. The customer may direct changes to be made that are outside of the contractor's original contract scope, and the contractor anticipates this by carrying additional personnel.

Objective manufacturing criteria generally are not used to achieve the most efficient production. Variable-type time allowances that are often the basis for staffing tend to create the appearance of a "cost reduction curve." There is customer emphasis on reduction curves which stimulates contractors to "sell" and emphasize reduction curves. Given these conditions which may also exist in other industries, the challenge to management and to other parties is to separate the wheat from the chaff and to identify the real learning curve if there is one.

ILLUSORY SAVINGS AND VERIFICATION

Illusory savings may be the result of errors in the selection of labour hour data to be used in plotting the curve. First, automation may lead to a reduction in labour input per unit. Second, a direct-labour savings may disguise a greater use of indirect labour. Third, a change in the "labour mix" through hiring more qualified workers may lead to savings in direct-labour hours and an increase in direct-labour cost. Finally, the savings in labour may be due to a change in volume rather than to learning. All this creates a problem of verification. The problem of verification pertains mainly to the possibility of obtaining inaccurate data for direct labour, and to the potential inability to isolate accurately the learning factor that led to the reduction in direct labour. As a result, the learning curve in its present state has been criticized as failing to be a "scientific tool."

NEGATIVE OR DEFEATIST ATTITUDES

The negative or defeatist attitudes of employees may act as a barrier to the implementation or acceptance of the learning curve. Attitudes which ignore, belittle, or negate the presence of learning threaten the applicability of the learning phenomenon. For the learning phenomenon to be used effectively, positive attitudes have to be generated from the employee.

Faith in the phenomenon is important. If progress is believed possible, then the learning phenomenon has a chance to occur. Open ended expectations and the absence of "ceiling psychology" are two factors most conducive to a learning effect. Some companies have been reported to have obtained more progress when the workers are not informed of the target rate. This is possible because the target set does not become a self-fulfilling prophecy. Finally, credibility in the phenomenon and its possibilities act as a major drive for its use. As Hirschmann states: If the premise is valid that learning performance can be an underlying natural characteristic, then such performance should be found not only for more types of activities already recognized as responsive, but also for operations not previously reported or believed possible. Petroleum refining is considered to have such operations. It is characterized by large investments in heavy equipment, and is so highly automated that learning is thought to be nonexistent or too small to be of value.

What Hirschmann is alluding to is progress by serendipity whereby the assumption that continual progress can occur may also create an atmosphere conducive to a learning phenomenon. He states again: Nevertheless, discovering such performance for operations previously considered unresponsive does provide additional tangible evidence that learning can be an underlying natural characteristic of organized activity. It does not merely extend the catalog of learning curves.

Instead, it can help to breed the correction that such performance should be found elsewhere, and thereby lead not only to scrutinizing all operations to see which additional ones are susceptible, but to assuming that all operations have learning curve potential and to devising ways of making this potential a reality. Thus, it is prudent to reflect learning potential in plans and forecasts. White goes further by suggesting the use of learning curve theory to predict expected improvement in advance and sets these goals as an incentive to accomplishment.

ANOMALIES IN THE LEARNING CURVE SHAPE

It is common practice to assume that improvement in direct-labour activity associated with a start-up will continue throughout the production history of the product. These assumptions are at best tenuous. For example, Asher found evidence of plateaus developing in the start-up histories of several postwar airframes produced in the United States. Similarly, Conway and Schultz found distinct steady-state conditions occurring at the end of several new product start-ups. It is generally more accepted that there are several variations to the smooth learning curve forms, mainly with respect to the start-up point. The steepness of some curves may be due to an assumed high labour requirement. For example, if the proportion of assembly work was supposed to be lower, the downward slope of the curve would not be as steep. In addition to the steepness, there may be anomalies to the learning curve shape. Hirschmann listed the following possible anomalies to the learning curve shape.

- A leveling off or a toe up may occur due to such factors as the closing of operations at the end of a contract. The costs may increase, which is a condition known in the industry as reverse learning.
- An aberration may also occur in the middle of the curve.

6

Computer Applications

USE OF COMPUTER SYSTEMS

Misuse of an automated information system is sometimes illegal, often unethical, and always reflects poor judgment or lack of care in following security rules and regulations. Misuse may, unintentionally, create security vulnerabilities or cause damage to important information. A pattern of inability or unwillingness to follow rules for the operation of computer systems raises serious concerns about an individual's reliability and trustworthiness. As we store more and more information in computer data bases, and as these data bases become more closely linked in networks, more people have broader access to more information than ever before. Computer technology has magnified many times the ability of a careless or disaffected employee to cause severe damage.

This topic discusses rules for using your computer. You should also read Computer Vulnerabilities, which describes in nontechnical language the security and other vulnerabilities of computer networks that make some of these rules necessary. Owing to the magnitude of problems that can be caused by misuse of computer systems, Misuse of Technical Information Systems is now one of the 13 criteria used in adjudicating approval and revocation of security clearances for access to classified information. Adjudicative Guidelines for Determining Access to Classified Information

Many aspects of computer use are governed by your organization's policy rather than by federal government regulation. Many government agencies and defence contractors specify the security procedures and prohibited or inappropriate activities discussed below.

SECURITY RULES

The following are basic rules for secure use of the computer:

- Do not enter into any computer system without authorization. Unauthorized entry into a protected or compartmented computer file is a serious security violation and is probably illegal. It can be a basis for revocation of your security clearance. Whether motivated by the challenge of penetrating the system or by simple curiosity to see what is there, unauthorized entry is a deliberate disregard for rules and regulations. It can cause you to be suspected of espionage. At a minimum, it violates the need-to-know principle and in some cases is an invasion of privacy.
- Do not store or process classified information on any system not explicitly approved for classified processing. See Security of Hard Drives.
- Do not attempt to circumvent or defeat security or auditing systems without prior authorization from the system administrator, other than as part of a system test or security research authorized in advance.
- Do not install any software on your computer without the approval of your system administrator.
- Do not use another individual's userid, password, or identity.
- Do not permit an unauthorized individual (including spouse, relative or friend) access to any sensitive computer network.
- Do not reveal your password to *anyone* —not even your computer system administrator.
- Do not respond to any telephone call from anyone whom you do not personally know who asks questions about your computer, how you use your computer, or about your userid or password.

- If you are the inadvertent recipient of classified material sent via e-mail or become aware of classified material on an open bulletin board or web site, you must report this to the security office.
- Do not modify or alter the operating system or configuration of any system without first obtaining permission from the owner or administrator of that system.
- Do not use your office computer system to gain unauthorized access to any other computer system.

INAPPROPRIATE USE

Many offices permit some, minimal personal use of office equipment when such personal use involves minimal expense to the organization, is performed on your personal non-work time, does not interfere with the office's mission, and does not violate standards of ethical conduct.

The following activities are considered to be misuse of office equipment:

- The creation, download, viewing, storage, copying, or transmission of sexually explicit or sexually oriented materials can cause you to be fired from your job. See discussion under E-Mail.
- Annoying or harassing another individual, for example through uninvited e-mail of a personal nature or using lewd or offensive language can cause you to be fired from your job. See discussion under E-Mail.
- Using the computer for commercial purposes or in support of "for-profit" activities or in support of other outside employment, business activity (*e.g.*, consulting for pay, sales or administration of business transactions, sale of goods or services), or gambling.
- Engaging in any outside fund-raising activity, endorsing any product or service, participating in any lobbying activity, or engaging in any prohibited partisan political activity.
- The creation, copying, transmission, or retrans-

mission of chain letters or other unauthorized mass mailings.

- Any activities that are illegal, inappropriate, or offensive to fellow employees or the public. Such activities include hate speech or material that ridicules others on the basis of race, creed, religion, colour, sex, disability, national origin, or sexual orientation.
- Use for posting office information to any external newsgroup, chat room, bulletin board, or other public forum without prior approval.
- Any personal use that could cause congestion, delay, or disruption of service to any office equipment. This includes sending pictures, video, or sound files or other large file attachments that can degrade computer network performance.
- The unauthorized acquisition, use, reproduction, transmission, or distribution of any controlled information. This includes copyrighted computer software; other copyrighted or trademarked material or material with intellectual property rights (beyond fair use); privacy information; and proprietary data or export-controlled data or software.

E-MAIL

There are two big problems with e-mail. One is increased risk of accidental security compromise. The other is sending inappropriate materials by e-mail, which has caused many people to be fired from their jobs.

SECURITY RISKS WITH E-MAIL

As a result of the Internet and e-mail, there has been a sharp increase in security incidents involving the accidental disclosure of classified and other sensitive information. One common problem occurs when individuals download a seemingly unclassified file from a classified system, and then fail to carefully review this file before sending it as an attachment to an e-mail message. Too often, the seemingly unclassified file actually has some classified material or classification markings that are not readily apparent when the file is viewed on line. Sending such material by e-mail is a security violation even if the recipient has an appropriate security clearance, as e-mail can easily be monitored by unauthorized persons. More important, even if the downloaded file really is unclassified, the electronic version of that file may have recoverable traces of classified information. This happens because data is stored in "blocks." If a file does not take up an entire block, the remainder of that block may have recoverable traces of data from other files. Your system administrator must follow an approved technical procedure for removing these traces before the file is treated as unclassified.

Some organizations have found it necessary to lock their computer drives to prevent any downloading of files from the classified system. If an individual wishes to download and retransmit an unclassified file from a classified system, the file must be downloaded and processed by the system administrator to remove electronic traces of other files before it is retransmitted.

INAPPROPRIATE MATERIALS

Sending e-mail is like sending a postcard through the mail. Just as the mailman and others have an opportunity to read a postcard, network eavesdroppers can read your e-mail as it passes through the Internet from computer to computer. E-mail is not like a telephone call, where your privacy rights are protected by law. The courts have repeatedly sided with employers who monitor their employees' e-mail or Internet use. In an American Management Association poll, 47% of major companies reported that they store and review their employees' e-mail. Organizations do this to protect themselves against lawsuits, because the organization can be held liable for abusive, harassing, or otherwise inappropriate messages sent over its computer network. In the same poll, 25% of companies reported that they have fired employees for misuse of the Internet or office e-mail.

In the past couple years, *The New York Times* fired 23 employees for exchanging off-colour e-mail. Xerox fired 40 people for inappropriate Internet use. Dow Chemical fired 24 employees and disciplined another 230 for sending or storing pornographic or violent material by e-mail. Several years ago, Chevron Corp. had to pay $2.2 million to plaintiffs who successfully brought a suit of sexual harassment, in part because an employee sent an e-mail to coworkers listing the reasons why beer is better than women.

SECURITY OF HARD DRIVES

Secrets in the computer require the same protection as secrets on paper. This is because information can be recovered from a computer hard drive even after the file has been deleted or erased by the computer user. It is estimated that about a third of the average hard drive contains information that has been "deleted" but is still recoverable. Computers on which classified information is prepared must be kept in facilities that meet specified physical security requirements for processing classified information. If necessary to prepare classified information on a computer in a non-secure environment, use a removable hard drive or laptop that is secured in an approved safe when not in use. Alternatively, use a typewriter.

Check with your security office concerning rules for traveling with a laptop on which classified or other sensitive information has been prepared. Laptop computers are a particular concern owing to their vulnerability to theft.

COMPUTER PASSWORDS

Passwords are used to authenticate an individual's right to have access to certain information. Your password is for your use only. Lending it to someone else is a security violation and may result in disciplinary action against both parties. Never disclose your password to anyone. Memorize it – do not put it in writing. If you leave your terminal unattended for any reason, log off or use a screen lock. Otherwise, someone else could use your computer to access information they are not authorized to have. You will be held responsible if someone else uses your password in connection with a system transaction. Do change your password regularly. Use a password with at least six and preferably eight characters and consisting of a mix of upper and lower case letters, numbers, and special characters such as punctuation marks This mix of various types of characters makes it more difficult for a hacker to use an automated tool called a "password cracker" to discover your password. Cracking passwords is a common means by which hackers gain unauthorized access to protected systems. For additional information on selecting a strong password and why this is so important, Passwords and the case studies in Computer Vulnerabilities.

SOCIAL ENGINEERING

"Social engineering" is hacker-speak for conning legitimate computer users into providing useful information that helps the hacker gain unauthorized access to their computer system. The hacker using social engineering usually poses as a legitimate person in the organization (maintenance technician, security officer, inexperienced computer user, VIP, etc.) and employs a plausible cover story to trick computer users into giving useful information. This is usually done by telephone, but it may also be done by forged e-mail messages or even in-person visits. Most people have an incorrect impression of computer break-ins. They think they are purely technical, the result of technical flaws in computer systems which the intruders are able to exploit. The truth is, however, that social engineering often plays a big part in helping an attacker slip through security barriers. Lack of security awareness or gullibility of computer users often provides an easy stepping stone into the protected system if the attacker has no authorized access to the system at all.

COMPUTER APPLICATIONS IN BUSINESS

Computer Applications in Business provides an overview of the integrated software packages most often used in the workplace. By the end of this course, you will have a sound understanding of the basic features and business applications for the word processor, spreadsheet, database, and presentation software in your choice of either Microsoft Works Suite or Microsoft Office Professional packages. This will teach you the basics in how to use computers to communicate. In the process of completing this course, you will also learn how to problem solve and use the Help function and online tutorial assistance for your software. Finally, as this is an online course, you will learn about using the Internet and e-mail.

DELIVERY METHOD

There is continuous enrolment for this course. Delivery is self-paced, allowing you the flexibility to proceed through the course according to your own schedule.

PREREQUISITES

None. Students will need access to a PC with full internet access and MS Office Professional (XP preferred) including Access database software or MS Works (the 2002 or newer Works 'Suite' with Word included is preferred). This course is not ideal for those using the MS Office 2007 version.

EXCLUSIONS

Students with credit for CMPT 109, 150 or a similar course may not take CMPT 119 for further credit.

OBJECTIVES

- Answer questions regarding your computer's hardware, software, and basic operations.
- Set up your computer for World Wide Web connection.
- Use e-mail to send messages and file attachments.
- Participate in on-line discussion groups.
- Describe the types of documents created with a word processing programme.
- List the principal features of a word processing programme.
- Create and format a business letter.
- Create and format a schedule containing a table.

- Design either a textual or a visual message for a public audience.
- Select and use style features to create new documents.
- Use the Help system to answer questions and troubleshoot problems.
- Describe the purposes of a spreadsheet and define its vocabulary.
- Set up and analyse itemized lists of numbers, such as the various types of budgets or financial statements.
- Perform and manipulate the calculations to achieve meaningful information.
- Present the numerical data in the spreadsheet in a graphical format.
- Conduct "what if" simulations of the numerical statements.
- Import spreadsheet reports and charts into word processing and/or database documents.
- Define the purpose of a database programme.
- Describe the components of a database.
- Plan a simple two-table database.
- Use wizards to enter and to search data, and to create a report.
- Enter data in a form.
- Merge data with a document.
- Create mailing labels.
- Analyse data in a database.
- Privacy issues related to databases.
- Plan a presentation.
- Apply good design principles to a presentation.
- Examine examples of a presentation.
- Describe the purpose of presentation software.
- Describe the components of a presentation.
- Create a presentation outline.
- Apply and modify a design template.
- Add clip art and charts to a presentation.
- Run a slide show.

Small, rural high schools are constantly trying to determine what type of computer training should be provided to students to meet the needs of business in the surrounding area. Many students in high schools today are not college bound and attempt to find local employment after graduation. Leaders in the community are also interested in retaining as many young people as possible in the area by helping them find local jobs through adequate high school training.

CHANGING FACE OF BUSINESS

Reports of shipments of personal computers to small businesses and home offices are growing at a 16% annual rate. The power of the computer, the fax machine and voice mail allow a small company to do almost anything a larger corporation does. New technology has streamlined every part of our business lives. The challenge for small firms is to apply these technologies appropriately. After investing in a computer, for example, most discover other peripherals they want to incorporate into their office systems.

The bottom line is that even small businesses can, and do, utilize computers and related technologies in their day-to-day operations. This means that even a high school graduate who does not plan to further his or her formal education should have some knowledge of computers.

In addition, it is important to bridge the gap between basic theory and computer applications.2 There is a strong correlation between high anxiety and reduced computer competence. Experience with computers in school tends to reduce anxiety on the job and leads to more productive workers. A good computer course also shows students how the computer can be utilized in many diverse fields.

IDENTIFYING SKILLS

Businesses must be periodically surveyed for information on the type of skills needed by their workers. In today's evolving world of work, required skills change as fast as the available technologies. In Nebraska, for example, the Manpower company surveyed offices from Lincoln west to the Colorado border by sending a questionnaire on office automation topics to over 2,500 businesses. The results indicated that word processing was the number one activity, using a spreadsheet was number two, and manipulating a database was number three. Lotus 1-23 was the most widely installed software. WordPerfect was the most popular word processing package, capturing 40% of those responding to their survey. Service companies were the largest number of respondents, with government second and retail/wholesale businesses third.

Previous to its decisions on what type of computers to purchase and which software packages to teach, Auburn High School needed to know similar information. They wanted to provide their students specific experience with the computers and applications being utilized by business and industry in the local geographic area. This would reassure their students that they would be employable after graduation. It would also assist the local communities by keeping young people in the area and not have them travel to find jobs elsewhere.

Upon the suggestion of Auburn's computer programming teacher, Claudette Stevens, a comprehensive survey of local area businesses was conducted in southeast Nebraska in two rural counties, Richardson and Nemaha. All of both counties' businesses were identified from the telephone book and local Chamber of Commerces, totalling 627. A random sample of 150 (approximately 25%) of these firms were contacted by telephone. All companies that were contacted agreed to answer the questions on the survey. Table 1 contains the exact numbers and results of the survey.

EXAMINING THE SURVEY RESULTS

Almost half of the small, rural businesses contacted (46%) are still not using computers. Of those using computers, over 68% said they purchased them mainly for accounting. However, most companies indicated they use computers for a variety of functions.

Surveyed companies reported using a total of 38 different software packages. The most common type of programme used was for accounting, the second most common was word processing, and the third most common software produced customer receipts. The questionnaire also dealt with the amount of knowledge new employees were expected to possess. Only one employer expected to hire a person with a bachelor's degree in computer science, and that job also required a four month period of intense training. A majority of companies expected to hire employees with basic knowledge on how to use the type of computer the firm owned. Some companies wanted potential employees to have an amount of keyboarding skills; other firms wanted general computer ability.

COMPUTER IN GOVERNMENT

LARGE-SCALE COMPUTER APPLICATIONS

Government use of computer applications need to be flexible enough to cope with holding a lot of data about the entire population of the country. Examples of government use of computer applications are public records systems, revenue collection and electronic voting.

Public Records Systems

- The Office of National Statistics holds census information on every person and household in England and Wales.
- Similarly, the General Register Office for Scotland holds census information for Scotland and the Northern Ireland Statistics and Research Agency holds census information for Northern Ireland.
- The Driver and Vehicle Licensing Agency holds records of all registered drivers and vehicles in England, Wales and Scotland.

Revenue Collection

- The U.K. Inland Revenue has one of the biggest I.T. systems in use by the U.K. government. It has to be capable of holding many years' worth of tax data for every person and company in the United Kingdom.
- If that wasn't complex enough, it has to be accessible

in real time-that is, whenever needed-to every Tax Office in the United Kingdom at the same time.

Electronic Voting (E-Voting)

- Electronic voting or e-voting is being tested, or is in use, in many countries and jurisdictions around the world.
- In the U.K., the Office of the Deputy Prime Minister hope to introducing electronic voting for general elections by about 2010, enabling citizens to vote from any polling station across the country rather than just their designated one.
- This would mean that every local authority's electoral register would have to be stored in a secure database, and on polling days every electronic polling booth would need to connect to the relevant electoral register, verify voter details and record who has voted in real time.

COMPUTER IN HEALTHCARE

INTRODUCTION

We discuss a core problem in healthcare. We indicate the technology necessary to make the transformation from partially informed 'financial' decision-making (managed costs) to better informed 'clinical' decision making (true managed care). We believe that using tools that address this core problem enable the delivery of the highest quality, lowest cost and most evidence based healthcare possible.

LANGUAGE' AS A CORE PROBLEM

To obtain information linking clinical actions to the costs of health care, clinicians and health enterprise managers require very specific tools: the computerized patient record (CPR) chief among them. But the CPR alone is insufficient, because standard methods of representing and communicating health data are missing. The complexity of the English language, which is formidable indeed, pales in comparison to the eclectic, ambiguous, redundant idiom of clinicians. The down side of the 'uncontrolled' parlance of medicine has been sharply accentuated by the computer age, because without standard vocabulary the ability to acquire knowledge about healing professions through information technology is painfully limited. The clinical applications available today have restricted utility because they cannot 'understand' each other. Today's information technology tools fail without 'controlled medical terminology' (CMT).

Christopher Chute of the Mayo clinic pointed out with elegant simplicity that for "clinical information systems to be broadly useful... comparable information...is needed.' Central to obtaining 'comparable information' is standardized language. Over the past two decades academicians have grappled with issues surrounding clinical terminology. We have learned from these efforts that there are several areas of our medical language and codes that must be integrated and managed if we are to leverage our health system information technology to benefit our profession and the health status of American society.

THE HEART OF THE PROBLEM

Despite the wide availability and acceptance of computer applications in some niches of medicine—such as lab systems that print clear reports and ICU monitors that check for irregular heart beats—the majority of these systems "know" very little about medicine. Critical knowledge, such as what should be done about a cardiac arrhythmia or unexpected lab results, still exists in the minds of practitioners and in the notes they write in patient charts. To date, healthcare IT has failed to get the knowledge into the machine.

The irony is that many of the mundane, repetitive tasks involved in caring for people can be more efficiently and securely handled by computers. Computers can do things more reliably than humans: they rarely make mistakes when they are given precise, correct instructions, and they never forget. And when they are given improved instructions they totally forget the old, inadequate methods of doing things (which we humans call habits) and move ahead. As recently highlighted by the Institute of Medicine of the National Academy of Sciences, human error and the lack of basic information are harming many people who seek aid in our healthcare system. A strong recommendation for greater reliance on technology arose from these findings. Physicians are the consummate users of medical information and health technology, so why do we fail to effectively harness the power of computers? One reason is that despite a firm understanding of how to gather clinical information and care for patients, we have used computers almost exclusively to deal with illogical rules on how to submit bills, order lab tests or document treatments in compliance with governmental or payor mandates.

Each of these practical tasks revolves around separate systems with their own codes or languages, none of which actually enhance the delivery of care nor communicate with each other. Although physicians are trained to document care and propose proper courses of treatment in 'the chart', we are unprepared to craft clinical notes to match-up with the more than 20,000 idiosyncratic billing codes.

This detraction from pure clinical thinking is but one of many reasons physicians are so unhappy with the changes in medical practice today. Add to this the fear of ungrounded malpractice claims, the barriers to efficient information transfer, the need to re-collect evidence for clinical decision making in an almost ludicrous fashion from encounter to encounter, the often poorly constructed 'report cards' based on utilization patterns rather than clinical effectiveness measurements, and one has just a preliminary grasp of the elements driving physicians to lash out at or leave their profession in droves.

At the same time, we, and the health plans we practice with, remain rightfully wary of the possibility of Medicare fraud charges because of coding errors. And despite all of the data collection and submission efforts we attend to, we still have no reliable way to recover accurate information about our efforts and efficacy because of the inherent faults of billing data sets.

CONTROLLED MEDICAL TERMINOLOGY

The Computer Based Patient Record Institute suggests that clinical terminology is: 'Standardized terms and their synonyms, which [allow one to] record patient findings, circumstances, events and interventions with sufficient detail to support clinical care, decision support, outcomes research and quality improvement; and can be efficiently mapped to broader classifications for administrative, regulatory, oversight and fiscal requirements.'

Work with existing terminologies has allowed several important observations:

- First, simple *'nomenclatures'* (lists) of terms have proven inadequate as CMT schemas because they are difficult to manage and nearly impossible to use for knowledge derivation.
- Second, *'classifications'*, which are better because they relate terms to each other in various ways, are still less robust than optimal for efficiently managing, updating and tracking term and concept changes.
- Third, *'knowledge based ontologies*, in which concepts and their terms are strictly defined and related to each other based on their definitions, seem to be best suited to accomplishing the controlled medical terminology task.

Ontologies provide a human readable yet machine processable conceptual framework that diverse computer systems may utilize for purposes of interoperability. A seamless bridge is built from our 'words' to the abstract concepts they represent in the computer. Note how closely such an approach approximates the dictum that 'the core utility of any language is to represent concepts by terms or words with meanings that are commonly understood.'

SOFTWARE TOOLS TO MANAGE CMT

Controlled medical terminology is optimally modeled and updated in knowledge-based 'ontologies'. A 'lexical runtime engine', formerly called a vocabulary server (VOSER), then serves up the relevant vocabulary to users of applications in the clinical environment. The ontology, housed in a lexicon *model,* implies the existence of a data structure that supports both the maintenance and use of controlled vocabulary data. The model is accessed via a *modeling environment,* which can be simple or complex. The measure of a modeling environment is simply its ability to convey the information contained within the model to its users.

Some of the core facilities provided by a modeling environment include:

- *Browsing*: A user interface for looking through the lexicon and moving from concept to concept in a logical fashion.
- *Searching*: Finding and navigating directly to a desired spot in the knowledge model without having "know where it is" at the start. A robust search interface allows rapid navigation to needed information.
- *Editing*: Making manual and or/bulk changes to the existing vocabulary for the purposes of local requirements. Editing systems should have some form of security to ensure the integrity of the underlying knowledge model.
- *Configuration Management and version control*: As changes are made to the lexicon, careful tracking of the changes is important.
- *List management*: While the vocabulary must be very rich in content as a whole, the user or application may only need or want a select portion of the 100,000+ concepts at a time. Lists are used to accomplish this task.

What is Wrong with the Billing Codes We Use Now

Attempts to cross map, catalogue, and unify medical terminology have occurred historically, resulting in multiple 'right' clinical vocabularies. Medicine ultimately found itself infiltrated by proprietary and diverging sets of 'standard vocabularies', some in the form of nomenclatures and others as classifications. Today there are over 100 vocabulary sets defined internationally for some purpose, and in the United States institutions must deal with from 5-10 of them just to meet reporting or reimbursement requirements!

In 1968, at the behest of the Department of Health and Human Services, the United States adopted ICD as the 'official code set', and realizing it was woefully inadequate, set about creating ICD-CM (Clinical Modifications). Third party insurers followed suit, but stirred in the equally inadequate CPT codes as requirements for clinical service reimbursement.

These chosen schemes, detailed below, lack accuracy, precision and cognitive coherence. But since the actual communication and documentation of care were largely unaffected by the new add-on coding regulations, clinical professionals swallowed hard and closed their eyes to the downstream effects such derisory coding schemes would have on their professional lives.

Progressive healthcare information system developers knew that billing codes were inadequate for electronic clinical documentation and that precise medical words were needed if analysis of information from automated medical records was to improve quality and service in healthcare. Rather than gravitate towards any existing clinical vocabulary standard, they elected to create their own 'dictionaries' or 'vocabulary sets'. Their methods represented an improvement over completely un-encoded or free text documentation (which is still the norm in many computer based patient records), but each vendor, working in isolation, created a terminology which could not be read or understood by other vendor systems. Thus the potential of data exchange and aggregation was impossible. Managing these highly proprietary code sets, and then trying to compare information gathered in one system to data from another proved quite expectedly problematic.

- *Code Set*: Diagnosis coding systems
  - *Overview*: ICD versions are *classifications*, thus one code typically represents a category into which several diseases may be mapped. There are several consequences of this arrangement: Large numbers of categories are too broad to be

clinically useful. A significant amount of clinical detail is lost when a paper-based medical record is coded, and the only way to retrieve the level of detail in the medical record is to review the chart manually (an expensive and time consuming task). ICD contains many ambiguous and redundant catch-all categories. The combination categories make the process of information retrieval using ICD codes extraordinarily complex. *Designing searches in systems with combination categories is a nightmare*

- *Code Set*: Procedure coding systems
  - *Overview*: There are three procedure-coding systems in use in the United States. They are volume 3 of ICD-9-CM, the American Medical Association's (AMA) Current Procedural Terminology (CPT), and the Health Care Financing Administration's Common Procedure Coding System (HCPCS). These systems have all of the weaknesses of the diagnosis coding systems discussed above.
- *Code Set*: Ambulatory Patient Classification (APC)
  - *Overview*: The APC is made up of groups of procedures such that the services within each group have comparable resource usage and are clinically similar. It is obvious that APC was developed and is best suited for billing. With CPT/HCPCS codes as elements, APC has the same shortcomings as those terminologies have, with the added burden of having been reorganized to fit a particular need, that of being a method for the calculation of payments.
- *Code Set*: UMLS
  - *Overview*: The Unified Medical Language System (UMLS) was developed by the National Library of Medicine (NLM) in an attempt to relate disparate medical vocabularies and facilitate the sharing of medical knowledge across information

systems. While initial efforts were directed at providing a linguistic framework for integrating clinical knowledge, additions covering more arcane coding systems have complemented its content, and now, the 11th edition of the UMLS Metathesaurus contains more than 60 source vocabularies. The UMLS Metathesaurus is a coding and language support tool, rather than a coding system per se; it was never intended as a common vocabulary for clinical use.

- *Code Set*: SNOMED and SNOMED-RT (Systematized Nomenclature of Medicine, with RT referring to 'Reference Terminology')
  – *Overview*: Under development by the College of American Pathology (CAP) for more than 30 years, SNOMED contains the best overall coverage of clinical content. The underlying granularity of SNOMED-RT allows expressiveness, and the organization of these granular terms into hierarchies with logical relationships, provides the basis for computational categorization and management of the vocabulary based on strict concept definitions. The heart of SNOMED-RT is its breadth of terminological coverage, its logical classification system, and its compositional nature based upon medically relevant and granular concept elements.
- *Code Set*: Logical Observation Identifier Names and Codes (LOINC)
  – *Overview*: LOINC is an example of how a modern, concept-based terminology can solve system integration problems and thus find widespread acceptance in the healthcare IT community. LOINC provides a set of standard codes for observations made by providers during the process of care. By far, its largest and most important domain is that of laboratory :ests, but it also includes such clinical observations such

as vital signs, intake and output measurements, temperature, EKG tracing measurements, and echocardiogram measurements.

- *Code Set*: Consumer Terminology
  - *Overview*: The need for a consumer-oriented terminology has been debated. When patients are able to access their clinical records online can the problem list, treatment plan and test results be represented in a way that is understandable to them? What happens when patients begin to use online applications that allow them? Will consumers be able to self-report their own health history in a way that is clinically acceptable? Will this information be machine-readable and linked to accepted clinical terminologies? With the new Internet-enabled e-Health environment, patients are realizing the promise of access to health records, access to insurance information, access to credible health content, and greater clinical and billing efficiency. In order to enable greater patient participation, however, the words of the patient must be treated with as much respect as the words of the health care professional.

CONTROLLED MEDICAL TERMINOLOGY AND CLINICAL INFONOMICS

The term *clinical infonomics* implies a new science in which care practices, health informatics and national economics are finally recognized as inseparable. Healthcare delivery is reliant on information technology because clinical decision-making, as well as the reengineering of business and clinical processes, depends on the immediate availability of current accurate information about patients, diseases and populations.

In fact, information technology, along with strong clinical leadership, are key to bringing about a badly needed shift in the entire care delivery system from one based on *cost*, to one based on *value*.

Never before have tools existed that could verify, validate, or debunk treatments, narrow practice variation to a more cost-effective mean, allow discovery and communication of optimal methods of diagnosis or therapy and literally *prove* the value of clinical interventions.

Iatrogenic injury has received a great deal of attention lately. During hospitalization in the US it is estimated that as many as a third of patients suffer from complications related to their care ; between 5% and 13% of hospital admissions result from the adverse effects of diagnosis or treatment , and some 70% of iatrogenic complications affecting more than 1.3 million hospitalized patients annually are preventable!

There are from 44,000 to 180,000 treatment related deaths in hospitals every year and of life threatening/serious adverse drug events, the most common failures relating to these errors are system errors involving drug knowledge dissemination, drug dosing, patient identity checking and patient information availability, suggesting inadequate systems, rather than individual inadequacy, as causes for error. In a survey of attendees conducted at the 2000 Healthcare Information Management and Systems Society, it was discovered that a startling 98% of respondents believed that controlled medical terminology would be important to mitigation of iatrogenic mishaps.

AS CARE PROVIDERS HOW DOES CMT BENEFIT US

Benefits include faster, more accurate billing, more informed patient management, faster, clearer and more precise documentation (the ultimate in 'decision support'), lower malpractice premiums and improved knowledge. We cannot develop nor exercise the ability to move healthcare forward, as clinicians or administrators, without the informatics tools, language and communication standards outlined above.

Without technology that "listens to and understands us" we cannot act in accordance with evidence based guidelines and principles, narrow practice variation and improve knowledge of appropriate and cost-effective techniques for managing health.

SO WHAT CAN ONE DO

The tools and language content sets exist today to help with this problem, but unless *controlled medical terminology* and the informatics infrastructure suggested above are widely embraced, we cannot possibly make good decisions about whether interventions are in a range of from 'possibly beneficial' to 'highly indicated', determine *physiologic from biologic outcomes* based on measurements, or assess clinician assessment versus patients perceived*health outcomes* (including pain, suffering, disfigurement, disability). Without a common language we cannot improve the quality of healthcare, no matter how many times we say the words, nor even approach evidence based medicine on anything but a microcosmic scale.

To get there, the steps one can take as an individual are relatively simple:

- Insist that clinical computing systems to be purchased for your ambulatory or in-patient environments be based upon a *controlled medical terminology*, (not 'our' standard terminology); and one which meets the requirements of good CMT.
- Seek greater understanding of the clinical systems that are being purchased for use by your group, because they are not going away; they are enormously helpful once you get over the initial fear of using them, and if you insist that they collect good information they will be tools you can use rather than weapons that can be used against you.
- Become familiar with E-mail interactions and the formalities surrounding them because they will become a norm in the future, and even a billable one at that , but do NOT become comfortable with the fact that these 'un-encoded' communications are sufficient, for all the same reasons un-encoded information in the medical record are insufficient.
- Don't be afraid of the change, in either the technology or the language. Having lived through it, and having helped many clinicians through the transition, we know it can be done to our own great advantage,

and to the benefit of healthcare in the United States population in entirety.

Without CMT-enabled health informatics technology we are 'sewing in the dark'; we have no standard methods for evaluating either our work or the preferences of our patients. Controlled medical terminology essentially 'turns on the lights'. Failing to move this direction with our language and information technology dooms us to control by those who have more data, but far less knowledge.

COMPUTER APPLICATIONS IN EDUCATION

A computer helps to manipulate data according to a list of instructions, called a programme. It can save a lot of data and produce the same, instantly. It is also called a universal information-processing machine. It is a common operating system used in corporate businesses, educational organizations and many research programmes. The computer technology has been used proficiently in various educational fields. There are many professional courses that programme their curriculum on computers.

It enables the students and teachers to methodically study or conduct classes. Most schools highlight the importance of computer education. They provide computer education to children, at a very young age. It helps them to learn and develop interest in the basics of computers. The main purpose is to make them comfortable using the system, as the future holds a bright promise for the technology. Many students become proficient and plan to pursue careers in the world of computers.

Computers are used in running school and college administrations, during the admission procedures, storing of official and student records. They are also used in syllabus planning and decision-making, controlling, assisting instructions and simulation. Computers are helpful in directing aptitude tests and achievement tests, at the time of entrance exams.

There is computer software designed to process performances related to teachers and employees promotion avenues. They also process records of salaries, examinations, schemes of examination, printing of papers and question papers, evaluation of answer sheets, mark sheets and certificates. Computers are used in colleges, by the professors, to conduct special classes and enable their students to adopt a methodical way of study. Students take more interest in the documented programmes, designed on different topics. Internet has provided a favourable means of pursuing courses from renowned universities, across the world. These facilities become available at a click of the mouse.

Computer Education provides detailed information on Computer Education, Computer Education Online, Computer Science Education, Computer Education Institute and more. Computer Education is affiliated with Computer Graphic Training. Over the years apprenticeship has undergone a desperate change. Acceptance accept confused from cardboard assignment to computer applications and Internet. In abounding of the educational institutions, acceptance assignment on apriorism or projects appliance desktop software. They abide these to advisers as e-mail accessories or hard-copy documents. Assorted computer programmes and applications are acclimated for authoritative presentations, projects, research, publication, etc. Nowadays a apprentice learns to address web pages, resumes, cards, newsletters, etc. with the use of computer systems. Various applications and accoutrement accept been alien by the advice technology. They accept revolutionized communication, abundance and accord amid agents and students. For instance, web conferencing, online chat processing, book administration are few such solutions. They accept enabled users to actualize and allotment documents. Coordination from anywhere is additionally possible. It facilitates teaching and learning. Acceptance additionally use assorted accoutrement like, PDF Software. It helps them to catechumen a Power Point, Excel or Chat book to Pdf book or carnality versa.

It is acclimated for presentations, thesis, etc. It is acclimated back absolute argument in one architecture has to be adapted into addition format. In this conversion, layout, style, graphics, images, etc. abide intact. The accoutrement are either chargeless or accept a price. If they appear with a amount they are affordable. Technical barriers are attenuated which helps acceptance and agents to coact with anniversary other. The acceptance additionally go for online learning. There are assorted online courses, tutorials and examinations. The online acquirements is an accessible to use tool. It has boundless accessibility and able features. The affection of the assignment gets bigger as able-bodied as the akin of cerebral engagement. The educators accommodate in abyss revisions and comments. With the use of chat processing the affection of apprentice autograph has improved. It is because acceptance tend to address added and get authentic end notes.

THINKING ABOUT SECURING YOUR HOME COMPUTER

Before diving into the tasks you need to do to secure your home computer, let's first think about the problem by relating it to something you already know how to do. In this way, you can apply your experience to this new area. So, think of your computer as you would your house, your apartment, or your condo. What do you know about how that living space works, what do you routinely do to keep it secure, and what have you installed to improve its security? (We'll use this "computer-is-like-a-house-and-the-things-in-it" analogy throughout, departing only a few times to make a point.)

For example, you know that if you have a loud conversation, folks outside your space can probably hear you. You also routinely lock the doors and close the windows when you leave, and you don't give the keys to just anyone. Some of you may install a security system to complement your practices. All of these are part of living in your home.

Let's now apply similar thinking to your home computer. E-mail, *instant messaging*, and most web traffic go across the Internet *in the clear*; that is, anyone who can capture that information can read it. These are *things you ought to know*. You should always select and use strong passwords and exercise due care when reading all e-mail, especially the unsolicited variety. *These are things you ought to do*. Finally, you can add a *firewall*, an anti-virus programme, *patches*, and file encryption to improve the level of security on your home computer, and we'll call these *things you ought to install*. The rest of this document describes the things you ought to know, do, and install to improve the security of your home computer.

THINGS YOU OUGHT TO KNOW

One starting point for solving home computer security problems is being aware of how the Internet and some of its technologies work. If you know how they work, you can evaluate solutions to the problems that come up. You can also use the Internet more safely and responsibly. In this section, we'll talk about two topics: trust and information in the clear as it crosses the Internet.

Trust

Human beings are trusting by nature. We trust much of what we hear on the radio, see on television, and read in the newspaper. We trust the labels on packages. We trust the mail we receive. We trust our parents, our partner or spouse, and our children. We trust our co-workers. In fact, those who don't trust much are thought to be cynical. Their opinions may be all too quickly ignored or dismissed.

The Internet was built on trust.[1] Back in the mid 1960s, computers were very expensive and slow by today's standards, but still quite useful. To share the expensive and scarce computers installed around the country, the U.S. government funded a research project to connect these computers together so that other researchers could use them remotely. This project was called the *Arpanet,* named after the government research agency – ARPA, the Advanced Research Projects Agency – that funded and managed the project.

Key to the ARPAnet was the level of trust placed in its users; there was little thought given to malicious activity. Computers communicated using a straightforward scheme that relied on everybody playing by the rules. The idea was to make sharing ideas and resources easy and as efficient as the technology of the day provided. This philosophy of trust colours many of the practices, procedures, and technologies that are still in place today. Only within the last few years, when Internet commerce (known as *e-commerce*) began to spread, it has become inadequate to rely principally on trust. Since the days of the ARPAnet, we've changed the way we use computer networks while others have changed the underlying technologies, all in an attempt to improve the security of the Internet and the trust we place on it.

Let's dig deeper into two examples of what we trust in our daily lives. When you receive mail through the post office, many envelopes and the letters in them contain the sender's address. Have you ever wondered if those addresses were valid; that is, do they match the address of the person or persons who really sent them? While you could check to see that those addresses are valid and refer to the person they name, it's not an easy task. How would you go about it? Would you call the phone number provided with the letter? That number could also be invalid, and the person that answers the phone could be as misleading as the original address. Perhaps you could call directory assistance or the police department that has jurisdiction over the town where the letter was supposedly from. They might be helpful, but that is likely to take lots of time. Most people wouldn't bother.

And it's not just return addresses either. How about advertisements, news stories, or the information printed on groceries? Suppose you were on a low-fat diet. You'd want to buy foods low in fat. To select the right foods, you'd read the product label at the grocery store. How do you know that the label information is valid? What's to say it's not forged? And how would you know? The Internet has many of the same issues, and e-mail is one of the best examples. In an e-mail message, an intruder can easily fabricate where the came from. But this information forging – called *spoofing* by intruders and security professionals – is not limited to just e-mail. In fact, the basic unit of information transferred on the Internet – called a *packet* – can also be easily forged or spoofed. What does this mean and why should you care? It means that any information you receive from some other computer on the Internet should not be trusted automatically and unconditionally. When you trust an e-mail message that turns out to have a harmful virus attached to it, your computer can be infected, your *files* destroyed, and your work lost. And that's why you should care. This is how the Internet works. It was built on trust. Over time, there have been technological changes that are worthy of a higher level of our trust than before. Nonetheless, a true sense of insecurity is better than a false sense of security. So, think about the information you trust. Be critical and cautious.

Information in the Clear

When you have a conversation with someone in your living space, everybody within earshot can hear the words and probably understand them. If your conversation is especially loud and your windows open, even passersby can hear. If you want privacy, you and your conversation partner need to go to another room and close the doors and windows.

The Internet works much the same way, except the room is much, much bigger. When you send e-mail, browse a web site, or chat online with someone, the conversation between you and that person does not go directly from your computer to his or her computer. Instead, it goes from your computer to another computer to still another computer and so on, eventually reaching his or her computer. Think of all of these computers as an Internet "room." Anyone, or, more accurately, any programme, in that Internet room that can hear that conversation can also probably understand it. Why? Because just like the conversation at home, most Internet conversations are in the clear, meaning that the information exchanged between computer systems is not concealed or hidden in any way.

Again, this is how the Internet works. You need to know that the information sent across the Internet may be at *risk* of others listening in, capturing what you send, and using it for their own benefit. Later, we'll talk about encryption as a way to address this problem. Encryption uses mathematics to conceal information. There are many programmes you can install to encrypt the information you send across the Internet.

WHAT SHOULD I DO TO SECURE MY HOME COMPUTER

Securing your home computer is not a trivial task. There are many topics to consider and many steps to follow. They take time to learn and do. If you can, read this entire document before you begin to secure your computer. You'll have a better understanding of the effort and all its facets. This ought to help you when you begin to tackle the tasks described here.

In the next part of this document, we describe two types of activities. Some you can do using the programmes that came with your computer: working with *passwords* and e-mail attachments, running programmes, and *backing up* your work. For other activities, you might need to obtain some specialized programmes: applying patches, and running anti-virus, firewall, and file encryption programmes. Though some vendors' products provide these features, we'll assume your computer doesn't have any of them so you'll need to add all of them. Here then is the list of tasks you need to do to secure your home computer. Their order is based on how intruders attack computers, beginning with the most-often used attack methods. By starting with the lower numbered tasks, you address the biggest problems you face in securing your home computer. Remember that most sections end with a reference to a web site that you can use to find an example of how to do the task on a Microsoft Windows 2000 computer.

INSTALL AND USE ANTI-VIRUS PROGRAMMES

If someone rang your doorbell and wanted to come into your living space to sell you something or to use your telephone, you'd need to make a decision whether or not to let them in. If they were a neighbour or someone you knew, you'd probably let them in. If you didn't know them but believed their story and found them to be otherwise acceptable, say they were neat and clean and not threatening, you'd probably also let them in, but you'd watch them closely while they were in your space. What are you doing here? You are profiling this person and then deciding what to do based on that profile. It's your responsibility to be concerned about who enters your living space. Further, if you have children, you've probably also taught them how to deal with strangers who come to your door.

Anti-virus programmes work much the same way. These programmes look at the contents of each file, searching for specific patterns that match a profile – called a *virus signature* – of something known to be harmful. For each file that matches a signature, the anti-virus programme typically provides several options on how to respond, such as removing the offending patterns or destroying the file. To understand how anti-virus programmes work, think about scam artists – people who visit your home to try to get you to buy a phony product or service, or to let them in. Once inside, they may try to steal your valuables or try to harm you in some way.

There are a variety of ways you might find out about a specific scam artist lurking in your neighbourhood. Perhaps you see a television report or read a newspaper article about them. They might include pictures and excerpts of the story the scam artist uses to scam their victims. The news report gives you a profile of someone you need to be on the lookout for. You watch for that person until either the story fades away or you hear that they've been caught. Anti-virus programmes work much the same way. When the anti-virus programme vendors learn about a new virus, they provide an updated set of virus signatures that include that new one. Through features provided by the updated anti-virus programme, your home computer also automatically learns of this new virus and begins checking each file for it, along with checking for all the older viruses. However, unlike scam artists, viruses never completely fade away. Their signatures remain part of the master version of all virus signatures.

Suppose a scam artist was at your front door. What would you do? Perhaps you'd not encourage them to come in nor buy their product but, at the same time, you'd try not to upset them. You'd politely listen to their story and then send them on their way. After you closed the door, you may call the police or the telephone number given in the report that initially brought them to your attention. With viruses, you often have the chance to react to them when they've been discovered on your home computer. Depending upon the specific characteristics of the virus, you might be able to clean the infected file. Or you might be forced to destroy the file and load a new copy from your backups or original distribution *media*. Your options depend upon your choice of anti-virus programme and the virus that's been detected.

In your living space, you look at those who come to your door and you look at what you receive in the mail. These are two of the ways that items can get into your living space, so you examine them, sometimes closely, sometimes not. Viruses can reach your computer in many ways, through floppy disks, *CD-ROMs*, e-mail, web sites, and *downloaded* files. All need to be checked for viruses each time you use them. In other words, when you insert a floppy disk into the drive, check it for viruses. When you receive e-mail, check it for viruses (remember to use the KRESV tests described in Task 3- *Use Care When Reading E-mail with Attachments*). When you download a file from the Internet, check it for viruses before using it. Your anti-virus programme may let you specify all of these as places to check for viruses each time you operate on them. Your anti-virus programme may also do this automatically. All you need to do is to open or run the file to cause it to be checked.

Just as you walk around your living space to see if everything is OK, you also need to "walk" around your home computer to see if there are any viruses lurking about. Most anti-virus programmes let you schedule periodic exams of all files on your home computer on a regular basis, daily for example. If you leave your computer turned on over night, think about scheduling a full-system review during that time. Some anti-virus programmes have more advanced features that extend their recognition capabilities beyond virus signatures. Sometimes a file won't match any of the known signatures, but it may have some of the characteristics of a virus. This is comparable to getting that "there's something not quite right here, so I'm not going to let them in" feeling as you greet someone at your door. These *heuristic*tests, as they're called, help you to keep up with new viruses that aren't yet defined in your list of virus signatures. An anti-virus programme is frequently an add-on to your home computer, though your newly purchased computer might include a trial version. At some point, say after 60 days, you must purchase it to continue using it.

To decide whether to make that purchase or to look elsewhere, use these steps for evaluating anti-virus programmes:

- *The Demand test*: Can you check a file on demand, for example, when you want to send an attachment as part of the KRESV tests?
- *The Update test*: Can you update the virus signatures automatically? Daily is best.
- *The Respond test*: What are all the ways that you can respond to an infected file? Can the virus checker clean a file?
- *The Check test*: Can you check every file that gets to your home computer, no matter how it gets there, and can those checks be automated?
- *The Heuristics test*: Does the virus checker do heuristics tests? How are these defined?

These tests – the DURCH tests – help you compare anti-virus programmes. Once you've made your selection, install it and use all of its capabilities all of the time. Intruders are the most successful in attacking all computers – not just home computers – when they use viruses and *worms*. Installing an anti-virus programme and keeping it up to date is among the best defences for your home computer. If your financial resources are limited, they are better spent purchasing a commercial anti-virus programme than anything else.

- Use a Checklist to help you think anti-virus issues.
- *Example: Operating an Anti-Virus Programme.*

KEEP YOUR SYSTEM PATCHED

If one of your appliances broke, you'd probably try to have

it repaired. You'd call a repairperson whom you hope could do the job. You'd get an estimate and then you'd either get it fixed or replace it. Your goal is to somehow restore the functions that the appliance provides. What do you do when a software "appliance" – a programme – or the *operating system* itself breaks? How do you restore the functions that they provide? Do you know whom to call or even where to look to determine what to do next?

Most vendors provide patches that are supposed to fix *bugs* in their products. Frequently these patches do what they're supposed to do. However, sometimes a patch fixes one problem but causes another. For example, did you ever have a repairperson fix an appliance but in the process, they scratched the floor or damaged a countertop during their visit? For a computer, the repair cycle might have to be repeated until a patch completely fixes a problem. Vendors often provide free patches on their web sites. When you purchase programmes, it's a good idea to see if and how the vendor supplies patches, and if and how they provide a way to ask questions about their products. Just as appliance vendors often sell extended warranties for their products, some software vendors may also sell support for theirs. Have you ever received a recall notice for your car or another product you've purchased? Vendors send these notices to product owners when a safety-related problem has been discovered. Registering your purchase through the warranty card gives the vendor the information they need to contact you if there is a recall. Programme vendors also provide a recall-like service. You can receive patch notices through e-mail by subscribing to mailing lists operated by the programs' vendors. Through this type of service, you can learn about problems with your computer even before you discover them and, hopefully, before intruders have the chance to exploit them. Consult the vendor's web site to see how to get e-mail notices about patches as soon as they're available.

Some vendors have gone beyond mailing lists. They provide programmes bundled with their systems that automatically contact their web sites looking for patches specifically for your home computer. These automatic updates tell you when patches are available, download them, and even install them. You can tailor the update features to do only want you want, such as just telling you something new is waiting but doing nothing more. While the patching process is getting easier, even to the point where it can be completely automated, it is not yet foolproof. In some cases, installing a patch can cause another seemingly unrelated programme to break. The challenge is to do as much homework as you can to learn what a patch is supposed to do and what problems it might cause once you've installed it.

This is a hard job. Often, the vendors don't tell you about problems their patches can cause. Why? Because it is simply impossible to test all possible programmes with all possible patches to discover unexpected side effects. Imagine doing that job and then continuing to do that for each new programme and patch that comes along. Vendors rely on their customers to tell them when something unexpected happens once a patch is installed. So, if this happens to you, let them know. Imagine then that you've either found a patch on the vendor's site or you've received notice that a patch is available. What do you do next?

Follow the steps below to evaluate a patch before you install it:

- *The Affected test*: Does this patch affect one of the programmes on your computer? If it doesn't affect your computer, you're done. Whew!
- *The Break test*: Can you tell from the vendor's web site or the patch's description if installing it breaks something else that you care about? If installation does break something, then you have to decide how to proceed. Try notifying the vendor of the programme that might break to learn what their strategy is for addressing this problem. Also, use your web browser to learn if anyone else has experienced this problem and what he or she did about it.
- *The Undo test*: Can you undo the patch? That is, can you restore your computer to the way it was before

you installed the patch? Currently, vendors are building most patches with an uninstall feature that enables you to remove a patch that has unwanted consequences. In addition, some computers also come with features that help you restore them to a previously known and working state should there be a problem. You need to know what your computer provides so that you can undo a patch if necessary.

Recall from the *Introduction* that intruders exploit vulnerabilities to gain access to home computers. How do intruders find out about these vulnerabilities? In many cases, they read the same vendor mailing lists and use the same automatic notification schemes that you use.

This means that you need to evaluate and install patches on your home computer as soon as they're available. The longer a vulnerability is known, the greater the chances are that an intruder will find it on your home computer and exploit it. With the ABU tests, you can quickly evaluate and install patches to keep intruders off your home computer.

One last thing: patches are usually distributed as programmes. This means that you need to use the DCAL steps described in before loading and installing a patch. Intruders often take advantage of vulnerabilities wherever they may be. In many cases, the vulnerabilities they exploit may have patches, but those patches were not installed.

For your home computer, make time to keep your programmes patched wherever possible. If you can't patch a programme, shop around for an equivalent programme and use it until the original programme is fixed or you've abandoned it in favour of something more reliable.

You can spend money on maintenance where you get patches for programmes, but that's usually not necessary. Since most vendors provide free patches, mailing lists, and automatic updates, keeping your computer patched usually only costs you time.

- Use a Worksheet to record your important patch information.
- *Example: Installing Patches.*

CARE WHILE READING E-MAIL

We've all heard stories about people receiving an item in the mail that in some way caused them harm. We've heard of letter bombs and exploding packages, and in 2001, we learned about Anthrax-laden letters. Although their frequency is low, they do make news. These unsolicited items are sent to unsuspecting recipients. They may contain a return address, a provocative envelope, or something else that encourages its receiver to open it. This technique is called *social engineering*. Because we are trusting and curious, social engineering is often effective.

In the case of the Anthrax letters addressed to United States senators, the envelopes contained a school's return address as an inducement to open them. What government official wouldn't want to serve their constituency by reading and responding to a letter supposedly sent by a class at a school, especially an elementary school? By opening the letter and subsequently spreading its lethal contents, the recipient complied with the wishes of the sender, a key foundation of social engineering. In the pre-Anthrax letter days, a mail handler might have given little thought to the contents of the letter or the validity of the return address. Those days are behind us.

You probably receive lots of mail each day, much of it unsolicited and containing unfamiliar but plausible return addresses. Some of this mail uses social engineering to tell you of a contest that you may have won or the details of a product that you might like. The sender is trying to encourage you to open the letter, read its contents, and interact with them in some way that is financially beneficial – to them. Even today, many of us open letters to learn what we've won or what fantastic deal awaits us. Since there are few consequences, there's no harm in opening them.

E-mail-borne viruses and worms operate much the same way, except there are consequences, sometimes significant ones. Malicious e-mail often contains a return address of someone we know and often has a provocative Subject line. This is social engineering at its finest – something we want to read from someone we know. E-mail viruses and worms are fairly common. If you've not received one, chances are you will. Here are steps you can use to help you decide what to do with every e-mail message with an attachment that you receive. You should only read a message that passes all of these tests.

- *The Know test*: Is the e-mail from someone that you know?
- *The Received test*: Have you received e-mail from this sender before?
- *The Expect test*: Were you expecting e-mail with an attachment from this sender?
- *The Sense test*: Does e-mail from the sender with the contents as described in the Subject line and the name of the attachment(s) make sense? For example, would you expect the sender – let's say your Mother – to send you an e-mail message with the Subject line "Here you have,;o)" that contains a message with attachment – let's say AnnaKournikova.jpg.vbs? A message like that probably doesn't make sense. In fact, it happens to be an instance of the Anna Kournikova worm, and reading it can damage your system.
- *The Virus test*: Does this e-mail contain a virus? To determine this, you need to install and use an anti-virus programme. That task is described in *Install and Use Anti-Virus Programmes.*

You should apply these five tests -- KRESV – to every piece of e-mail with an attachment that you receive. If any test fails, toss that e-mail. If they all pass, then you still need to exercise care and watch for unexpected results as you read it.

Now, given the KRESV tests, imagine that you want to send e-mail with an attachment to someone with whom you've never corresponded – what should you do? Here's a set of steps to follow to begin an e-mail dialogue with someone.

- Since the recipient doesn't already Know you, you need to send them an introductory e-mail. It must not contain an attachment. Basically, you're introducing yourself and asking their permission to send e-mail with an attachment that they may otherwise be suspicious of. Tell them who you are, what you'd like to do, and ask for permission to continue.

- This introductory e-mail qualifies as the mail Received from you.
- Hopefully, they'll respond; and if they do, honour their wishes. If they choose not to receive e-mail with an attachment from you, don't send one. If you never hear from them, try your introductory e-mail one more time.
- If they accept your offer to receive e-mail with an attachment, send it off. They will Know you and will have Received e-mail from you before. They will also Expect this e-mail with an attachment, so you've satisfied the first three requirements of the KRESV tests.
- Whatever you send should make Sense to them. Don't use a provocative Subject line or any other social engineering practice to encourage them to read your e-mail.
- Check the attachments for Viruses. This is again based on having virus-checking programmes, and we'll discuss that later.

The KRESV tests help you focus on the most important issues when sending and receiving e-mail with attachments. Use it every time you send e-mail, but be aware that there is no foolproof scheme for working with e-mail, or security in general.

You still need to exercise care. While an anti-virus programme alerts you to many viruses that may find their way to your home computer, there will always be a lag between when a virus is discovered and when anti-virus programme vendors provide the new virus signature. This means that you shouldn't rely entirely on your anti-virus programmes. You must continue to exercise care when reading e-mail.

- Use a checklist to help you make decisions about opening e-mail attachments.

USE A FIREWALL PROGRAMME

This section describes a firewall, its importance to your home computer strategy, and a way to think about the job you need to do. We're going to depart from our "computer-is-like-a-house-and-the-things-in-it" analogy to use another that you are probably also familiar with: an office building. Have you ever visited a business where you first stopped at the reception desk to interact with a security guard? That guard's job is to assess everybody who wishes to enter or leave the building to decide if they should continue on or be stopped. The guard keeps the unwanted out and permits only appropriate people and objects to enter and leave the business's premises.

Let's dig deeper into this analogy. When someone enters a building, the security guard usually greets them. If they have an appropriate identification badge, they show it to the guard or swipe it through a reader. If all is OK, they pass through the guard's checkpoint. However, if something's wrong or if they are a visitor, they must first stop at the guard desk. The guard asks whom they wish to see. The guard may also ask for identification such as a driver's license or their company ID. The guard reviews the list of expected guests to see if this person is approved to visit the party in question. If the guard decides everything is all right, the visitor may pass. The visitor usually signs a logbook with their name, the company they represent, whom they are seeing, and the time of day.

On a computer, the firewall acts much like a guard when it looks at network traffic destined for or received from another computer. The firewall determines if that traffic should continue on to its destination or be stopped. The firewall "guard" is important because it keeps the unwanted out and permits only appropriate traffic to enter and leave the computer. To do this job, the firewall has to look at every piece of information – every packet – that tries to enter or leave a computer. Each packet is labeled with where it came from and where it wants to go. Some packets are allowed to go anywhere (the employee with the ID badge) while others can only go to specific places (visitors for a specific person). If the firewall allows the packet to proceed (being acceptable according to the rules), it moves the packet on its way to the destination. In most cases, the firewall records where the packet came from, where it's going, and when it was seen.

For people entering a building, this is similar to the ID card system keeping track of who enters or the visitor signing the visitor's log. The building's guard may do a few more tasks before deciding that the person can pass. If the person is a visitor and is not on the visitors list, the guard calls the employee being visited to announce the visitor's arrival and to ask if they may pass. If the employee accepts the visitor, they may proceed. The guard may also give the visitor a badge that identifies them as a visitor. That badge may limit where in the building they can go and indicate if they need to be escorted. Finally, no matter whether the person is a visitor or an employee, the guard may inspect their briefcase or computer case before they pass. The firewall can also check whether a given packet should pass, allowing the computer's user to respond to unanticipated network traffic (just as the guard does with the unexpected visitor).

Individual packets can be allowed to pass, or the firewall can be changed to allow all future packets of the same type to pass. Some firewalls have advanced capabilities that make it possible to direct packets to a different destination and perhaps even have their contents concealed inside other packets (similar to the visitor being escorted). Finally, firewalls can filter packets based not only on their point of origin or destination, but also on their content (inspecting the briefcase or computer case before being allowed to pass). Back to the office building, when employees leave the building, they may also have to swipe their ID card to show that they've left. A visitor signs out and returns their temporary badge. Both may be subject to having their possessions inspected before being allowed to leave.

Firewalls can also recognize and record when a computer-to-computer connection ends. If the connection was temporary (like a visitor), the firewall rules can change to deny future similar connections until the system's user authorizes them (just as visitors must re-identify themselves and be re-approved by an employee). Finally, outgoing connections can also be filtered according to content (again, similar to inspecting possessions at the exit).

What does this all mean? It means that with a firewall, you can control which packets are allowed to enter your home computer and which are allowed to leave. That's the easy part. The hard part is deciding the details about the packets that are allowed to enter and exit your home computer. If your firewall supports content filtering, you also need to learn which content to allow and which not to allow. To help you get a handle on this harder task, let's return to our security guard analogy. Imagine that you are that security guard and it's your first day on the job. You have to decide who's allowed in, who's allowed out, and what people can bring into and take out of the building. How do you do this? One strategy is to be very conservative: let no one in or out and let no possessions in or out. This is very simple, very easy to achieve, but not particularly helpful to the business if none of its employees or visitors can get in or out. Nor is it helpful if they can't bring anything with them. With this type of strategy, your tenure as a security guard may be short-lived. If you try this, you quickly learn that you need to change your strategy to allow people in and out only if they have acceptable identification and possessions using some agreed-to criteria. Add the requirement that if you don't meet the precise criteria for admittance, you don't get in.

With most firewalls, you can do the same thing. You can programme your firewall to let nothing in and nothing out. Period. This is a *deny-all*firewall strategy and it does work, though it effectively disconnects you from the Internet. It is impractical for most home computers. You can do what the security guard did: review each packet (employee or visitor) to see where it's coming from and where it's going. Some firewall products let you easily review each packet so that you can decide what to do with it. When you are shopping for a firewall, look for this review feature because it can be quite helpful. Practically speaking, it isn't easy to decide which traffic is all right and which is not all right. Any feature that makes this job easier helps you achieve your goal of securing your home computer. Just like the security guard who learns that anybody with a company photo ID is allowed to pass, you too can create firewall rules that allow traffic to pass without reviewing each packet each time. For example, you may choose to allow your Internet browsers to visit any web site. This rule would define the source of that traffic to be your browsers (Netscape Navigator and Microsoft Internet Explorer, for example) and the destination location to be any web server. This means that anybody using your home computer could visit any Internet web site, as long as that web server used the well-known standard locations.

Now that you have an idea of what your firewall security guard is trying to do, you need a method for gathering information and programming your firewall.

Here is a set of steps to use to do just that:

- *The Programme test*: What's the programme that wants to make a connection to the Internet? Although many programmes may need to make the same type of connection to the same Internet destination, you need to know the name of each. Avoid general rules that allow all programmes to make a connection. This often results in unwanted and unchecked behaviour.
- The Location test: What's the Internet location of the computer system to which your computer wants to connect? Locations consist of an address and a port number. Sometimes a programme is allowed to connect to any Internet location, such as a web browser connecting to any web server. Again, you want to limit programmes so that they only connect to specific locations where possible.
- The Allowed test: Is this connection allowed or denied? Your firewall rules will contain some of each.
- The Temporary test: Is this connection temporary or permanent? For example, if you're going to connect to this specific location more than five times each time you use the computer, you probably want to make the connection permanent. This means that you

ought to add a rule to your firewall rules. If you aren't going to make this connection often, you should define it as temporary.

With each connection, apply the PLAT tests to get the information you need to build a firewall rule. The answer to the PLAT tests tells you if you need to include a new firewall rule for this new connection. For most firewall programmes, you can temporarily allow a connection but avoid making it permanent by not including it in your rules. Where possible, allow only temporary connections. As you run each programme on your home computer, you'll learn how it uses the Internet. Slowly you'll begin to build the set of rules that define what traffic is allowed into and out of your computer. By only letting in and out what you approve and denying all else, you will strike a practical balance between allowing everything and allowing nothing in or out.

Along the way, you may come across exceptions to your rules. For example, you might decide that anybody who uses your home computer can visit any web site *except* a chosen few web sites. This is analogous to the security guard letting every employee pass except a few who need more attention first. To do this with firewall rules, the exception rules must be listed before the general rules. For example, this means that the web sites whose connections are not allowed must be listed before the rules that allow all connections to any web site.

Why? Most firewall programmes search their rules starting from the first through the last. When the firewall finds a rule that matches the packet being examined, the firewall honours it, does what the rule says, and looks no further. For example, if the firewall finds the general rule allowing any web site connections first, it honours this rule and doesn't look further for rules that might deny such a connection. So, the order of firewall rules is important. Many firewalls can be programmed to require a password before changing the rules. This extra level of protection safeguards against unwanted changes no matter their source, that is, you, an intruder, or another user. Follow the guidance in assigning a password to your firewall. Finally, make a backup of your firewall rules.

You've probably taken a lot of time to build and tune them to match how your home computer is used. These rules are important to your computer's security, so back them up using the guidance in *Make Backups of Important Files and Folders.*

Firewalls come in two general types: hardware and software (programmes). The software versions also come in two types: free versions and commercial versions (ones that you purchase). At a minimum, you should use one of the free versions on your home computer. This is especially important if you have a laptop that you connect to your home network as well as a network at a hotel, a conference, or your office.

If you can afford a hardware firewall, you should install one of these too. We've recommended this as something to do later. (Firewall programmes are on our list of recommended actions, and hardware firewalls are The same issues apply to the hardware versions that apply to the software versions. Many can also be password protected against unwanted changes. Search the Internet with your browser to see what's available and what they cost. The price of hardware firewalls is coming down as the demand grows. A firewall is your security guard that stands between your home computer and the Internet. It lets you control which traffic your computer accepts. It also controls which of your programmes can connect to the Internet. With a firewall, you define which connections between your computer and other computers on the Internet are allowed and which are denied. There are free firewall products that provide the capabilities you need to secure your home computer. Commercial versions have even more features that can further protect your computer.

Firewalls are an important part of your home computer's security defences:

- Use a worksheet to record your firewall decisions.
- *Example*: *Operating a Firewall Programme.*

MAKE BACKUPS OF IMPORTANT FILES AND FOLDERS

Whether you know it or not, you've divided everything you own into two broad categories: those items you can replace and those you can't. For the items you can't replace, you've probably stored them in a safe place, either somewhere in your living space or elsewhere, in a lockbox at a bank, for example. In either case, you've probably also bought insurance that provides the funds you'd need to buy replacements. Your insurance policy covers almost everything you own.

On your home computer, have you similarly divided everything into the same categories? What have you done about the items – files in this case – that you can't replace? Examples are the files that make up your checking account records, that novel you've been writing for the past few years, and those pictures you took last summer with your digital camera.

What happens if your computer malfunctions or is destroyed by a successful attacker? Are those files gone forever? Now think about your car for a moment. Do you have a spare tire? Is it inflated? When was the last time you used it? Can you imagine buying a car without a spare tire? Even if you bought a used car without a spare, how soon did you buy a spare so that you'd have one when you needed it?

Think back to your home computer. Do you have a "spare tire," meaning a way to continue computing when you have a "blowout" caused by a malfunction or an intruder? Said another way, can you back up your files onto some other media so that you can recover them if you need to? If you'd never buy a car without a spare tire, why did you buy a computer without a device to back up your files?

When deciding what to do about backing up files on your computer, ask these questions:

- *The Files question*: What files should you back up? The files you select are those that you can neither easily recreate nor reinstall from somewhere else, such as the CD-ROMs or the floppy disks that came with your computer.

Be realistic. That check register you printed does not constitute a backup from which you can easily recreate the files needed by your checking account programme. You're probably not going to re-enter all that data if the files are destroyed. Just as you protect your irreplaceable valuables, back up the files you cannot replace, easily or otherwise.

- The Often question: How often should you back them up? In the best of all cases, you should back up a file every time it changes. If you don't, you'll have to reintroduce all the changes that happened since your last backup. Just as you store your precious jewelry in a lockbox at the local bank lest the lucky robber find it in your jewelry box, you need to store your files safely (back them up) after every use (change in the file) lest an intruder destroys the file or there's a system catastrophe.
- The Media question: Where should you back them up to; that is, what media should you use to hold backed up files? The answer is: whatever you have. It's a question of how many of that media you have to use and how convenient it is. For example, most computers have a floppy disk drive. You could back up your irreplaceable files to floppies. That process just takes lots of time and may not be as convenient as using another media. Larger capacity removable disk drives and writable CD-ROMs also work well, take less time, and are more convenient.

If you don't have a backup device, there are alternatives. There are Internet services that let you back up your files to another Internet computer.

Some of these services provide "transparent access" to the backups. That is, they look like another hard drive attached to your computer. You use the file copy scheme that your computer provides to back up files and recover them from backed up storage. To find these services, do some Internet searches using your browser.

Remember that the information you transfer across the Internet could be viewed and captured by others; that is, the information is in the clear. Be sensitive to that if you use an Internet-based backup computer. In addition, you need to be able to trust the information when you recover a file from that service.

- The Store question: Where should you store that media once it contains your backed up files? No matter how you back up your files, you need to be concerned about where those backed up copies live.

You already know that intruders try to break into your home computer to gain access to your files and your computer's resources. Another way to gain access to the same information is by stealing your backups. It is more difficult, though, since a robber must physically be where your backups are, whereas an intruder can access your home computer from literally anywhere in the world. The key is to know where the media is that contains your backed up files.

Just like important papers stored in a fireproof container at your house, you also need to be concerned about your backups being destroyed if your living space is destroyed or damaged. This means that you ought to keep a copy of your backed up files in a fireproof container or somewhere beyond your living space, your office for example. It is the eternal compromise between security and usability. If you need to recover a file and the backed up copies are at the office, that's inconvenient. However, while storing them at home is more convenient and more usable, they share the same risks that your computer faces should your living space be destroyed. Be aware of the issues and make a conscious decision, perhaps keeping copies in both places.

If you have that spare tire for your car or a lockbox for your valuables, you've already planned for the worst that can happen around your living space. Continue that good practice by backing up your critical files onto media that you can safely store elsewhere. Do those backups often enough that you can capture the changes you've made. With the FOMS questions, you have a structured approach to use to back up your critical files. You've now planned for the worst.

As you computerize the routine aspects of your daily life, making backup copies of important files and folders becomes critical. Even if you can't store the backup copies in a fireproof container or somewhere outside your home, make backups anyway. Any backup is better than none.

- Use a worksheet to record your important information about backups.

USE STRONG PASSWORDS

Your living space has doors and windows, and perhaps most of the time they're locked. For each lock that uses a key, chances are that each key is different. You know to lock up and not to share the keys with strangers, and probably not with most of your friends. You should not hide keys under the mat or in a flowerpot on your front porch. Passwords for computers are much the same. For each computer and service you use (online purchasing, for example), you should have a password. Each password should be unique and unrelated to any of your other passwords. You shouldn't write them down nor should you share them with anyone, even your best friends. Take a look at your front door key. It's pretty complicated. There are lots of notches and grooves.

If there weren't so many possible variations, a thief could easily make a key for every possible combination and then try each on your front door. This trial-and-error method, (for computers, called *brute force*) is likely to be effective even if it takes a long time. Nonetheless, no matter how complicated, if the thief gets hold of your key, he or she can copy it and use that copy to open your door.

A password can also be complicated. Most schemes let you use any combination of letters, both upper and lower case, and numbers; and some also let you use punctuation marks. Lengths can vary. You can create a password to be as complicated as you want. The key (no pun intended) is to be able to remember this password whenever you need it without having to write it down to jog your memory.

Like the thief at your door, computer intruders also use trial-and-error, or brute-force techniques, to discover passwords. By bombarding a login scheme with all the words in a dictionary, they may "discover" the password that unlocks it. If they know something about you, such as your spouse's name, the kind of car you drive, or your interests, clever intruders can narrow the range of possible passwords and try those first. They are often successful. Even slight variations, such as adding a digit onto the end of a word or replacing the letter o (oh) with the digit 0 (zero), don't protect passwords. Intruders know we use tricks like this to make our passwords more difficult to guess.

Just like the front door key, even a complicated password can be copied and the copy reused. Remember the earlier discussion about information on the Internet being in the clear? Suppose that really strong password you took a long time to create – the one that's 14 characters long and contains 6 letters, 4 numbers, and 4 punctuation marks, all in random order – goes across the Internet in the clear. An intruder may be able to see it, save it, and use it. This is called *sniffing* and it is a common intruder practice. The point is that you need to follow the practice of using a unique password with every account you have. Below is a set of steps that you can use to help you create passwords for your accounts:

- The Strong test: Is the password as strong (meaning length and content) as the rules allow?
- The Unique test: Is the password unique and unrelated to any of your other passwords?
- The Practical test: Can you remember it without having to write it down?
- The Recent test: Have you changed it recently?

In spite of the SUPR tests, you need to be aware that sniffing happens, and even the best of passwords can be captured and used by an intruder. You should use passwords not only on your home computer but also for services you use elsewhere on the Internet. All should have the strongest passwords you can use and remember, and each password should be unique and unrelated to all other passwords.

A strong password is a password that is longer than it is short, that uses combinations of uppercase and lowercase letters, numbers, and punctuation, and that is usually not a word found in a dictionary. Also remember that no matter how strong a password is, it can still be captured if an intruder can see it "in the clear" somewhere on the Internet.

- Use a worksheet to help you manage your passwords.

USE CARE WHEN DOWNLOADING AND INSTALLING PROGRAMMES

When you buy an appliance, you give little thought to it doing you or your house any harm. Why? Because there are organizations likeUnderwriters Laboratories that set standards and certify products. When you see a certifier's label, you have more confidence that a product will be safer than a competing product that does not carry the same label. You're willing to accept the risk because you believe the product has met some standards and has been certified by a respected authority.

Unfortunately, the Internet is not the same. There are neither standards nor many certification organizations. Anyone who writes a programme can distribute it through any means available, such as through the web or by sending you a copy. Speaking of that, have you ever received a CD-ROM in the mail? How do you know that it contains what the label says? The answer is: you don't know. More importantly, it's difficult to know. No matter how you acquire a programme, it runs on your computer at the mercy of the program's author. Anything, any operation, any task that you can do, this programme can also do. If you're allowed to remove any file, the programme can too. If you can send e-mail, the programme can too. If you can install or remove a programme, the programme can too. Anything you can do, the intruder can do also, through the programme you've just installed and run.

Sometimes there's no explanation of what a programme is supposed to do or what it actually does. There may be no user's guide. There may be no way to contact the author. You're on your own, trying to weigh a program's benefits against the risk of the harm that it might cause. What's the problem you're trying to solve here? You are trying to determine if the programme you've just found satisfies your needs (say it provides a service that you want or you're just experimenting) without causing harm to your computer and ultimately the information you have on the computer. How do you decide if a programme is what it says it is? How do you gauge the risk to you and your computer by running this programme?

You address these same risk issues when you purchase an appliance; you may just not have realised that's what you were doing. When you make that purchase, you buy from either a local store you know or a national chain with an established reputation. If there's a problem with your purchase, you can take it back to the store and exchange it or get your money back. If it causes you harm, you can seek relief through the legal system. The reputation of the merchant, the refund/return policy, and the availability of the legal system reduce your risk to a point where you make the purchase.

Apply these same practices when you buy a programme. You should:

- Learn as much as you can about the product and what it does before you purchase it.
- Understand the refund/return policy before you make your purchase.
- Buy from a local store that you already know or a national chain with an established reputation.

Presently, it is not as clear what the legal system's role is for a programme that causes harm or does not work as advertised. In the meantime, the LUB practices are a good first step. Today's Internet has a feature that standard products don't have, or at least have but to a lesser extent. This feature is free programmes. There is a multitude of free programmes available for all types of systems, with more available each day. The challenge is to decide which programmes deserve your confidence and are, therefore, worth the risk of installing and running on your home computer. So then, how do you decide if a programme is worth it?

To decide if you should install and run a programme on your home computer, follow these steps:

- The Do test: What does the programme do? You should be able to read a clear description of what the programme does. This description could be on the web site where you can download it or on the CD-ROM you use to install it. You need to realise that that if the programme was written with malicious intent, the author/intruder isn't going to tell you that the programme will harm your system. They will probably try to mislead you. So, learn what you can, but consider the source and consider whether you can trust that information.

- The Changes test: What files are installed and what other changes are made on your system when you install and run the programme? Again, to do this test, you may have to ask the author/intruder how their programme changes your system. Consider the source.
- The Author test: Who is the author? (Can you use e-mail, telephone, letter, or some other means to contact them?) Once you get this information, use it to try to contact them to verify that the contact information works. Your interactions with them may give you more clues about the programme and its potential effects on your computer and you.
- The Learn test: Has anybody else used this programme, and what can you learn from him or her? Try some Internet searches using your web browser. Somebody has probably used this programme before you, so learn what you can before you install it.

If you can't determine these things – the DCAL tests for short – about the programme you'd like to install, then strongly consider whether it's worth the risk. Only you can decide what's best. Whatever you do, be prepared to rebuild your computer from scratch in case the programme goes awry and destroys it. Task 5- *Make Backups of Important Files and Folders* tells you how to make a copy of your important information should you need it. Your anti-virus programme prevents some of the problems caused by downloading and installing programmes. However, you need to remember that there's a lag between recognizing a virus and when your computer also knows about it. Even if that nifty programme you've just downloaded doesn't contain a virus, it may behave in an unexpected way. You should continue to exercise care and do your homework when downloading, installing, and running new programmes.

- Use a worksheet to record important information about programmes you install on your computer.

INSTALL AND USE A HARDWARE FIREWALL

Complement your firewall programme by installing a hardware firewall. Together, these two firewalls stand between your home computer and the Internet. This is another place where your money is well spent. Please go to Task 4- *Install and Use a Firewall Programme* to learn more about firewalls. That section concentrates primarily on firewall programmes, but much of the information applies to hardware firewalls as well. To find out what hardware firewall products are available, search the Internet with your web browser.

- Use a worksheet to record the ruleset for your hardware firewall.

TELEWORKING

DEFINITION

The European Trade Union Confederation (ETUC), the Union of Industrial and Employers' Confederations of Europe/ the European Union of Crafts and Small and Medium-Sized Enterprises (UNICE/UEAPME), and the Centre of Enterprises with Public Participation (ECPE) have signed a framework agreement on telework aimed at ensuring greater security for teleworkers employed in the EU. This agreement is of particular importance because it is the first European agreement put in place by the social partners themselves.

The agreement aims at establishing a general framework at European level concerning the employment conditions of teleworkers and at reconciling the needs for flexibility and security shared by employers and workers. It grants teleworkers the same overall level of protection as workers who carry out their activities at the employer's premises.

The agreement defines telework as a form of organising and/or performing work, using information technology, in the context of an employment contract/relationship, where work, which could also be performed at the employer's premises, is carried out away from those premises on a regular basis. Since telework covers a wide and fast evolving spectrum of circumstances, the social partners have chosen a definition of telework that includes various forms of regular telework. The agreement focuses on several key areas in which the specific nature of telework must be taken into account, viz:

Voluntary Nature of Teleworking

Telework is voluntary for the worker and the employer concerned. Telework may be required as part of a worker's initial job description or it may be engaged in as a voluntary arrangement subsequently. In both cases, the employer provides the teleworker with relevant written information in accordance with Directive 91/533/EEC;

Employment Conditions

Teleworkers benefit from the same rights as comparable workers at the employer's premises. These rights are guaranteed by applicable legislation and collective agreements. In order to take into account the particularities of telework, specific agreements may be necessary;

Data Protection

The employer is responsible for taking the appropriate measures to ensure the protection of data used and processed by the teleworker for professional purposes. The employer informs the teleworker in particular of any restrictions on the use of equipment and of sanctions in the case of non-compliance;

Privacy

The employer respects the teleworker's privacy. If any kind of monitoring system is put in place, it needs to be proportionate to the objective and introduced in accordance with Directive 90/270 on visual display units;

Equipment

As a general rule, the employer is responsible for

providing, installing and maintaining the equipment necessary for regular telework unless the teleworker uses his/her own equipment. The employer has the liability, in accordance with national legislation and collective agreements, regarding costs for loss and damage to the equipment and data used by the teleworker.

Health and Safety

The employer is responsible for the protection of the occupational health and safety of the teleworker in accordance with Directive 89/391 and relevant daughter directives, national legislation and collective agreements. In order to verify that the applicable health and safety provisions are correctly employed, the employer, workers' representatives and/or relevant authorities have access to the telework place, within the limits of national legislation and collective agreements. If the teleworker is working at home, such access is subject to prior notification and his/her agreement. The teleworker is entitled to request inspection visits;

Organisation of Work

Within the framework of applicable legislation, collective agreements and company rules, the teleworker manages the organisation of his/her working time. The workload and performance standards of the teleworker are equivalent to those of comparable workers at the employer's premises;

Training of Teleworkers

Teleworkers have the same access to training and career development as comparable workers at the employer's premises and are subject to the same appraisal policies as these are their workers. Teleworkers receive appropriate training targeted at the technical equipment at their disposal and at the characteristics of this form of work organisation;

The Collective Rights of Teleworkers

Teleworkers have the same collective rights as workers at the employer's premises. No obstacles are put to communicating with workers' representatives.

IMPLEMENTATION AND FOLLOW-UP

This European framework agreement will be implemented within three years after the date of signature by the members of UNICE/UEAPME, CEEP and ETUC (and the Liaison Committee EUROCADRES/CEC). Member organisations will report on the implementation of this agreement to an ad-hoc group set up by the signatory parties, under the responsibility of the Social Dialogue Committee. Within four years after the date of signature of this agreement, this ad-hoc group will prepare a joint report on the implementation measures taken. The signatory parties will review the agreement five years after the date of signature if requested by one of the signatory parties.

CONTEXT

This new agreement directly supports the strategy defined at the Lisbon European Council and the transition to a knowledge-based economy and society, in line with the Lisbon objectives. In July 1997, the European Commission adopted a raft of policy recommendations on the labour market and the social dimension of the information society. The recommendations included commitments to promote teleworking in Europe and to study teleworking within the Commission. In 1998 a pilot project was launched by the Directorate General for Employment, Social Affairs and Equal Opportunities and the Directorate-General for the Information Society. It includes three telework types of a part-time nature: working both from home and in the office, working whilst on the move during official missions, and occasional work in another Commission building.

The promotion of telework opportunities is one of the components of the Commission's proposals for an employment strategy in the information society. The Commission supports the work of the social partners with a view to establishing framework conditions and practical rules so as to allow telework to be introduced on a large scale.

WHAT IS TELEWORKING

Telework occurs when information and communications

technologies (ICTs) are applied to enable work to be done at a distance from the place where the work results are needed or where the work would conventionally have been done.

It includes:

- Home-based telework or "telecommuting", when an employee or contractor works at home instead of travelling to an employer's or a customer's premises.
- Mobile telework, when executives, professionals or service staffs using ICTs to enable them to spend more time with customers and to deliver "on the road" a range of services and capabilities that previously would have involved office based staff or visits to the company offices;
- Telecentres, providing local office facilities for people who prefer not to work at home but wish to avoid the cost, time and inconvenience of commuting;
- Telecottages, which provide local communities with access to skills development, high performance ICTs, and the networking and socialisation aspects of work that may be missed by a home based worker.
- Functional relocation, where business functions that previously were located close to the customer are concentrated and delivered at a distance; examples include both "front office" (selling activities previously done in the High Street, now delivered by phone or computer networks) and "back office" (service and maintenance work previously done "on site", which may now be done anywhere in the world using remote access to systems).

Telework also affects some kinds of "outsourcing", in that many kinds of work can now be done from thousands of miles away and "outsourced" across national borders. Telework has also been said to include "dispersed team working", in which (for example) an engineering company uses three or more teams in different time zones to work 24 hours a day on a time-sensitive customer tender, with each team "passing the baton" to the next at the end of its working day. As well as affecting the individual and the enterprise telework has significant economic and trade implications, for example many jobs in computer programing that might previously have been done in California or in Sweden are now done in Bangalore. Understanding telework in all its ramifications is essential to the future of work and jobs.

ELECTRONIC MAIL

INTRODUCTION

Electronic mail, or E-mail, is one of the most important Internet services. Until the advent of the World-Wide Web, it was also the most popular. It's also the most personal mainstream service: your E-mail reflects your own personality, so it's important to convey the correct impression in your electronic mail. For many people, electronic mail is still a novel experience. Many people sign up for an e-mail account, get some mail programme like Eudora or one of the Microsoft mail programmes, play around for a while, and then just about forget it, leaving mail to collect unanswered. Even big companies are offenders here.

In those cases where such people do send or answer mail, the quality of the message is frequently poor. They often contain misspellings, irrelevant quotes, or poor layout ("formatting"). Don't underestimate the effect of such a mail message. Your mail message is all that many people see of you, and if it's poorly formatted, one line per paragraph, badly spelt, or full of errors, it will give people a poor impression of you. E-mail use is just now becoming mainstream, but many hackers have been using it for 20 years or more.

In the impersonal world of the Internet, your mail messages are the most tangible thing about you. Send out a well thought out, clear and legible message, and you will leave a good impression. Send out a badly formulated, badly formatted and badly spelt message, and you will leave a bad impression. So what's good formatting and what's bad formatting? That's partially a matter of opinion (and self-expression), of course, but there are a number of Internet Standards which define what a message should look like.

Unfortunately, Microsoft is trying to impose its own "standard" on the world. I can't give a link to it, because they haven't published their "standard".

Problems in mail fall into a number of categories. Select the link for more details of each category:

- Format problems. In extreme cases, messages can be barely legible. Microsoft "Outlook" seems to have taken this problem to new heights.
- Character set problems. Traditionally, Mail was written in US-ASCII, a character set which only suffices to represent English correctly. Even most of the optional English letters, such as æ and French accents é, è and friends are missing.
- Message layout issues. These are entirely in your hands, and they reflect most on your personality. Use them well and you'll make a good impression. Use them badly and you'll make a bad impression. Who decides what good and bad are? The reader does, and you don't get a say in the matter.

In this document, I used text-mode UNIX mail readers to illustrate the problems. You may not find them as pretty as Microsoft mailers, and all the whiz-bang icons are missing. This is my personal choice: I use mail readers to read and send mail, and not for web browsing or writing documents. This discussion doesn't relate only to text-mode mailers, though—take a look at the page about UNIX graphic mode mailers if you prefer them.

One of the most prominent uses of networking since the first networks were devised, has been electronic mail. It started as a simple service that copied a file from one machine to another, and appended it to the recipient's *mailbox* file. Basically, this is still what e-mail is all about, although an ever growing net with its complex routing requirements and its ever increasing load of messages has made a more elaborate scheme necessary. Various standards of mail exchange have been devised. Sites on the Internet adhere to one laid out in RFC-822, augmented by some RFCs that describe a machine-independent way of transferring special characters, and the like. Much thought has also been given recently to "multi-media mail", which deals with including pictures and sound in mail messages. Another standard, X.400, has been defined by CCITT. Quite a number of mail transport programmes have been implemented for systems. One of the best-known is the University of Berkeley's sendmail, which is used on a number of platforms. The original author was Eric Allman, who is now actively working on the sendmail team again. There are two ports of sendmail-5.56c available, one of which will be described.

The mail agent most commonly used with is smail-3.1.28, written and copyrighted by Curt Landon Noll and Ronald S.-Karr. This is the one included in most distributions. In the following, we will refer to it simply as smail, although there are other versions of it which are entirely different, and which we don't describe here. Compared to sendmail, smail is rather young. When handling mail for a small site without complicated routing requirements, their capabilities are pretty close. For large sites, however, sendmail always wins, because its configuration scheme is much more flexible. Both smail and sendmail support a set of configuration files that have to be customised. Apart from the information that is required to make the mail subsystem run (such as the local hostname), there are many more parameters that may be tuned.

Sendmail's main configuration file is very hard to understand at first. It looks as if your cat had taken a nap on your keyboard with the shift key pressed. smail configuration files are more structured and easier to understand than sendmail's, but don't give the user as much power in tuning the mailer's behaviour. However, for small UUCP or Internet sites the work required in setting up any of them is roughly the same.

USING MAILER

Your choice of MUA ("mailer") is personal—maybe. You can only choose from what's available. If you use UNIX or a compatible operating system, there are dozens of mailers available, some of them good. I personally prefer mutt. If you use Microsoft, you'll also find several mailers, but most of them are bad, at least from the point of view of what the recipient sees.

My personal hate list (in order of decreasing capability to annoy) is:

- Lotus Notes
- Microsoft "Outlook" Express
- Microsoft "Outlook"

Netscape Communicator is better, but not much. None of these mailers is capable of both producing correct formats and not mutilating quoted text. "Outlook" Express apparently insists on displaying in a proportionally spaced font, so you can't even decide where to insert a manual line break. Most of them discard headers, which may contain important information—it's rather like receiving conventional ("snail mail") letters without the envelope.

MAIL MESSAGE

A Mail message generally consists of a message body, which is the text the sender wrote, and special data specifying recipients, transport medium, etc., very much like what you see when you look at a letter's envelope. This administrative data falls into two categories; in the first category is any data that is specific to the transport medium, like the address of sender and recipient. It is therefore called *the envelope.* It may be transformed by the transport software as the message is passed along.

The second variety is any data necessary for handling the mail message, which is not particular to any transport mechanism, such as the message's subject line, a list of all recipients, and the date the message was sent. In many networks, it has become standard to prepend this data to the mail message, forming the so-called *mail header*. It is offset from the *mail body* by an empty line. Most mail transport software in the world uses a header format outlined in a RFC-822. Its original purpose was to specify a standard for use on the ARPANET, but since it was designed to be independent from any environment, it has been easily adapted to other networks, including many UUCP-based networks.

RFC-822 however is only the greatest common denominator. More recent standards have been conceived to cope with growing needs as, for example, data encryption, international character set support, and multi-media mail extensions (MIME). In all these standards, the header consists of several lines, separated by newline characters. A line is made up of a field name, beginning in column one, and the field itself, offset by a colon and white space. The format and semantics of each field vary depending on the field name. A header field may be continued across a newline, if the next line begins with a TAB. Fields can appear in any order.

A typical mail header may look like this:

```
From brewhq.swb.de!ora.com!andyo Wed Apr 13
00:17:03 1994
Return-Path:
Received: from brewhq.swb.de by monad.swb.de
with uucp
  (Smail3.1.28.1 #6) id m0pqqlT-00023aB; Wed,
  13 Apr
94 00:17
Received: from ora.com (ruby.ora.com) by
brewhq.swb.de with
smtp
  (Smail3.1.28.1 #28.6) id; Tue, 12 Apr 94 2
Received: by ruby.ora.com (8.6.8/8.6.4) id
RAA26438; Tue, 12
Apr 94
Date: Tue, 12 Apr 1994 15:56:49-0400
Message-Id: <199404121956.PAA07787@ruby>
From: andyo@ora.com (Andy Oram)
To: okir@monad.swb.de
Subject: Re: Your RPC section
```

Usually, all necessary header fields are generated by the mailer interface you use, like elm, pine, mush, or mailx. Some however are optional, and may be added by the user. elm, for example, allows you to edit part of the message header. Others are added by the mail transport software. A list of common header fields and their meaning are given below:

- *From*: This contains the sender's e-mail address, and possibly the "real name". A complete zoo of formats is used here.
- *To*: This is the recipient's e-mail address.

- *Subject*: Describes the content of the mail in a few words. At least that's what it should do.
- *Date*: The date the mail was sent.
- *Reply-To*: Specifies the address the sender wants the recipient's reply directed to. This may be useful if you have several accounts, but want to receive the bulk of mail only on the one you use most frequently. This field is optional.
- *Organization*: The organization that owns the machine from which the mail originates. If your machine is owned by you privately, either leave this out, or insert "private" or some complete non-sense. This field is optional.
- *Message-ID*: A string generated by mail transport on the originating system. It is unique to this message.
- *Received*: Every site that processes your mail (including the machines of sender and recipient) inserts such a field into the header, giving its site name, a message id, time and date it received the message, which site it is from, and which transport software was used. This is so that you can trace which route the message took, and can complain to the person responsible if something went wrong.
- *X-anything*: No mail-related programmes should complain about any header which starts with X-. It is used to implement additional features that have not yet made it into an RFC, or never will. This is used by the Linux Activists mailing list, for example, where the channel is selected by the X-Mn-Key: header field.

The one exception to this structure is the very first line. It starts with the keyword From which is followed by a blank instead of a colon. To distinguish it from the ordinary From: field, it is frequently referred to as From_. It contains the route the message has taken in UUCP bang-path style (explained below), time and date when it was received by the last machine having processed it, and an optional part specifying which host it was received from. Since this field is regenerated by every system that processes the message, it is sometimes subsumed under the envelope data. The From_ field is there for backward compatibility with some older mailers, but is not used very much anymore, except by mail user interfaces that rely on it to mark the beginning of a message in the user's mailbox. To avoid potential trouble with lines in the message body that begin with "From ", too, it has become standard procedure to escape any such occurrence by preceding it with

MAIL DELIVERED

Generally, you will compose mail using a mailer interface like mail or mailx; or more sophisticated ones like elm, mush, or pine. These programmes are called *mail user agents*, or MUA's for short. If you send a mail message, the interface programme will in most cases hand it to another programme for delivery. This is called the *mail transport agent*, or MTA. On some systems, there are different mail transport agents for local and remote delivery; on others, there is only one. The command for remote delivery is usually called rmail, the other is called lmail (if it exists). Local delivery of mail is, of course, more than just appending the incoming message to the recipient's mailbox. Usually, the local MTA will understand aliasing (setting up local recipient addresses pointing to other addresses), and forwarding (redirecting a user's mail to some other destination). Also, messages that cannot be delivered must usually be *bounced*, that is, returned to the sender along with some error message.

For remote delivery, the transport software used depends on the nature of the link. If the mail must be delivered over a network using TCP/IP, SMTP is commonly used. SMTP stands for Simple Mail Transfer Protocol, and is defined in RFC-788 and RFC-821. SMTP usually connects to the recipient's machine directly, negotiating the message transfer with the remote side's SMTP daemon.

In UUCP networks, mail will usually not be delivered directly, but rather be forwarded to the destination host by a number of intermediate systems. To send a message over a UUCP link, the sending MTA will usually execute rmail on the forwarding system using uux, and feed it the message on standard input. Since this is done for each message separately, it may produce a considerable work load on a major mail hub, as well as clutter the UUCP spool queues with hundreds of small files taking up an unproportional amount of disk space. Some MTAs therefore allow you to collect several messages for a remote system in a single batch file. The batch file contains the SMTP commands that the local host would normally issue if a direct SMTP connection was used. This is called BSMTP, or *batched* SMTP. The batch is then fed to the rsmtp or bsmtp programme on the remote system, which will process the input as if a normal SMTP connection had occurred.

E-MAIL ADDRESSES

For electronic mail, an address is made up of at least the name of a machine handling the person's mail, and a user identification recognized by this system. This may be the recipient's login name, but may also be anything else. Other mail addressing schemes, like X.400, use a more general set of "attributes" which are used to look up the recipient's host in an X.500 directory server. The way a machine name is interpreted, *i.e.* at which site your message will finally wind up, and how to combine this name with the recipient's user name greatly depends on the network you are on. Internet sites adhere to the RFC-822 standard, which requires a notation of user@host.domain, where host.domain is the host's fully qualified domain name. The middle thing is called an "at" sign. Because this notation does not involve a route to the destination host but gives the (unique) hostname instead, this is called an *absolute* address.

In the original UUCP environment, the prevalent form was path!host!user, where path described a sequence of hosts the message had to travel before reaching the destination host. This construct is called the *bang path* notation, because an exclamation mark is loosely called a "bang". Today, many UUCP-based networks have adopted RFC-822, and will understand this type of address. Now, these two types of addressing don't mix too well. Assume an address of hostA!user@hostB. It is not clear whether the '@' sign takes precedence over the path, or vice versa: do we have to send the message to hostB, which mails it to hostA!user, or should it be sent to hostA, which forwards it to user@hostB? Addresses that mix different types of address operators are called *hybrid addresses*. Most notorious is the above example. It is usually resolved by giving the '@' sign precedence over the path. In the above example, this means sending the message to hostB first. However, there is a way to specify routes in RFC-822-conformant ways: <@hostA,@hostB:user@hostC> denotes the address of user on hostC, where hostC is to be reached through hostA and hostB (in that order). This type of address is frequently called a *route-addr address*.

Then, there is the '%' address operator: user% host B@hostA will first be sent to hostA, which expands the rightmost (in this case, only) per cent sign to an '@' sign. The address is now user@hostB, and the mailer will happily forward your message to hostB which delivers it to user. This type of address is sometimes referred to as "Ye Olde ARPANET Kludge", and its use is discouraged. Nevertheless, many mail transport agents generate this type of address. Other networks have still different means of addressing. DECnet-based networks, for example, use two colons as an address separator, yielding an address of host:user.Lastly, the X.400 standard uses an entirely different scheme, by describing a recipient by a set of attribute-value pairs, like country and organization. On FidoNet, each user is identified by a code like 2:320/204.9, consisting of four numbers denoting zone (2 is for Europe), net (320 being Paris and Banlieue), node (the local hub), and point (the individual user's PC). Fidonet addresses can be mapped to RFC-822; the above would be written as Thomas.Quinot@p9.f204.n320.z2.fidonet.org. Now didn't I say domain names are easy to remember?

There are some implications to using these different types of addressing which will be described throughout the following sections. In a RFC-822 environment, however, you will rarely use anything else than absolute addresses like user@host.domain.

Bibliography

Axtell, R.: *Gestures: The Do's and Taboos of Body Language Around the World*, New York: John Wiley & Sons, 2005.

Ball, G.: *Software Agents*, Cambridge, MA: MIT Press, 1999.

Cassell, J.: *Believable Communicating Agents: The Relationship Between Verbal and Nonverbal Behavior in Autonomous Communicating Agents*, Cambridge, MA: ACM Press, 2007.

Cialdini, R.: *Influence: The Psychology of Persuasion*, New York: Quill, 2005.

Foner, L.: *A Sociological Case Study*, Cambridge, MA: MIT Media Lab, 2003.

Gauvin, JF.: *Posting your References on the Web*, New York: John Wiley and Sons, 2000.

Grice, H.: *Logic and Conversation*, New York: Academic Press, 2007.

Grosch, A.: *Textual Database Software*, New Jersey: Prentice Hall, 2007.

Herman, J.: *A Speech Interface to a Personalized Information Agent*, Cambridge, MA: MIT Media Lab, 2001.

Laurel, B.: *The Art of Human Computer Interface Design*, New York: Springer-Verlag, 1999.

Lundeen, G.: *Software for Managing Personal Files*, Princeton: Princeton University Press, 2005.

Maes, P.: *Agents that Reduce Work Overload and Information Overload*, London: Academic Press, 2005.

Marx, M.: *Toward Effective Conversational Messaging*, Brazil: Manning Publications, 2003.

Nass, C.: *The Media Equation: How People Treat Computers, Televisions, and New Media as Real People and Places*, Cambridge: Cambridge University Press, 2004.

Negroponte, N.: *The Art of Human-Computer Interface Design,* New York: John & Sons Publication, 2001.

Oren, T.: *The Art of Human-computer Interface Design,* London: Cambridge University, 2003.

Picard, R.: *Affective Computing,* Cambridge: The MIT Press, 2006.

Puglia, V.: *TBMS Database Power Unleashed,* New Jersey: Prentice Hall, 2005.

Raeder, A.: *Library Master for Databases,* New Jersey: Prentice Hall, 2006.

Schmandt, C.: *Voice Communication with Computers: Conversational Systems,* New York: Van Nostrand Reinhold, 2008.

Thomas, F.: *The Illusion of Life,* New York: Abbeville Press, 1998.

Index